Getting Started with Project Management Using Microsoft® Project 2016

Amy Kinser

KRISTYN A. JACOBSON

D
Id
Sub
Clas
LC re

Boston Col s Indianapolis New York S
Dubai Lo Madrid Milan Munich Paris Mon
Paulo Sydney Hong Kong Seoul Singap

Editorial Director: Andrew Gilfillan
Senior Portfolio Manager: Samantha McAfee Lewis
Team Lead, Project Management: Laura Burgess
Project Manager: Anne Garcia
Development Editor: Vonda Keator, Keator & Pen
Portfolio Management Assistant: Michael Campbell
Director of Product Marketing: Maggie Waples
Director of Field Marketing: Leigh Ann Sims
Product Marketing Manager: Kaylee Carlson
Field Marketing Managers: Joanna Conley & Molly Schmidt
Marketing Assistant: Kelli Fisher
Senior Operations Specialist: Maura Zaldivar-Garcia
Senior Art Director: Mary Siener
Manager, Permissions: Gina Cheselka
Interior and Cover Design: Studio Montage
Cover Photo: Rawpixel.com/Shutterstock
Associate Director of Design: Blair Brown
MyLab Product Model Manager: Eric Hakanson
Vice President, Product Management, MyLab: Jason Fournier
Digital Product Manager: Heather Darby
Media Project Manager, Production: John Cassar
Full-Service Project Management: Cenveo Publisher Services
Composition: Cenveo Publisher Services
Chapter Opener Images: art_of_sun/shutterstock

Credits and acknowledgments borrowed from other sources and reproduced, with permission, in this textbook appear on appropriate page within text.

Pearson Education Ltd., London
Pearson Education Singapore, Pte. Ltd
Pearson Education, Canada, Inc.
Pearson Education–Japan
Pearson Education Australia PTY, Limited
Pearson Education North Asia Ltd., Hong Kong
Pearson Educación de Mexico, S.A. de C.V.
Pearson Education Malaysia, Pte. Ltd

Names: Kinser, Amy, author. | Jacobson, Kristyn A., author.
Title: Your office getting started with project management using microsoft(r) project 2016 / Amy Kinser, Kristyn A. Jacobson.
escription: Hoboken : Pearson, [2016]
entifiers: LCCN 2016048316 | ISBN 0134480929
jects: LCSH: Microsoft Project. | Project management—Computer programs.
sification: LCC HD69.P75 K564 2016 | DDC 658.4/04—8553--dc23
cord available at https://lccn.loc.gov/2016048316

arson

6 2019
ISBN-10: 0134480929
ISBN-13: 9780134480923

Dedications

I dedicate this series to my Kinser Boyz for their unwavering love, support, and patience; to my parents and sister for their love; to my students for inspiring me; to Sam for believing in me; and to the instructors I hope this series will inspire!

Amy S. Kinser

I dedicate this book to my loving parents, Jeron and Ranee', for their unending support, guidance, and encouragement.

Kristyn A. Jacobson

About the Authors

Amy S. Kinser, Esq., Series Editor

Amy holds a B.A. degree in Chemistry with a Business minor from Indiana University and a J.D. from the Maurer School of Law, also at Indiana University. After working as an environmental chemist, starting her own technology consulting company, and practicing intellectual property law, she has spent the past 15 years teaching technology at the Kelley School of Business in Bloomington, Indiana. Currently, she serves as the Director of Computer Skills and Senior Lecturer at the Kelley School of Business at Indiana University. She also loves spending time with her two sons, Aidan and J. Matthew, and her husband J. Eric.

Kristyn A. Jacobson

Kristyn holds an M.S. in Education from the University of Wisconsin-La Crosse and a B.S. in Business Education from the University of Wisconsin-Eau Claire. She has been a faculty member and department chair of the Business Technology department at Madison College in Madison, Wisconsin, for over 14 years. She also serves as the curriculum coordinator for Microsoft Excel beginning, intermediate, and advanced level courses for the college. As well as teaching, Kristyn provides training to businesses on the Microsoft Office Suite including MS Project, project management, customer service, personal productivity, and time management. Prior to teaching at Madison College, she taught at a business college in Des Moines, Iowa, where she helped implement their online learning program while also teaching traditional business courses.

Contents

Acknowledgments

The ***Your Office*** team would like to thank the following reviewers who have invested time and energy to help shape this series from the very beginning, providing us with invaluable feedback through their comments, suggestions, and constructive criticism.

We'd like to thank all of our conscientious reviewers, including those who contributed to our previous editions:

Sven Aelterman
Troy University

Nitin Aggarwal
San Jose State University

Heather Albinger
Waukesha County Technical College

Angel Alexander
Piedmont Technical College

Melody Alexander
Ball State University

Karen Allen
Community College of Rhode Island

Maureen Allen
Elon University

Wilma Andrews
Virginia Commonwealth University

Mazhar Anik
Owens Community College

David Antol
Harford Community College

Kirk Atkinson
Western Kentucky University

Barbara Baker
Indiana Wesleyan University

Kristi Berg
Minot State University

Kavuri Bharath
Old Dominion University

Ann Blackman
Parkland College

Jeanann Boyce
Montgomery College

Lynn Brooks
Tyler Junior College

Cheryl Brown
Delgado Community
College West
Bank Campus

Bonnie Buchanan
Central Ohio Technical College

Peggy Burrus
Red Rocks Community College

Richard Cacace
Pensacola State College

Margo Chaney
Carroll Community College

Shanan Chappell
College of the Albemarle, North Carolina

Kuan-Chou Chen
Purdue University, Calumet

David Childress
Ashland Community and Technical College

Keh-Wen Chuang
Purdue University North Central

Suzanne Clayton
Drake University

Amy Clubb
Portland Community College

Bruce Collins
Davenport University

Linda Collins
Mesa Community College

Margaret Cooksey
Tallahassee Community College

Charmayne Cullom
University of Northern Colorado

Christy Culver
Marion Technical College

Juliana Cypert
Tarrant County College

Harold Davis
Southeastern Louisiana University

Jeff Davis
Jamestown Community College

Jennifer Day
Sinclair Community College

Anna Degtyareva
Mt. San Antonio College

Beth Deinert
Southeast Community College

Kathleen DeNisco
Erie Community College

Donald Dershem
Mountain View College

Sallie Dodson
Radford University

Joseph F. Domagala
Duquesne University

Bambi Edwards
Craven Community College

Elaine Emanuel
Mt. San Antonio College

Diane Endres
Ancilla College

Nancy Evans
Indiana University, Purdue University, Indianapolis

Christa Fairman
Arizona Western College

Marni Ferner
University of North Carolina, Wilmington

Paula Fisher
Central New Mexico Community College

Linda Fried
University of Colorado, Denver

Diana Friedman
Riverside Community College

Susan Fry
Boise State University

Virginia Fullwood
Texas A&M University, Commerce

Janos Fustos
Metropolitan State College of Denver

John Fyfe
University of Illinois at Chicago

Saiid Ganjalizadeh
The Catholic University of America

Randolph Garvin
Tyler Junior College

Diane Glowacki
Tarrant County College

Jerome Gonnella
Northern Kentucky University

Lorie Goodgine
Tennessee Technology Center in Paris

Connie Grimes
Morehead State University

Debbie Gross
Ohio State University

Babita Gupta
California State University, Monterey Bay

Lewis Hall
Riverside City College

Jane Hammer
Valley City State University

Marie Hartlein
Montgomery County Community College

Darren Hayes
Pace University

Paul Hayes
Eastern New Mexico University

Mary Hedberg
Johnson County Community College

Lynda Henrie
LDS Business College

Deedee Herrera
Dodge City Community College

Marilyn Hibbert
Salt Lake Community College

Jan Hime
University of Nebraska, Lincoln

Cheryl Hinds
Norfolk State University

Mary Kay Hinkson
Fox Valley Technical College

Margaret Hohly
Cerritos College

Brian Holbert
Spring Hill College

Susan Holland
Southeast Community College

Anita Hollander
University of Tennessee, Knoxville

Emily Holliday
Campbell University

Stacy Hollins
St. Louis Community College Florissant Valley

Mike Horn
State University of New York, Geneseo

Christie Hovey
Lincoln Land Community College

Margaret Hvatum
St. Louis Community College Meramec

Jean Insinga
Middlesex Community College

Kristyn Jacobson
Madison College

Jon (Sean) Jasperson
Texas A&M University

Glen Jenewein
Kaplan University

Gina Jerry
Santa Monica College

Dana Johnson
North Dakota State University

Mary Johnson
Mt. San Antonio College

Linda Johnsonius
Murray State University

Carla Jones
Middle Tennessee State University

Susan Jones
Utah State University

Nenad Jukic
Loyola University, Chicago

Sali Kaceli
Philadelphia Biblical University

Sue Kanda
Baker College of Auburn Hills

Robert Kansa
Macomb Community College

Susumu Kasai
Salt Lake Community College

Linda Kavanaugh
Robert Morris University

Debby Keen
University of Kentucky

Mike Kelly
Community College of Rhode Island

Melody Kiang
California State University, Long Beach

Lori Kielty
College of Central Florida

Richard Kirk
Pensacola State College

Dawn Konicek
Blackhawk Tech

John Kucharczuk
Centennial College

David Largent
Ball State University

Frank Lee
Fairmont State University

Luis Leon
The University of Tennessee at Chattanooga

Freda Leonard
Delgado Community College

Julie Lewis
Baker College, Allen Park

Suhong Li
Bryant Unversity

Renee Lightner
Florida State College

John Lombardi
South University

Rhonda Lucas
Spring Hill College

Adriana Lumpkin
Midland College

Lynne Lyon
Durham College

Nicole Lytle
California State University, San Bernardino

Donna Madsen
Kirkwood Community College

Susan Maggio
Community College of Baltimore County

Michelle Mallon
Ohio State University

Kim Manning
Tallahassee Community College

Paul Martin
Harrisburg Area Community College

Cheryl Martucci
Diablo Valley College

Sebena Masline
Florida State College of Jacksonville

Sherry Massoni
Harford Community College

Lee McClain
Western Washington University

Sandra McCormack
Monroe Community College

Sue McCrory
Missouri State University

Barbara Miller
University of Notre Dame

Johnette Moody
Arkansas Tech University

Michael O. Moorman
Saint Leo University

Kathleen Morris
University of Alabama

Alysse Morton
Westminster College

Elobaid Muna
University of Maryland Eastern Shore

Jackie Myers
Sinclair Community College

Russell Myers
El Paso Community College

Bernie Negrete
Cerritos College

Melissa Nemeth
Indiana University, Purdue University, Indianapolis

Jennifer Nightingale
Duquesne University

Kathie O'Brien
North Idaho College

Michael Ogawa
University of Hawaii

Janet Olfert
North Dakota State University

Rene Pack
Arizona Western College

Patsy Parker
Southwest Oklahoma State Unversity

Laurie Patterson
University of North Carolina, Wilmington

Alicia Pearlman
Baker College

Diane Perreault
Sierra College and California State University, Sacramento

Theresa Phinney
Texas A&M University

Vickie Pickett
Midland College

Marcia Polanis
Forsyth Technical Community College

Rose Pollard
Southeast Community College

Stephen Pomeroy
Norwich University

Leonard Presby
William Paterson University

Donna Reavis
Delta Career Education

Eris Reddoch
Pensacola State College

James Reddoch
Pensacola State College

Michael Redmond
La Salle University

Terri Rentfro
John A. Logan College

Vicki Robertson
Southwest Tennessee Community College

Jennifer Robinson
Trident Technical College

Dianne Ross
University of Louisiana at Lafayette

Ann Rowlette
Liberty University

Amy Rutledge
Oakland University

Candace Ryder
Colorado State University

Joann Segovia
Winona State University

Eileen Shifflett
James Madison University

Sandeep Shiva
Old Dominion University

Robert Sindt
Johnson County Community College

Cindi Smatt
Texas A&M University

Edward Souza
Hawaii Pacific University

Nora Spencer
Fullerton College

Alicia Stonesifer
La Salle University

Jenny Lee Svelund
University of Utah

Cheryl Sypniewski
Macomb Community College

Arta Szathmary
Bucks County Community College

Nasser Tadayon
Southern Utah University

Asela Thomason
California State University Long Beach

Nicole Thompson
Carteret Community College

Terri Tiedeman
Southeast Community College, Nebraska

Lewis Todd
Belhaven University

Barb Tollinger
Sinclair Community College

Allen Truell
Ball State University

Erhan Uskup
Houston Community College

Lucia Vanderpool
Baptist College of Health Sciences

Michelle Vlaich-Lee
Greenville Technical College

Barry Walker
Monroe Community College

Rosalyn Warren
Enterprise State Community College

Sonia Washington
Prince George's Community College

Eric Weinstein
Suffolk County Community College

Jill Weiss
Florida International University

Lorna Wells
Salt Lake Community College

Rosalie Westerberg
Clover Park Technical College

Clemetee Whaley
Southwest Tennessee Community College

Kenneth Whitten
Florida State College of Jacksonville

MaryLou Wilson
Piedmont Technical College

John Windsor
University of North Texas

Kathy Winters
University of Tennessee, Chattanooga

Nancy Woolridge
Fullerton College

Jensen Zhao
Ball State University

Martha Zimmer
University of Evansville

Molly Zimmer
University of Evansville

Mary Anne Zlotow
College of DuPage

Matthew Zullo
Wake Technical Community College

Additionally, we'd like to thank our MyITLab team for their review and collaboration with our text authors:

LeeAnn Bates
MyITLab content author

Jennifer Hurley
MyITLab content author

Becca Lowe
Media Producer

Ralph Moore
MyITLab content author

Jerri Williams
MyITLab content author

Preface

Real World Problem Solving for Business and Beyond

The *Your Office* series provides the foundation for students to learn real world problem solving for use in business and beyond. Students are exposed to hands-on technical content that is woven into realistic business scenarios and focuses on using Microsoft Office as a decision-making tool.

Real world business exposure is a competitive advantage.

The series features a unique running business scenario—the Painted Paradise Resort & Spa—that connects all of the cases together and exposes students to using Microsoft Office to solve problems relating to business areas such as finance and accounting, production and operations, sales and marketing, and more. Look for the icons identifying the business application of each case.

Active learning occurs in context.

Each chapter introduces a realistic business case for students to complete via hands-on steps that are easily identified in blue-shaded boxes. Each blue box teaches a skill and comes complete with video, interactive, and live auto-graded support with automatic feedback.

Coursework that is relevant to students and their future careers.

Real World Advice, Real World Interview Videos, and Real World Success Stories are woven throughout the text and in the student resources. These share how former students use the Microsoft Office concepts they learned in this class and had success in a variety of careers.

Outcomes matter.

Whether it's getting a good grade in this course, learning how to use Excel to be successful in other courses, or learning business skills that will support success in a future job, every student has an outcome in mind. And outcomes matter. That is why we added a Business Unit opener to focus on the outcomes students will achieve by working through the cases and content of each chapter as well as the Capstone at the end of each unit.

No matter what career students may choose to pursue in life, this series will give them the foundation to succeed. And as they learn these valuable problem-solving and decision-making skills while becoming proficient in using Microsoft Office as a tool, they will achieve their intended outcomes, making a positive impact on their lives.

Key Features

Business Application Icons

Customer Service

Finance & Accounting

General Business

Human Resources

Information Technology

Production & Operations

Sales & Marketing

Research & Development

Soft Skills

The **Outcomes focus** allows students and instructors to focus on higher-level learning goals and how those can be achieved through particular objectives and skills.

- **Outcomes** are written at the course level and the business unit level.
- **Chapter Objectives list** identifies the learning objectives to be achieved as students work through the chapter. Page numbers are included for easy reference. These are revisited in the Concepts Check at the end of the chapter.
- **MOS Certification Guide** for instructors and students directs anyone interested in prepping for the MOS exam to the specific series resources to find all content required for the test.

The **real world focus** reminds students that what they are learning is practical and useful the minute they leave the classroom.

- **Real World Success** features in the chapter opener share anecdotes from real former students, describing how knowledge of Office has helped them be successful in their lives.
- **Real World Advice boxes** offer notes on best practices for general use of important Office skills. The goal is to advise students as a manager might in a future job.
- **Business Application icons** appear with every case in the text and clearly identify which business application students are being exposed to (finance, marketing, operations, etc.).

Features for active learning help students learn by doing and immerse them in the business world using Microsoft Office.

- **Blue boxes** represent the hands-on portion of the chapter and help students quickly identify what steps they need to take to complete the chapter Prepare Case. This material is easily distinguishable from explanatory text by the blue-shaded background.
- **Starting and ending files** appear before every case in the text. Starting files identify exactly which student data files are needed to complete each case. Ending files are provided to show students the naming conventions they should use when saving their files. Each file icon is color coded by application.
- **Side Note** conveys a brief tip or piece of information aligned visually with a step in the chapter, quickly providing key information to students completing that particular step.
- **Consider This** offers critical thinking questions and topics for discussion, set apart as a boxed feature, allowing students to step back from the project and think about the application of what they are learning and how these concepts might be used in the future.
- **Soft Skills icons** appear with other boxed features and identify specific places where students are being exposed to lessons on soft skills.

Study aids help students review and retain the material so they can recall it at a moment's notice.

- **Quick Reference boxes** summarize generic or alternative instructions on how to accomplish a task. This feature enables students to quickly find important skills.
- **Concept Check** review questions, which appear at the end of the chapter, require students to demonstrate their understanding of the objectives.

- **Visual Summary** offers a review of the objectives learned in the chapter using images from the completed solution file, mapped to the chapter objectives with callouts and page references, so students can easily find the section of text to refer to for a refresher.

Extensive cases allow students to progress from a basic understanding of Office through to proficiency.

- **Chapters all conclude with Practice, Problem Solve, and Perform Cases** to allow full mastery at the chapter level. Alternative versions of these cases are available in Instructor Resources.
- **Business Unit Capstones all include More Practice, Problem Solve, and Perform Cases** that require students to synthesize objectives from the two previous chapters to extend their mastery of the content. Alternative versions of these cases are available in Instructor Resources.
- **More Grader Projects** are offered with this edition, including Prepare cases as well as Problem Solve cases at both the chapter and business unit capstone levels.

Resources

Instructor Resources

The Instructor's Resource Center, available at www.pearsonhighered.com/irc includes the following:

- Annotated Solution Files with Scorecards, which assist with grading the Prepare, Practice, Problem Solve, and Perform cases
- Data and solution files
- Rubrics for Perform cases in Microsoft Word format, which enable instructors to easily grade open-ended assignments with no definite solution
- PowerPoint presentations with notes for each chapter
- Lesson plans that provide a detailed blueprint to achieve chapter learning objectives and outcomes and best use the unique structure of the business units
- Complete test bank, also available in TestGen format
- Additional Practice, Problem Solve, and Perform cases to provide variety and choice in exercises at both the chapter and business unit levels
- Scripted Lectures, which provide instructors with a lecture outline that mirrors the chapter Prepare case

Student Resources

Student Data Files

Access the student data files needed to complete the cases in this textbook at www.pearsonhighered.com/youroffice.

Available in MyITLab

- **Audio PowerPoints** provide a lecture review of the chapter content and include narration.
- **eText** is available in some MyITLab courses.

MyITLab for Office 2016 is a solution designed by professors for professors that allows easy delivery of Office courses with defensible assessment and outcomes-based training. The new **Your Office 2016** system will seamlessly integrate online assessment, training, and projects with MyITLab for Microsoft Office 2016!

Dear Students,

If you want an edge over the competition, make it personal. Whether you love sports, travel, the stock market, or ballet, your passion is personal to you. Capitalizing on your passion leads to success. You live in a global marketplace, and your competition is global. The honors students in China exceed the total number of students in North America. Skills can help set you apart, but passion will make you stand above. ***Your Office*** is the tool to harness your passion's true potential.

In prior generations, personalization in a professional setting was discouraged. You had a "work" life and a "home" life. As the Series Editor, I write to you about the vision for ***Your Office*** from my laptop, on my couch, in the middle of the night when inspiration struck me. My classroom and living room are my office. Life has changed from generations before us.

So, let's get personal. My degrees are not in technology, but chemistry and law. I helped put myself through school by working full time in various jobs, including a successful technology consulting business that continues today. My generation did not grow up with computers, but I did. My father was a network administrator for the military. So, I was learning to program in Basic before anyone had played Nintendo's Duck Hunt or Tetris. Technology has always been one of my passions from a young age. In fact, I now tell my husband: don't buy me jewelry for my birthday, buy me the latest gadget on the market!

In my first law position, I was known as the Office guru to the extent that no one gave me a law assignment for the first two months. Once I submitted the assignment, my supervisor remarked, "Wow, you don't just know how to leverage technology, but you really know the law too." I can tell you novel-sized stories from countless prior students in countless industries who gained an edge from using Office as a tool. Bringing technology to your passion makes you well rounded and a cut above the rest, no matter the industry or position.

I am most passionate about teaching, in particular teaching technology. I come from many generations of teachers, including my mother who is a kindergarten teacher. For over 12 years, I have found my dream job passing on my passion for teaching, technology, law, science, music, and life in general at the Kelley School of Business at Indiana University. I have tried to pass on the key to engaging passion to my students. I have helped them see what differentiates them from all the other bright students vying for the same jobs.

Microsoft Office is a tool. All of your competition will have learned Microsoft Office to some degree or another. Some will have learned it to an advanced level. Knowing Microsoft Office is important, but it is also fundamental. Without it, you will not be considered for a position.

Today, you step into your first of many future roles bringing Microsoft Office to your dream job working for Painted Paradise Resort & Spa. You will delve into the business side of the resort and learn how to use ***Your Office*** to maximum benefit.

Don't let the context of a business fool you. If you don't think of yourself as a business person, you have no need to worry. Whether you realize it or not, everything is business. If you want to be a nurse, you are entering the health care industry. If you want to be a football player in the NFL, you are entering the business of sports as entertainment. In fact, if you want to be a stay-at-home parent, you are entering the business of a family household where ***Your Office*** still gives you an advantage. For example, you will be able to prepare a budget in Excel and analyze what you need to do to afford a trip to Disney World!

At Painted Paradise Resort & Spa, you will learn how to make Office yours through four learning levels designed to maximize your understanding. You will Prepare, Practice, and Problem Solve your tasks. Then, you will astound when you Perform your new talents. You will be challenged through Consider This questions and gain insight through Real World Advice.

There is something more. You want success in what you are passionate about in your life. It is personal for you. In this position at Painted Paradise Resort & Spa, you will gain your personal competitive advantage that will stay with you for the rest of your life—***Your Office***.

Sincerely,
Amy Kinser
Series Editor

Painted Paradise

RESORT & SPA

Painted Paradise

Red Bluff Golf Course & Pro Shop

Welcome to the Team!

Welcome to your new office at Painted Paradise Resort & Spa, where we specialize in painting perfect getaways. As the Chief Technology Officer, I am excited to have staff dedicated to the Microsoft Office integration between all the areas of the resort. Our team is passionate about our paradise, and I hope you find this to be your dream position here!

Painted Paradise is a resort and spa in New Mexico catering to business people, romantics, families, and anyone who just needs to get away. Inside our resort are many distinct areas. Many of these areas operate as businesses in their own right but must integrate with the other areas of the resort. The main areas of the resort are as follows.

- The **Hotel** is overseen by our Chief Executive Officer, William Mattingly, and is at the core of our business. The hotel offers a variety of accommodations, ranging from individual rooms to a grand villa suite. Further, the hotel offers packages including spa, golf, and special events.

  Room rates vary according to size, season, demand, and discount. The hotel has discounts for typical groups, such as AARP. The hotel also has a loyalty program where guests can earn free nights based on frequency of visits. Guests may charge anything from the resort to the room.

- **Red Bluff Golf Course** is a private world-class golf course and pro shop. The golf course has services such as golf lessons from the famous golf pro John Schilling and playing packages. Also, the golf course attracts local residents. This requires variety in pricing schemes to accommodate both local and hotel guests. The pro shop sells many retail items online.

  The golf course can also be reserved for special events and tournaments. These special events can be in conjunction with a wedding, conference, meetings, or other events covered by the event planning and catering area of the resort.

- **Turquoise Oasis Spa** is a full-service spa. Spa services include haircuts, pedicures, massages, facials, body wraps, waxing, and various other spa services—typical to exotic. Further, the spa offers private consultation, weight training (in the fitness center), a water bar, meditation areas, and steam rooms. Spa services are offered both in the spa and in the resort guest's room.

  Turquoise Oasis Spa uses top-of-the-line products and some house-brand products. The retail side offers products ranging from candles to age-defying home treatments. These products can also be purchased online. Many of the hotel guests who fall in love with the house-brand soaps, lotions, candles, and other items appreciate being able to buy more at any time.

  The spa offers a multitude of packages including special hotel room packages that include spa treatments. Local residents also use the spa. So, the spa guests are not limited to hotel guests. Thus, the packages also include pricing attractive to the local community.

- **Painted Treasures Gift Shop** has an array of items available for purchase, from toiletries to clothes to presents for loved ones back home including a healthy section of kids' toys for traveling business people. The gift shop sells a small sampling from the spa, golf course pro shop, and local New Mexico culture. The gift shop also has a small section of snacks and drinks. The gift shop has numerous part-time employees including students from the local college.
- The **Event Planning & Catering** area is central to attracting customers to the resort. From weddings to conferences, the resort is a popular destination. The resort has a substantial number of staff dedicated to planning, coordinating, setting up, catering, and maintaining these events. The resort has several facilities that can accommodate large groups. Packages and prices vary by size, room, and other services such as catering. Further, the Event Planning & Catering team works closely with local vendors for floral decorations, photography, and other event or wedding typical needs. However, all catering must go through the resort (no outside catering permitted). Lastly, the resort stocks several choices of decorations, table arrangements, and centerpieces. These range from professional, simple, themed, and luxurious.
- **Indigo5** and the **Silver Moon Lounge**, a world-class restaurant and lounge that is overseen by the well-known Chef Robin Sanchez. The cuisine is balanced and modern. From steaks to pasta to local southwestern meals, Indigo5 attracts local patrons in addition to resort guests. While the catering function is separate from the restaurant—though menu items may be shared—the restaurant does support all room service for the resort. The resort also has smaller food venues onsite such as the Terra Cotta Brew coffee shop in the lobby.

Currently, these areas are using Office to various degrees. In some areas, paper and pencil are still used for most business functions. Others have been lucky enough to have some technology savvy team members start Microsoft Office Solutions.

Using your skills, I am confident that you can help us integrate and use Microsoft Office on a whole new level! I hope you are excited to call Painted Paradise Resort & Spa ***Your Office***.

Looking forward to working with you more closely!

Aidan Matthews
Aidan Matthews
Chief Technology Officer

Microsoft Project 2016

Chapter 1 | PLAN A PROJECT

OBJECTIVES

Prepare Case

Painted Paradise Golf Resort—Annual Charity Golf Tournament

The Painted Paradise Golf Resort will be holding its annual charity golf tournament to raise money for the purchase of textbooks to be donated to selected elementary schools in Santa Fe, New Mexico. The vice president (VP) of special projects, Julie Rholfing, has assigned Patti Rochelle, the tournament planning manager, to be the project manager of this event. Julie has asked Patti to use Microsoft Project 2016 to begin planning this year's tournament. Before Patti can begin entering in the tasks that need to be completed for the tournament, she must first understand the Project 2016 window, Project 2016 views, and the Project 2016 calendar. You will help Patti get started with the setup of this project.

Nmedia/fotolia

Student data files needed for this workshop:

 No data file needed

You will save your file as:

 pm01ch01CharityGolfTournament_LastFirst.mpp

Preparing a Project Plan

It is common today to work with teams or with groups of people to reach a desired outcome. Outcomes can be reached by brainstorming, communicating, planning, and then completing the plan as defined. Whether you work on a team or work alone, taking the time to plan before acting may help improve your chances of success. The process of planning and following through with a plan is project management.

In this chapter, you will be introduced to project management terminology and processes. Then you will learn how to get started using Project 2016, a project planning application often used to help create detailed project plans.

Understand Project Management and Microsoft Project Terminology

Project management is a process of initiating, planning, executing, monitoring, and closing a project's tasks and resources in order to accomplish a project's goal. A **project goal** is the desired result of a project upon completion. A project's goal is met when project tasks are completed on time, on budget, and within the scope of a given project. All projects, large or small, should follow the project management process groups, as shown in Table 1, to reach project success.

Process Group	Responsibility
Initiating	Set a project goal; identify a project schedule; define a project budget
Planning	Enter project tasks; determine task relationships; assign project resources
Executing	Produce results; report results
Monitoring and Control	Update tasks as in progress or completed; manage resources
Closing	Analyze performance; prepare final reports

Table 1 Project management process groups

REAL WORLD ADVICE **Resources for Project Managers**

If you are new to project management, you are not alone! There are many resources available for project managers who seek assistance with project management information and practices. One resource is *A Guide to the Project Management Body of Knowledge* (*PMBOK® Guide*). This guide defines project management terminology and presents industry standard guidelines for managing projects.

Another resource is the Project Management Institute (PMI). By joining PMI, project managers can get access to PMI publications, stay updated on global standards, have networking opportunities with other project managers, and have access to project management tools and templates to help manage projects. PMI also provides training and access to the Project Management Professional (PMP) certification.

Office.microsoft.com offers videos on Project 2016. This is a helpful resource for project managers who may be new to using the software.

A **project manager** is the person responsible for overseeing all the details of the project plan. The project manager works to create a plan that will lead to project success. A project manager also motivates project team members to achieve the project goals. Project managers may choose to use project planning software such as Project 2016 to help them plan and achieve project success. Project planning software keeps track of tasks, the duration to complete tasks, scheduled dates, project resources, and project costs organized in one location for a more efficient way of managing a project. It is a tool that allows project managers to track, analyze, and summarize project information.

In order to use project planning software, it is important to understand terminology associated with the software. A **task** is an activity that is completed to reach a project goal. For example, when planning for a charity golf tournament, a task could be "set tournament date and time" or "prepare preliminary budget."

Task duration is the prediction of time it will take to complete a task. Task durations in Project can be entered in minutes, hours, days, weeks, months, and years. For example, it may be determined it takes two days to "set tournament date and time" but two weeks to "prepare preliminary budget."

A **predecessor task** is a task that must be completed before the next task can start. A task that has a predecessor is called a **successor task**. Project managers often use the term task dependency when referring to how the predecessor or successor tasks are connected. A **task dependency** is a relationship between two tasks that defines which task(s) have to finish before the next task(s) can start. A task dependency is often called a task link.

Since not all tasks are the same in a project, scheduling them the same way may not be an option. Therefore, some tasks may have constraints applied. A **constraint** is a limitation set on a task. For example, a task of "create tournament website" may have a constraint of "finish no later than" a certain date to ensure the website is up and running in time to gather enough registrations for the event. Constraints on tasks affect how the task is scheduled. Setting constraints on tasks will determine how Project 2016 will schedule a task. Besides setting specific date constraints on a task, the following task constraints can be set on an individual task:

- As late as possible
- As soon as possible
- Finish no earlier than
- Finish no later than
- Must finish on
- Must start on
- Start no earlier than
- Start no later than

A **resource** is work, a material, or a cost associated with a project task. **Work resources** are people and equipment. **Material resources** are resources consumed during the project. **Cost resources** are independent costs associated with a task. For example, a task of "provide transportation from the airport" may have a cost of "$2,000 limousine service." Project managers assign resources to project tasks to help determine a project's schedule and a project's cost.

The **scope** of a project is what must be completed to deliver a specific product or service. The project scope includes the meeting of project goals, tasks, and deadlines set. Project managers use planning software such as Project 2016 to prevent deviating from the scope of a project.

A **milestone** is a task that is used to communicate project progress or mark a significant point in a project such as the end of a project phase. Milestones are entered into the Project 2016 software as a task with zero duration. For example, a milestone for the charity golf tournament could be "tournament website goes live." By default, Project 2016 displays a milestone as a diamond in the Gantt chart. A **Gantt chart** is a graphical representation of tasks where tasks are shown against a timeline displayed as horizontal bars in which the length of the bar is determined by the activities durations and start/finish dates.

Starting a Project

You have been asked to work on the planning team for the Painted Paradise Golf Resort Charity Golf Tournament. Your role on the team will be to set up a project plan in Project 2016. To get started, you will open and save a project.

In this exercise, you will start, save, close, and open a project.

To Begin, Save, Close, and Open a Project

a. On the taskbar, click **Ask me anything** or **Search the web and Windows**. Type proj.

b. Click **Project 2016** in the search results. The Project Start screen is displayed.

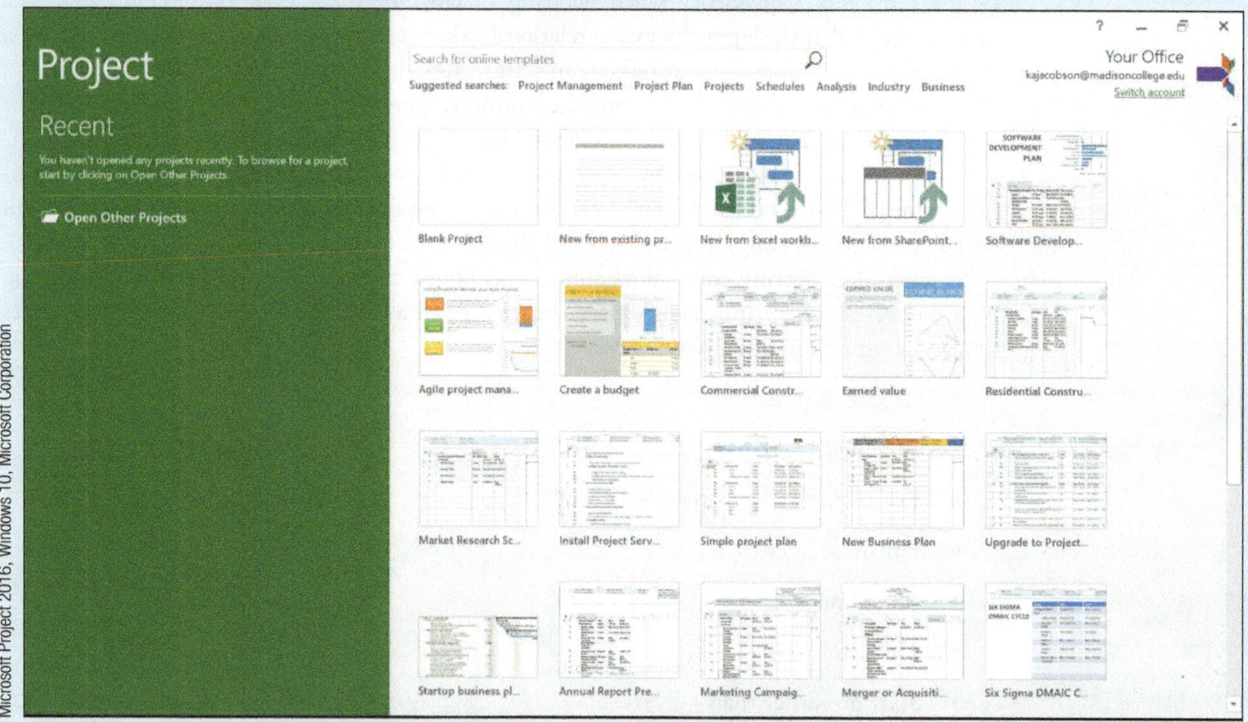

Figure 1 Creating a new project

c. Click **Blank Project** to open a new blank project.

d. Click the **File** tab, and then click **Save As**.

e. Click **Browse**, and then navigate to the location where you are saving your files.

f. Click in the **File name** box, and then type pm01ch01CharityGolfTournament_LastFirst, using your last name and first name. Click **Save**.

g. Click the **File** tab, and then click **Close**. The project file will close, but the Project application will remain open.

Troubleshooting

If Project 2016 closed completely, perform steps a–b again. Click the File tab, and then click Open. Browse to where you store your files, and then click pm01ch01CharityGolfTournament_LastFirst.mpp. Click Open. You could also perform step a–b again, and then click the file name in the left pane to reopen the file.

h. In the Navigation Pane, click **Open**, and then browse, if necessary, to locate **pm01ch01CharityGolfTournament_LastFirst.mpp**.

i. Click **pm01ch01CharityGolfTournament_LastFirst.mpp**, and then click **Open** to reopen your project file.

Explore the Project 2016 Window

When opening a new Project 2016 file, the default view is the Gantt Chart view, as shown in Figure 2. There may be slight differences with the view of your Project 2016 window. You will learn how to adjust the Project 2016 window in this chapter.

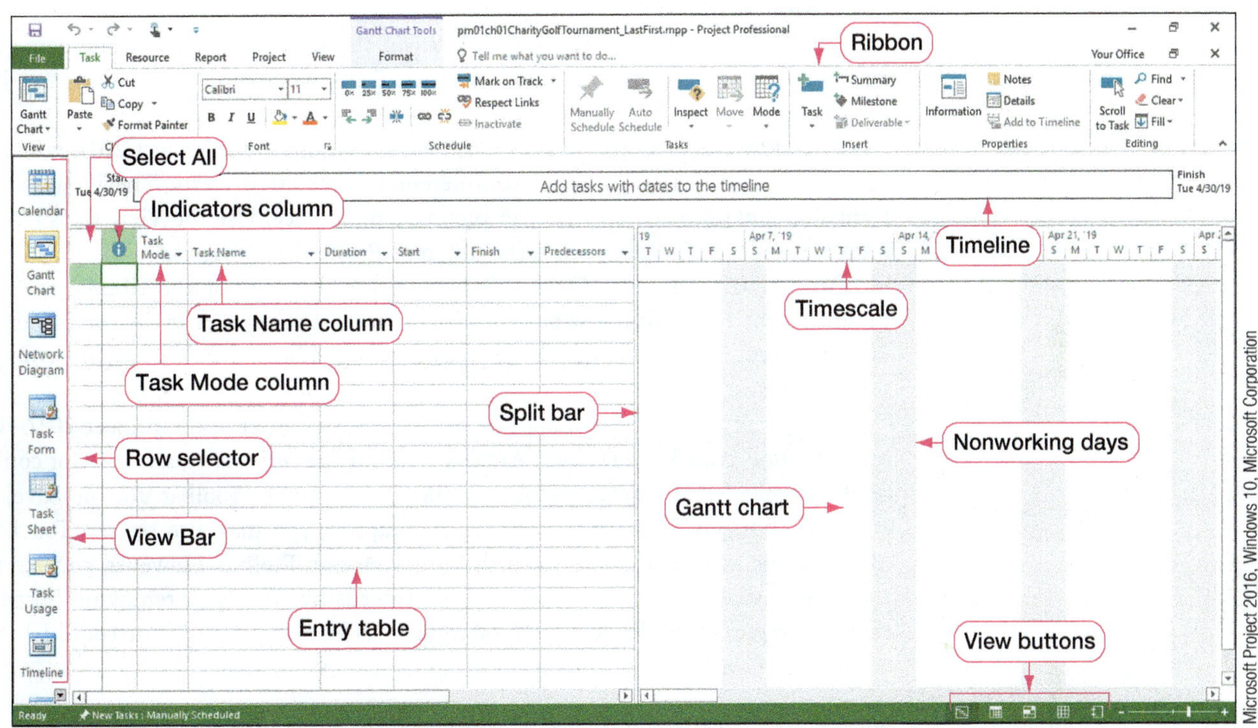

Figure 2 Project 2016 window

Gantt Chart view lists task details in the Entry table on the left side of the window and displays each task graphically in the Gantt chart on the right side of the window. In the Gantt chart, a project's tasks are shown against a timeline. The activities are displayed as horizontal bars in which the length of the bar is determined by the duration of the activities and start/finish dates. The **Entry table** is used to enter task information and is located to the left of the Gantt chart. The Entry table contains columns and rows similar to Microsoft Excel 2016. The Entry table is used to record project tasks, durations, predecessors, and resources. Each task becomes a new row in the Entry table. A vertical **split bar** separates the Entry table and the Gantt chart. If desired, the split bar can be dragged to resize the panes.

A **row selector** is the box containing the row number of a task in the Entry table. The **Select All** button is a button that selects all tasks and task information in the Entry table.

The **Timeline** is a visual representation of the project from start to finish. The Timeline is displayed above the Entry table and Gantt chart and below the ribbon. You can choose what to display on the Timeline. If the Timeline is added, it will be visible in the other Project 2016 views as well. The **timescale** is located above the Gantt chart. The timescale displays the unit of measure that determines the length of the Gantt bars in the Gantt chart.

The light gray vertical bars in the Gantt chart represent nonworking days. A **nonworking day** is a day during which Project 2016 will not schedule work to occur. Therefore, if a task starts at 8:00 AM on a Friday and has a three-day duration, Project 2016 would schedule the task for Friday 8:00 AM–5:00 PM, Monday 8:00 AM–5:00 PM, and Tuesday 8:00 AM–5:00 PM.

The **Indicators column** is a column in the Entry table that will display an icon that provides further information about a task. For example, if the constraint of a specific date is set to a task, a calendar icon would appear in the Indicators column.

The **Task Mode column** indicates the mode in which Project 2016 will schedule tasks, either manually or automatically. A task's mode can be adjusted by using the Task Mode arrow within the Task Mode column.

The **Task Name column** is a location in the Entry table where the name of each task is entered. One task is entered per row. Task names should be descriptive but not too wordy.

The **View Bar** is a vertical bar on the left-hand side of the Project 2016 window that contains buttons for quick access to different Project 2016 views. The View Bar can be turned on and off based on a project planner's preference. Use the View Bar's navigation buttons to easily navigate within the different Project 2016 views.

Project 2016 uses the Office 2016 design and layout of the ribbon as shown in Figure 2. The ribbon is a row of tabs with buttons that appears at the top of the Project 2016 window. The ribbon may be open as shown in Figure 2 or may also be collapsed to save screen space.

The Quick Access Toolbar appears in the top-left corner of the Project 2016 window as shown in Figure 3. The **Quick Access Toolbar** is a series of small icons for commonly used commands. The default icons on the Quick Access Toolbar are the Save, Undo, and Redo buttons. If using a touch-enabled laptop, you may also see the Touch/Mouse Mode button as a default button on the Quick Access Toolbar. However, you can modify the Quick Access Toolbar to fit your project needs by adding or removing buttons. For example, reports from Project 2016 often need to be printed, and time could be saved by adding the Print Preview button to the Quick Access Toolbar.

Modifying the Quick Access Toolbar and Collapsing the Ribbon

Since you are sharing the project with other team members, you want to be sure you always have proper spelling in your project plan. Project 2016 does not automatically check for proper spelling; therefore, you decide to add the Spelling button to your project's Quick Access Toolbar.

In this exercise, you will modify the Quick Access Toolbar and collapse the ribbon.

To Modify the Quick Access Toolbar and Collapse the Ribbon

SIDE NOTE

View Bar

If the View Bar is not visible on the left-hand side of the Project 2016 window, right-click the vertical text GANTT CHART on the left-hand side of the window and click View Bar.

a. Click the **Quick Access Toolbar** arrow.

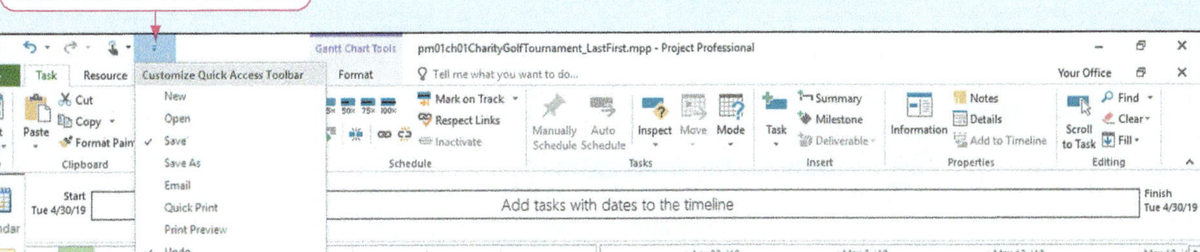

Microsoft Project 2016, Windows 10, Microsoft Corporation

Figure 3 Quick Access Toolbar shortcut menu

b. Click **More Commands**.

c. Click the **Choose commands from** arrow.

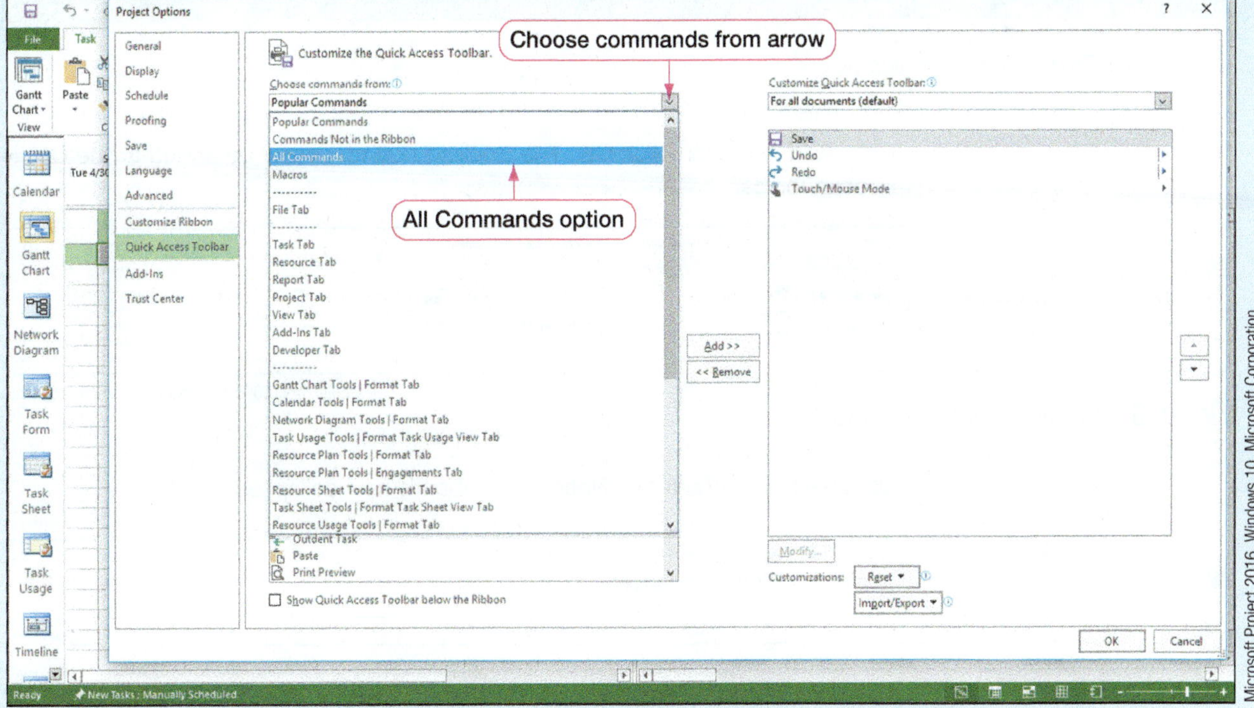

Microsoft Project 2016, Windows 10, Microsoft Corporation

Figure 4 Project Options dialog box to customize the Quick Access Toolbar

SIDE NOTE

Modifying the Quick Access Toolbar

You can also add buttons to the Quick Access Toolbar by right-clicking a button on the ribbon and clicking **Add to Quick Access Toolbar**.

d. Click **All Commands**, and then scroll through the list of commands. Click **Spelling**.

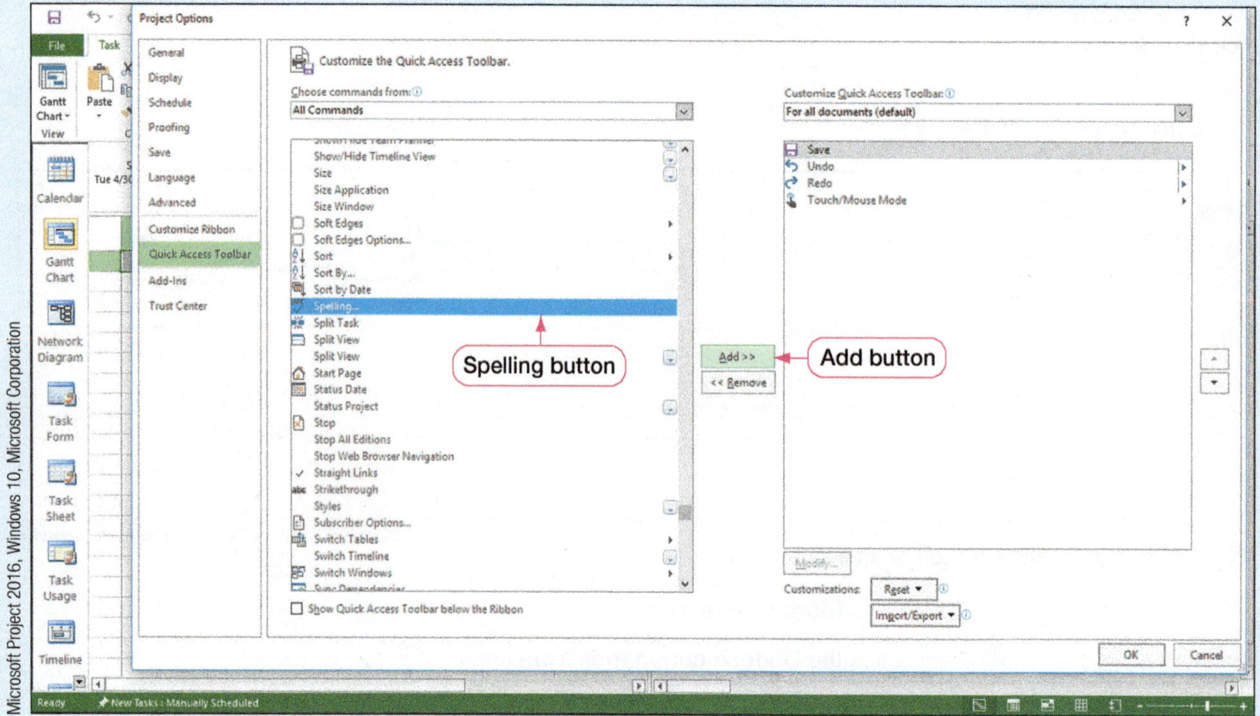

Microsoft Project 2016, Windows 10, Microsoft Corporation

Figure 5 Project Options dialog box

e. Click **Add**, and then click **OK**. The Spelling button will be added to the Quick Access Toolbar.

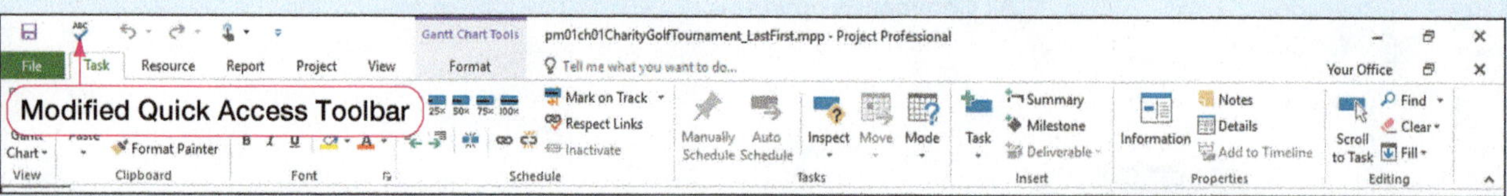

Microsoft Project 2016, Windows 10, Microsoft Corporation

Figure 6 Modified Quick Access Toolbar

f. Double-click the **Task** tab. Notice the ribbon is now collapsed.

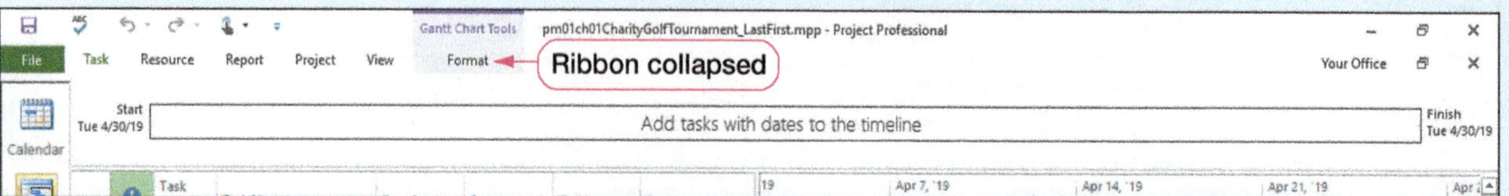

Microsoft Project 2016, Windows 10, Microsoft Corporation

Figure 7 Ribbon collapsed

g. Double-click the **Task** tab again to show the ribbon.

h. Right-click the **Task** tab.

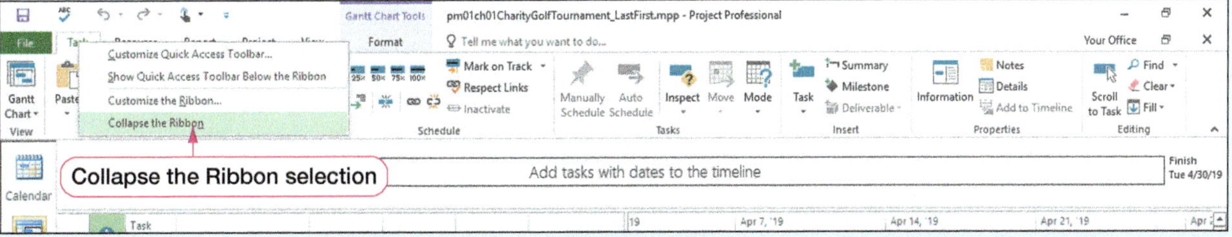

Figure 8 Collapsing the ribbon

i. Click **Collapse the Ribbon**. The ribbon is now collapsed.

j. Right-click the **Task** tab again. Click **Collapse the Ribbon** to show the ribbon.

k. On the Quick Access Toolbar, click **Save**.

Prepare a Project Schedule

Project 2016 has a complex scheduling engine, so to understand how it will calculate a project's schedule, it is important to review the Project Information dialog box. The Project Information button is found in the Properties group on the Project tab. Click the Project Information button to open the Project Information dialog box.

The **Project Information dialog box** is used to update various aspects of a project such as the project's start date or finish date, current date, status date, project base calendar, etc. Before entering specific task information for a project, the project's information should be identified. First, one must select whether the project will be scheduled from Start date or from Finish date. Project **Start date** is the date Project 2016 uses to schedule tasks that will calculate the project's Finish date. Scheduling a project by Start date is the most commonly used scheduling method. Project **Finish date** is the date Project 2016 uses to schedule tasks that will calculate the project's Start date. Scheduling projects by Finish date, while less common, helps determine the latest date a project can start and still finish by that finish date. A project can only be scheduled by Start date or Finish date, not by both. Start date is the default in the software.

If a project is set to calculate by Start date, as shown in Figure 9, all tasks will be scheduled to begin as soon as possible. If you schedule by Start date, Project 2016 will

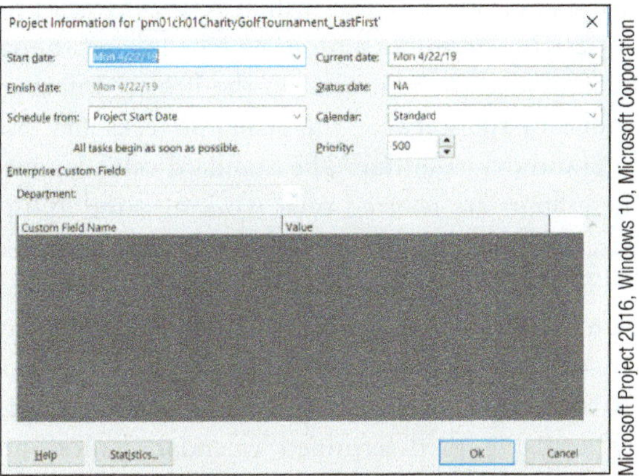

Figure 9 Project Information dialog box

calculate when the project should finish. The Finish date would be determined by individual tasks, task durations, task predecessors, and resources assigned to tasks.

If a project is set to calculate by Finish date, all tasks will be scheduled to begin as late as possible, as shown in Figure 10. If the project is scheduled by Finish date, Project 2016 will determine the date you must begin your project to be able to complete the project by the set finish date. The Start date would be determined by individual tasks, task durations, task predecessors, and resources assigned to tasks.

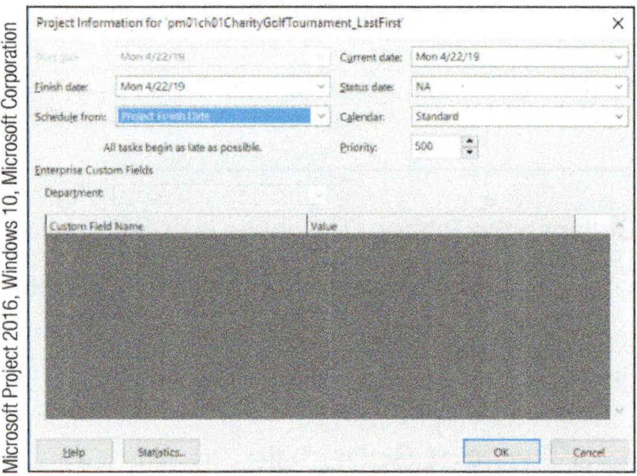

Microsoft Project 2016, Windows 10, Microsoft Corporation

Figure 10 Project Scheduled by Finish date

CONSIDER THIS | Scheduling by Finish Date

While most projects are scheduled by Start date, you may need to schedule your project by Finish date to determine the latest date you can start the project. If you schedule a project by Finish date, it may be wise to switch back to scheduling from the Start date when work on the project begins. Projects scheduled by Start date help to show the progress of your project and to keep track of factors and situations that might cause the Finish date to change.

The **Current date** is today's date as determined by your computer's clock. The current date can be changed by entering a new date in the Current date section of the Project Information dialog box or by clicking the arrow for Current date and selecting a new date.

The **Status date** is the date set to run reports on a project's progress. For example, if a weekly team meeting is on Monday morning to review the current status of the project for the week ahead, the Status date may be set to the Friday before the Monday morning meeting. To run status reports, a project baseline must be set. A **baseline** is a record of each task at a point in time from which you will track project progress.

Project 2016 determines a project's schedule off the base calendar. A base calendar is the calendar applied to the project in the Project Information dialog box and provides a template for how the software will schedule tasks and resources. The default base calendar is the **Standard calendar**. The Standard calendar specifies hours in which work can occur. These hours are referred to as working time. If a project is set to schedule based on the Standard calendar, all tasks and each resource are scheduled according to this calendar. The Standard calendar is based on a 40-hour work week with an 8-hour work day (8:00 AM to 12:00 PM and 1:00 PM to 5:00 PM) Monday through Friday. Saturday and Sunday are considered nonworking days. If you recall, nonworking days are days which Project 2016 will not schedule any work to be completed.

Other available predetermined calendar choices are shown in Figure 11. The **24 Hours calendar** assigns a schedule with continuous work. This type of calendar may be assigned to a project that must work around the clock—for example, a mechanical process. The **Night Shift calendar** assigns a schedule that is sometimes referred to as the "graveyard" shift schedule of Monday night through Saturday morning, 11:00 PM to 8:00 AM, with an hour off for break time.

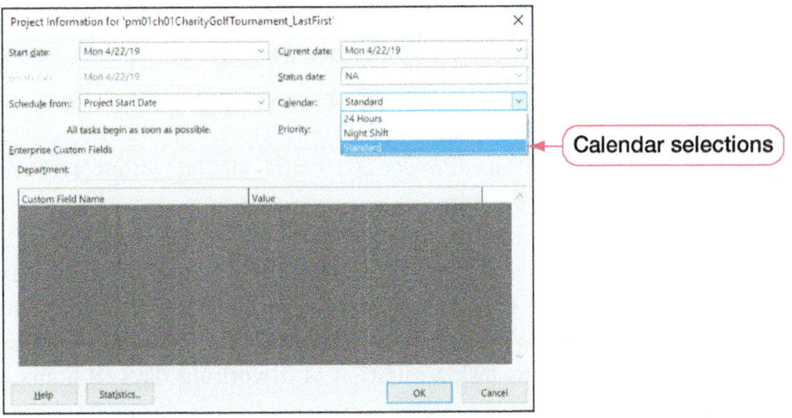

Figure 11 Project calendar choices

Project managers can set the priority of a project in the Project Information dialog box. The priority of a project is determined on a scale of 1 to 1,000 with 1 being the lowest priority and 1,000 being the highest priority. A project with a priority of 1,000 is considered more important than a project with a priority of 100. Priorities are only used when project managers are trying to balance resource assignments among tasks and projects.

Preparing a Project Schedule Using the Project Information Dialog Box

Patti Rochelle has asked you to help determine the date for the charity golf tournament. Therefore, you will use Project 2016 to help calculate a possible tournament date. You will begin planning the project at the end of April; therefore, Patti has asked you to plan the project start date as of April 30, 2019.

In this exercise, you will change project information.

SIDE NOTE

Selecting a Start Date

You can also select a start date by using the Start date arrow and scrolling through the calendar until you see the desired date.

To Change the Project Information

a. Click the **Project** tab, and then click **Project Information**.

b. In the Start date field, type April 30, 2019. In the Current date field, type April 23, 2019.

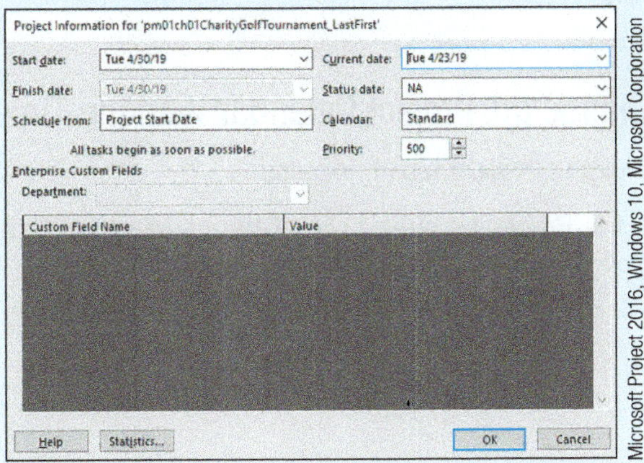

Figure 12 Project Information dialog box with modified start and current date

c. Verify the **Standard Calendar** is selected, and then click **OK**.

d. **Save** the project.

Modify a Project Calendar

Once a base calendar has been assigned to a project, it is important the base calendar accurately reflects the working time hours a project team is available to work on the project. If not, Project 2016 will calculate an incorrect project schedule that may lead to a project's failure.

Take the charity golf tournament as an example. If the base calendar of the project is the Standard calendar, Project 2016 will schedule all tasks on a 40-hour-per-week working time schedule. If the task of "prepare preliminary budget" is entered with a 1-week duration, Project 2016 will schedule 40 hours of work to the task. Project 2016 will assign this task a duration of 5 working days (8 hours per day for 5 days for a total of 40 hours).

Now imagine there are only 20 hours available each week to dedicate to this project due to other commitments (not the 40 hours as set by the base Standard calendar). If this is the case, the Standard calendar must be modified to reflect the actual working time available. If modifications to the calendar are not made, Project 2016 will schedule the work incorrectly. To review how Project 2016 schedules tasks based on a project's calendar, refer to Table 2.

Calendar	Task Duration	Working Time
Standard calendar with a 40-hour work week	1 week duration = 40 hours of work	5 days (40 hours/8 hours per day = 5 days)
Modified Standard calendar with a 20-hour work week	1 week duration = 40 hours of work	10 days (40 hours/4 hours per day = 10 days)

Table 2 Duration and start or finish dates

Modifying a Project Calendar

It is possible to adjust the Standard calendar to meet your project needs. Patti Rochelle, the project manager for the charity golf tournament, and her project team are only available to work on this project Tuesday through Friday 8:00 AM to 12:00 PM (16 hours per week). You will need to adjust the base Standard calendar to reflect the actual working time available.

To Change the Project Calendar Working Time

a. Click the **Project** tab, if necessary.

b. In the Properties group, click **Change Working Time** to open the Change Working Time dialog box for the Standard calendar.

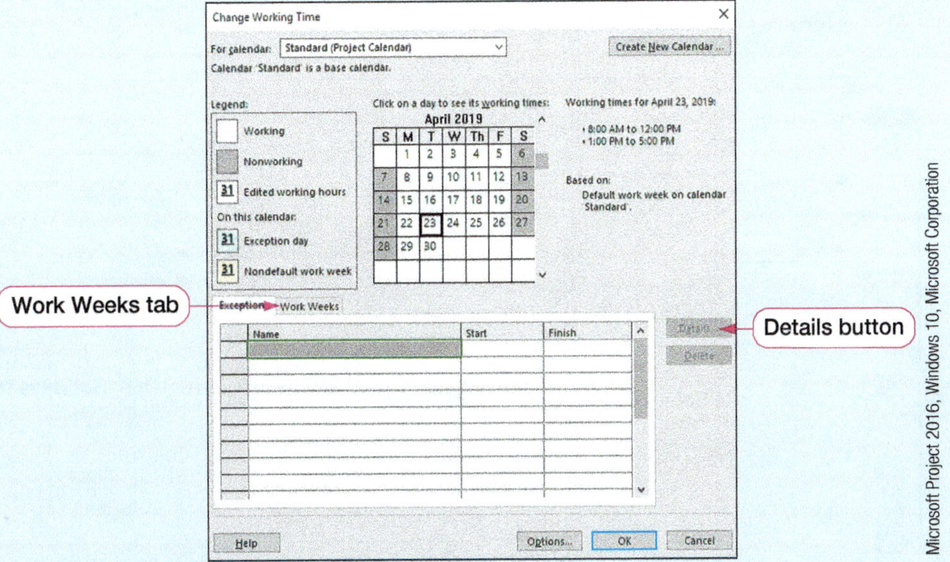

Microsoft Project 2016, Windows 10, Microsoft Corporation

Figure 13 Change Working Time dialog box

c. Click the **Work Weeks** tab in the bottom section of the dialog box, and then click the **Details** button. The Details for dialog box opens.

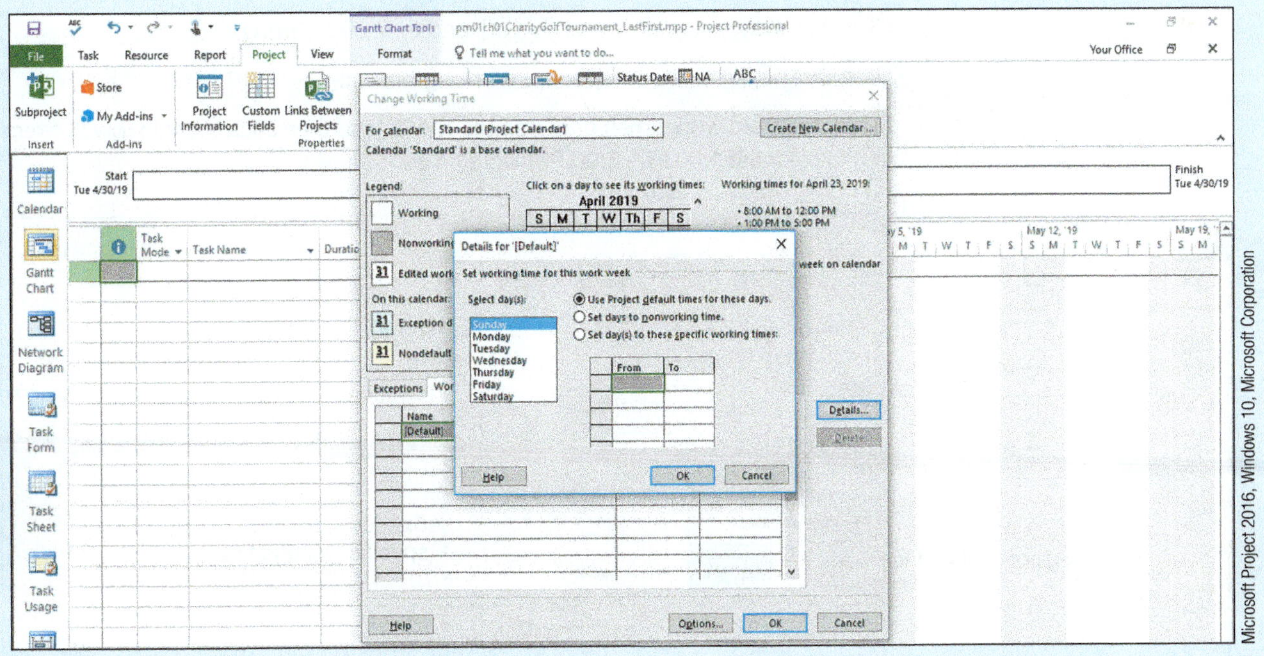

Microsoft Project 2016, Windows 10, Microsoft Corporation

Figure 14 Calendar Details dialog box

d. In the Details for dialog box, click **Monday**, and then click **Set days to nonworking time.**

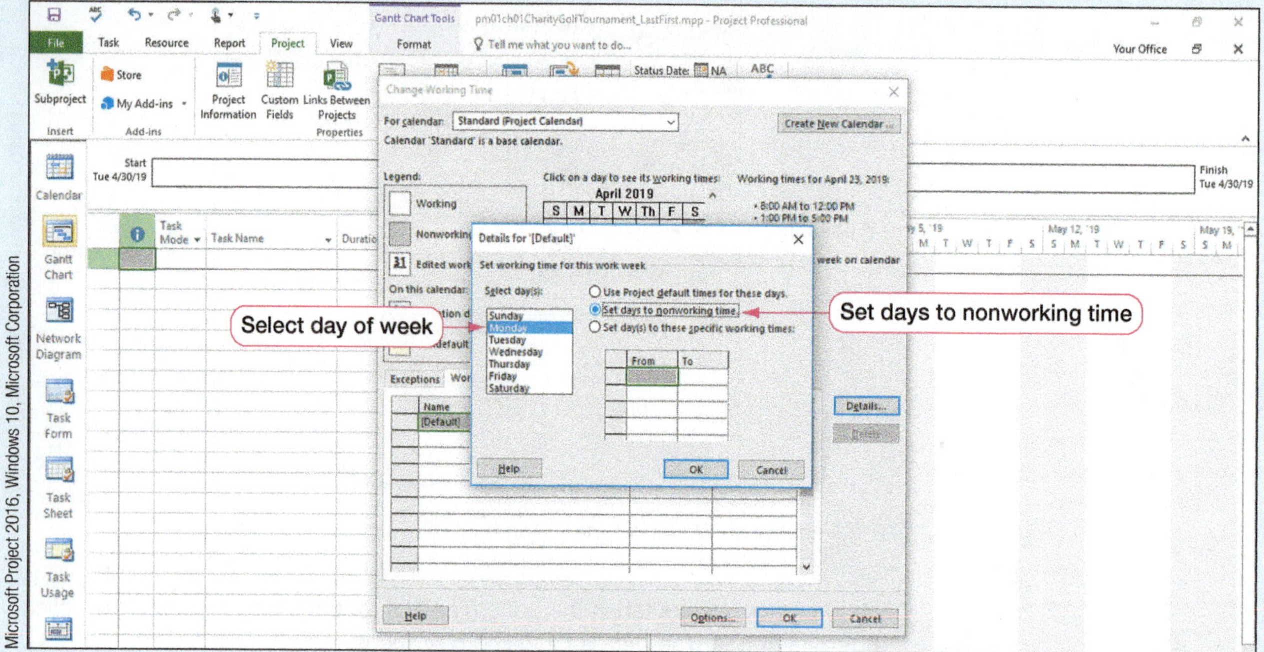

Figure 15 Mondays set to nonworking days

e. Click **Tuesday**, press and hold Shift, and then click **Friday**.

f. Click **Set day(s) to these specific working times:**.

g. In the specified work times grid, point to row 2, and then click the **2** in row 2. Press Del to clear the 1:00 PM–5:00 PM work times.

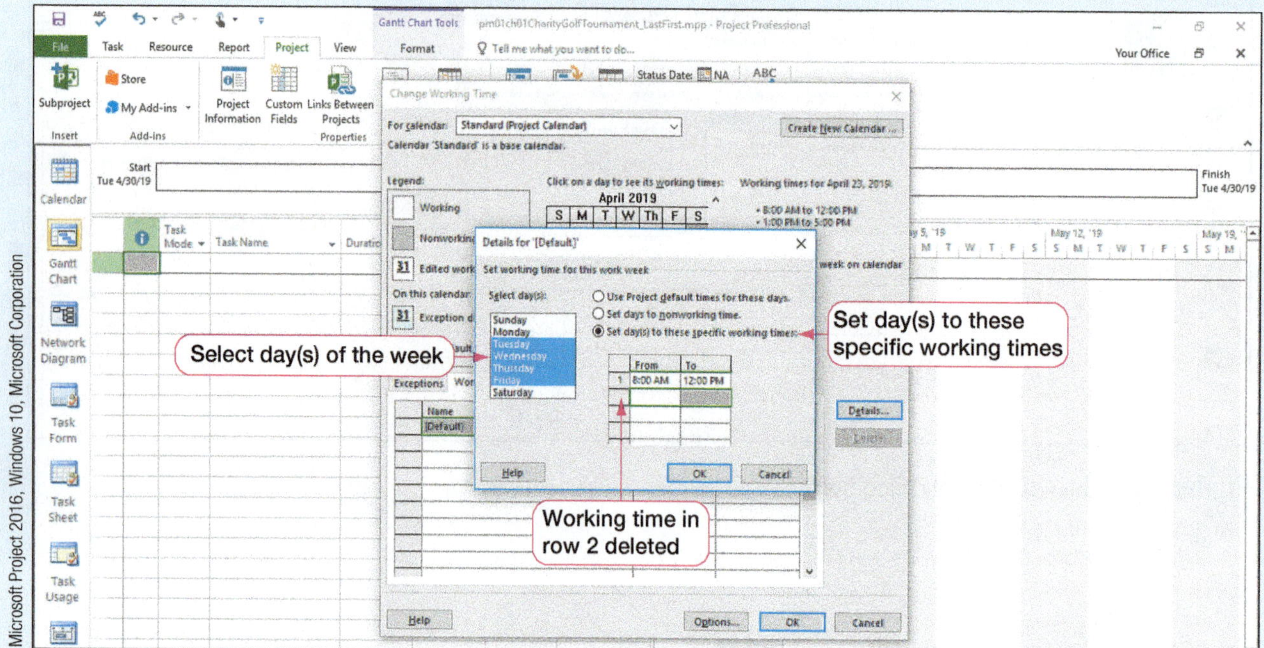

Figure 16 Specific working time for days of the week

h. Click **OK**. The base calendar has now been changed to reflect that Mondays are nonworking days and Tuesday–Friday working hours are 8:00 AM–12:00 PM.

> **Troubleshooting**
>
> If necessary, scroll through the calendar in the Change Working Time dialog box until you see April 2019.

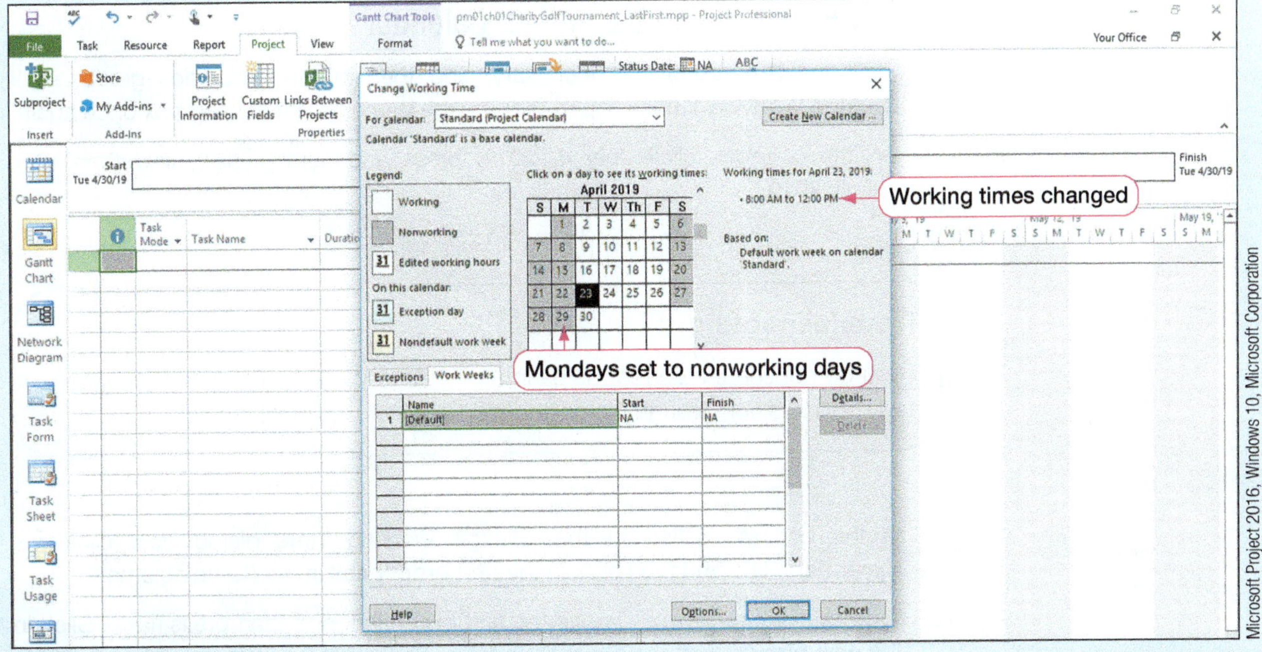

Figure 17 Change Working Time dialog box

i. Click **OK** to close the Change Working Time dialog box, and then **Save** the project.

REAL WORLD ADVICE — **Working with Microsoft Project 2016 Around the Globe**

In today's global economy, it is likely you will work for a company that has locations in different states or even countries. Therefore, when preparing your project calendar, consideration must be given to where your project team members reside. Although many countries consider a typical work week Monday through Friday with Saturday and Sunday as nonworking days, some countries may work on a 6-day work week or even a 4-day work week. So that Project 2016 has accurate information when creating a project's schedule, it is important that the base calendar accurately reflects the availability of all project team members.

Adding Exceptions to the Project Calendar

Since all organizations do not observe the same holidays, Project 2016 does not include holidays in the Project calendars. If your organization and/or project team observes holidays, you should account for them in the project's calendar. If holidays are not accounted for, Project 2016 cannot factor them into the project's schedule and therefore may miscalculate the project schedule by assigning work on a nonworking day. Holidays can be added to a project calendar by creating exceptions to a project's base calendar.

Patti Rochelle, the project manager for the charity golf tournament, has clarified that the following holidays will be observed by the project staff: July 4-5, 2019, and September 3, 2019. Therefore, you will need to make these days nonworking days in the project's calendar by adding exceptions to the project's calendar.

In this exercise, you will add exceptions to the project calendar.

To Add Exceptions to the Project Calendar

a. Click the **Project** tab, if necessary, and then in the Properties group, click **Change Working Time** to open the Change Working Time dialog box once again.

b. On the calendar, click **July 4, 2019**, press and hold Shift, and then click **July 5, 2019**.

Troubleshooting

If you do not see the correct dates in the Change Working Time calendar, you may need to scroll through the calendar until July 2019 is visible.

c. In the bottom section of the Change Working Time dialog box, click the **Exceptions** tab, and then click in the **first empty cell** in the Name column.

d. Type US Independence Day as the first exception, and then press Tab. Click in the next blank row of the Exceptions table. Verify that the dates of July 4-5, 2019, have been changed to nonworking days.

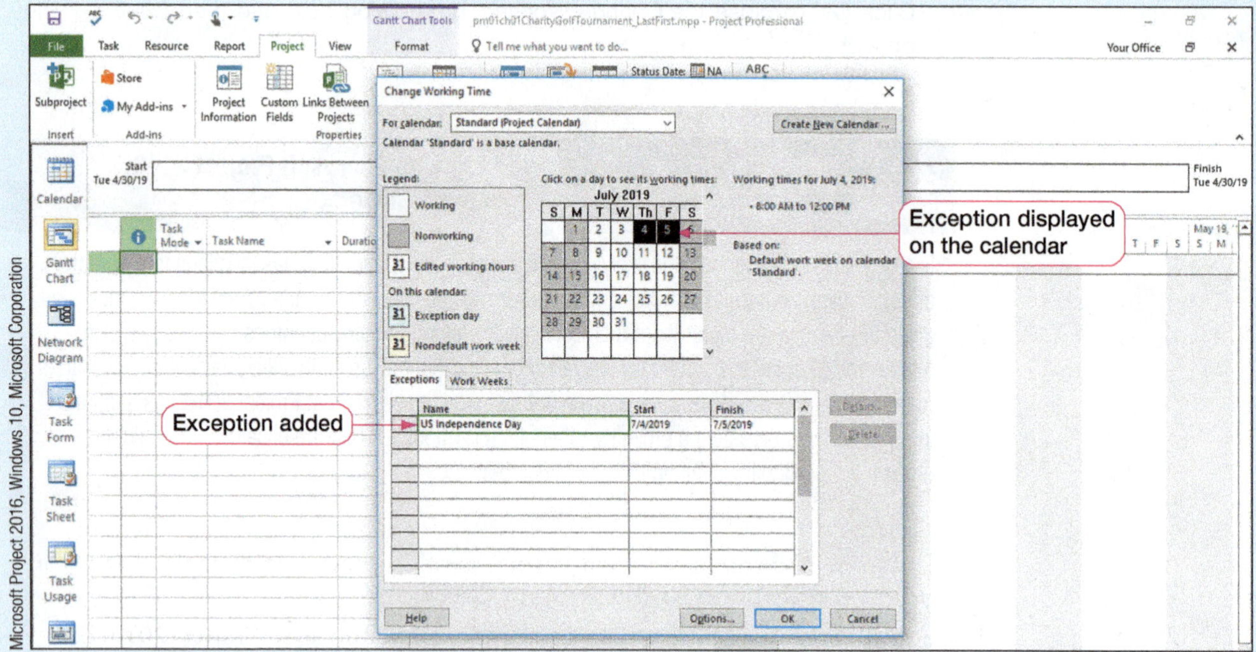

Figure 18 Calendar exception added

e. Click in the **next empty cell** in the Exceptions Name column, and then type Company Picnic.

f. Press Tab, and then click in the **Start** column.

g. Click the **Start** column arrow to display the date picker, change the Start date to September 3, 2019, and then press Tab. Click the **Finish** column to verify that September 3, 2019, is a nonworking day.

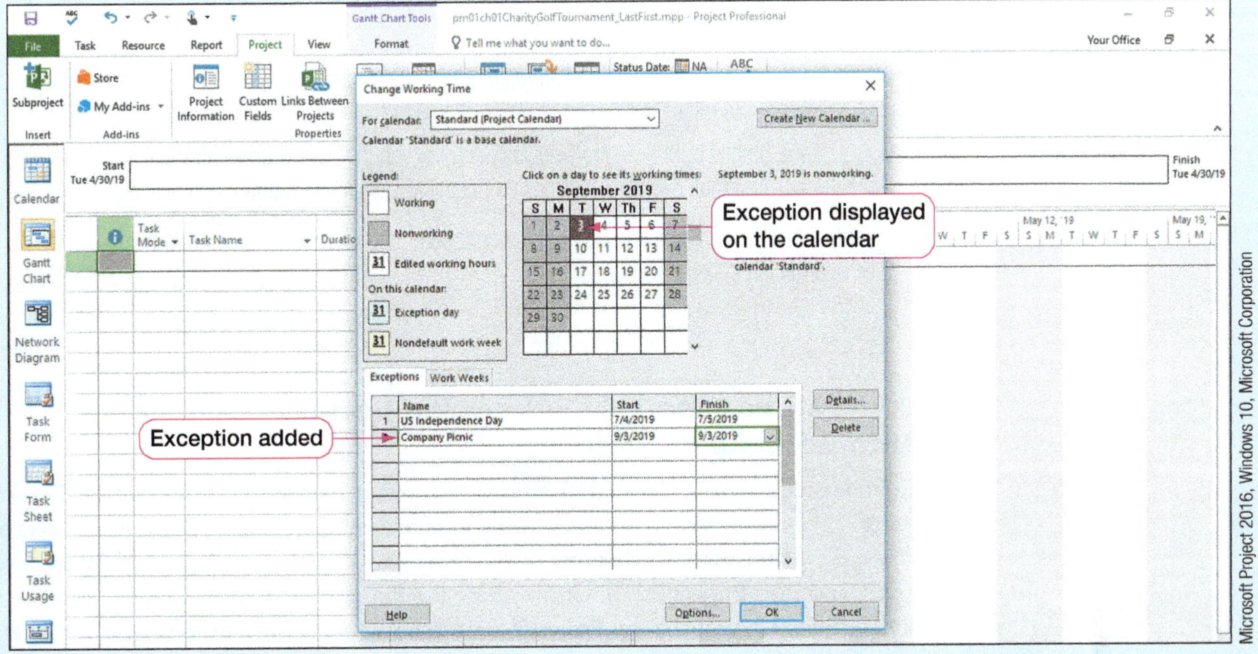

Figure 19 Calendar exception added

Troubleshooting

If an exception is not appearing as a nonworking day in the calendar, click the Exception row in the Exceptions Name box, and then click the Details button. Set the selected Exception day to Nonworking, and then click OK.

h. Click **OK** to close the Change Working Time dialog box, and then **Save** the project.

REAL WORLD ADVICE Task Calendars

One size does not fit all when it comes to Project 2016 calendars! To make sure Project 2016 is creating an accurate schedule, individual tasks may need to be completed outside of the base calendar working time. For example, if the charity golf tournament's base calendar is set to working times of Tuesday–Friday, 8:00 AM to 12:00 PM, but training for event staff needs to occur from 1:00 PM to 5:00 PM, a task calendar can be created to reflect the training times of 1:00 PM to 5:00 PM. Once a task calendar is created, the calendar is applied to the appropriate task(s), and Project 2016 is then able to schedule those particular tasks outside of the base calendar working times. Task calendars can be created for any task that does not follow the working and nonworking times set on the project's base calendar.

QUICK REFERENCE	Creating a Task Calendar

To create a task calendar, click the Project tab, and then:

1. Click Change Working Time in the Properties group.
2. Click the Create New Calendar button, and then enter a name for the task calendar. Click OK.
3. Click the Work Weeks tab.
4. Click the next empty cell in the Name column. Enter a descriptive name and press Tab, and then click in the Start cell.
5. Click the Details button. In the Details dialog box, choose the appropriate option for your task calendar. Edit the From and To times as necessary. Click OK in both dialog boxes.

Once the new task calendar is created, it would need to be assigned to specific tasks using the Task Information dialog box.

Understand Manually Scheduled Versus Auto Scheduled Projects

To understand how Project 2016 schedules tasks, it is important to identify if tasks are being scheduled manually or automatically. The default in Project 2016 is for tasks to be **Manually Scheduled**. In this mode, you enter a task duration and the task Start date for a task, and then Project 2016 will calculate the Finish date. In other words, task dates are not calculated or adjusted by Project's 2016 scheduling engine, even if changes to related tasks are made. Project managers who desire more control over the project schedule may elect to use manual scheduling.

If a project manager wants to take advantage of Project's 2016 scheduling engine, however, the project would likely be set to Auto Scheduled. If a project is set to **Auto Scheduled**, the project schedule is calculated based on the project's calendar, project tasks and task durations, task dependencies, resource assignments, and any constraint dates assigned to tasks. Auto scheduled projects are more structured than manually scheduled projects.

Figure 20 displays how Project 2016 is scheduling the two tasks differently. Because Task 1 is being Manually Scheduled, it has no Start date or Finish date calculated by Project 2016 even though a duration of two days has been assigned to the task. Task 2 is set to Auto Scheduled, and therefore, the Start date and Finish date are calculated by Project 2016 based on the project's calendar and the task duration. Also note the differences in the Gantt bars in the Gantt chart from Manually Scheduled to Auto Scheduled tasks.

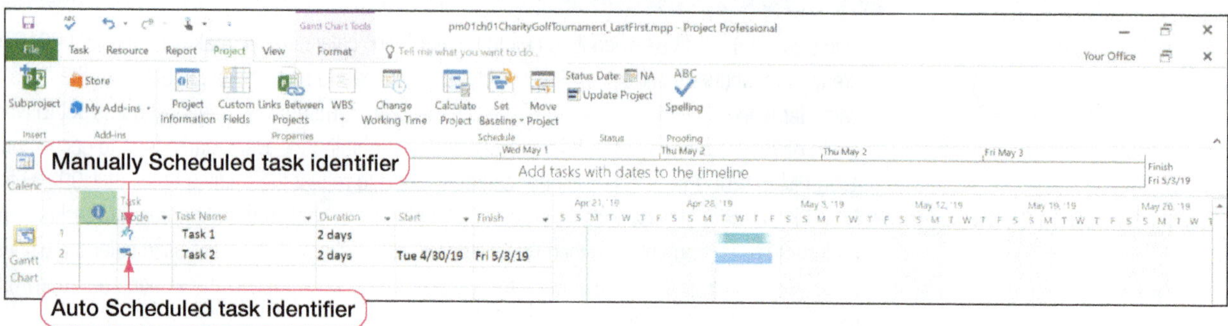

Microsoft Project 2016, Windows 10, Microsoft Corporation

Figure 20 Manually Scheduled versus Auto Scheduled tasks

Table 3 explains additional differences between a manual scheduling and automatic scheduling of project tasks.

	Manual Scheduling	Automatic Scheduling
Duration	Can be number, date, or text information, such as "4 days" or "a few days"	Only numbers can be used that represent length and units, such as "4 days" or "2 weeks"
Project Calendar	Ignored by Project	Used by Project to determine a project's schedule
Constraints	Ignored by Project	Used by Project to determine task Start or Finish date
Task Relationships (links)	Can be assigned but won't change the task schedule	Can be assigned and will change the schedule of a task
Resources	Can be assigned to tasks but won't change the task schedule	Can be assigned to tasks. Used by Project to help determine best schedule

Table 3 Manual scheduling versus automatic scheduling

Auto Scheduling a Project

A project can be set to Auto Scheduled so that all tasks, unless otherwise specified, are scheduled by Project's scheduling engine. If a project is set to Auto Scheduled, individual tasks can be changed to Manually Scheduled, if necessary. A project set to Manually Scheduled will allow the project manager to determine the Start and Finish dates of a project's tasks. If a project is set to Manually Scheduled, individual tasks can be set to Auto Scheduled. To change individual tasks, click the Task tab and then click Auto Schedule in the Tasks group or click the arrow in the Task Mode column.

You are asked to set the project to Auto Scheduled so that Project 2016 can help you determine when it is possible to hold the charity golf tournament. In this exercise, you will change a project to Auto Scheduled.

PM01.05

To Change a Project to Auto Scheduled

a. Click **New Tasks: Manually Scheduled** on the status bar.

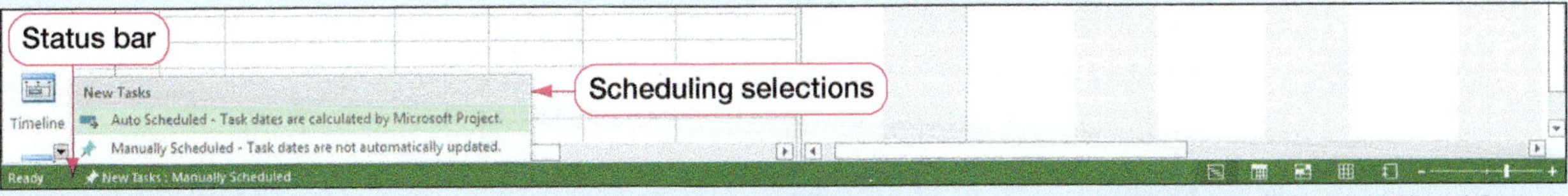

Microsoft Project 2016, Windows 10, Microsoft Corporation

Figure 21 Project status bar

b. Click **Auto Scheduled – Task dates are calculated by Microsoft Project**. All tasks will now be calculated by Project 2016 unless set individually to Manually Scheduled.

c. **Save** the project. If you need to take a break before finishing this chapter, now is a good time.

> **SIDE NOTE**
> **Task Mode Column**
> The Task Mode column in the Entry table will reflect how a task is being scheduled once a task is entered.

Creating a Project Plan

Understanding project management terminology, exploring the Project 2016 window, adjusting the Project 2016 calendar, and choosing a scheduling method are just the start to creating a project plan. Time also needs to be spent on identifying project tasks, task durations, task dependencies, and task constraints.

Identify and Enter Project Tasks

Tasks are activities that must be completed to accomplish a project goal. Tasks are entered into the Entry table in Gantt Chart view but can also be entered in the Network Diagram view and the Calendar view. Task names should be concise, and each task should be entered on a separate row in the Entry table. Tasks are assigned durations by the project's manager. In Project 2016, the default for a duration of one day is eight hours. Even if the project schedule is set to a 20-hour work week versus a 40-hour work week, Project 2016 still calculates one day as eight hours by default.

Durations help Project 2016 to calculate a task's Start (or Finish) date if a project is set to Auto Scheduled. Durations can be entered into the software using the following abbreviations:

QUICK REFERENCE	Entering Task Durations
Duration Abbreviation	**Result Duration**
1 min	1 minute
1 h	1 hour
1 d	1 day (default) or 8 hours
1 w	1 week
1 mon	1 month

Each task in a project is unique from other tasks within the same project, even if the tasks are related in some way. Information about a single task can be found in the Task Information dialog box by selecting the Information button on the Task tab. The **Task Information** dialog box includes all the details for a single task. Project managers can use the Task Information dialog box to view and update task details such as resource assignments, predecessors, and task calendar. Information for a task is divided into six categories (tabs): General, Predecessors, Resources, Advanced, Notes, and Custom Fields, as shown in Figure 22. You can also use the Task Information dialog box to make changes to a task.

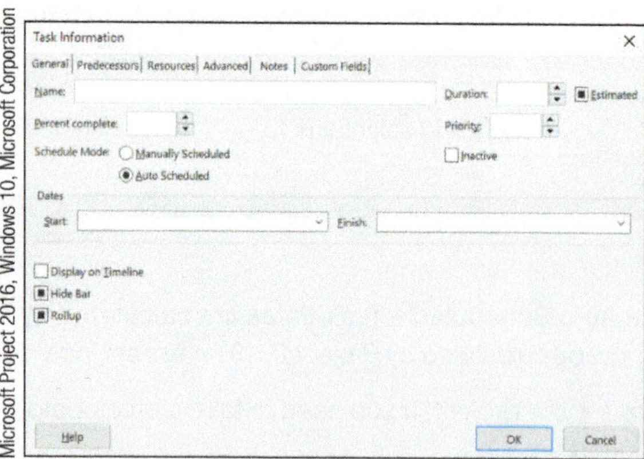

Microsoft Project 2016, Windows 10, Microsoft Corporation

Figure 22 Task Information dialog box

Task names should be brief; therefore, more information may need to be added to a task for clarification. This can be done with a task **Note**. A task Note acts as a sticky note for a task and can be added on the Notes tab in the Task Information dialog box. A Note can provide more information on a task such as a web link, a phone number, or even an embedded file, such as an Excel spreadsheet, that provides further information on the task.

Navigating around an Entry table uses keystrokes similar to those used in other Microsoft applications.

QUICK REFERENCE **Navigating the Entry Table**

Keyboard Shortcut	Moves the Active Cell
↑	Up one row in the same column
↓	Down one row in the same column
→	One column to the right
←	One column to the left
Enter	Down one row in same column
Shift + Enter	Up one row in same column
Home	First column of the current row
End	Last column of the current row
Ctrl + Home	First column and row
Ctrl + End	Last column of the last row
PgUp	Up one screen
PgDn	Down one screen
Tab	One column to right
Shift + Tab	One column to left

Entering Project Tasks

Now that you have prepared your project plan by adjusting the project calendar, and setting the project to schedule automatically and by start date, you are ready to create your project plan. Patti Rochelle, the charity golf tournament planning manager, has given you a list of tasks to enter into the project's Entry table.

In this exercise, you will enter project tasks.

SIDE NOTE
Text Wrap
Project 2016 has a Wrap Text feature for task names. If the name is longer than the column, the text will wrap within the cell.

To Enter Project Tasks

a. If you took a break, open the pm01ch01CharityGolfTournament_LastFirst project.

b. Click in the **Task Name** cell in row 1. Type Set tournament objectives.

c. Press Tab. The default value of 1 day? will appear in the Duration column.

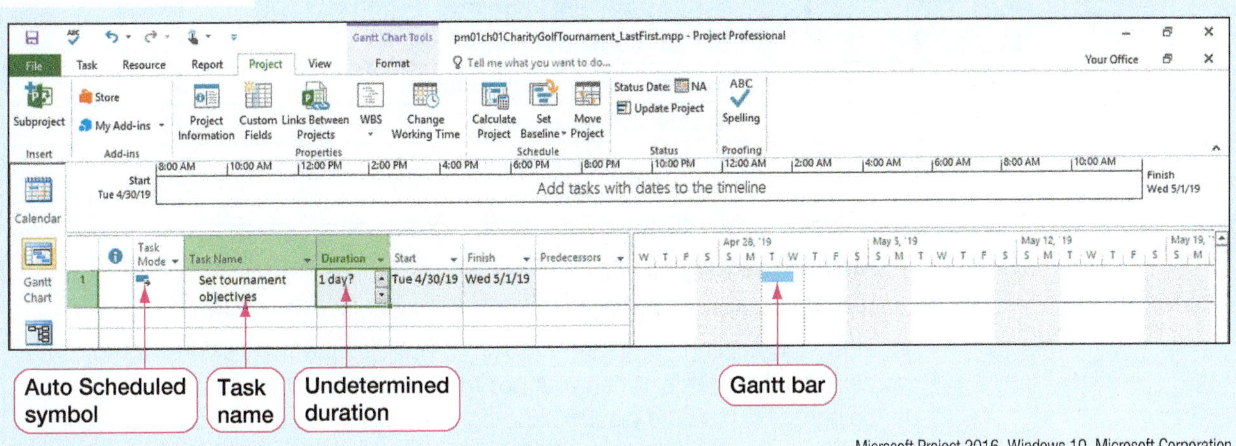

Microsoft Project 2016, Windows 10, Microsoft Corporation

Figure 23 Entry table with new task default duration

> **SIDE NOTE**
> **Project-Scheduled Changes**
> Whenever changes are made to affect a start or finish date of a task(s), those dates will be highlighted with a light colored background.

d. Type **6h** in the Duration column. Press Tab. Notice how Project 2016 assigns a Start date and Finish date because your project is set to Auto Scheduled. The task is scheduled over two days because there are only four hours available in a day to complete a task. Note the Auto Scheduled symbol in the Task Mode column.

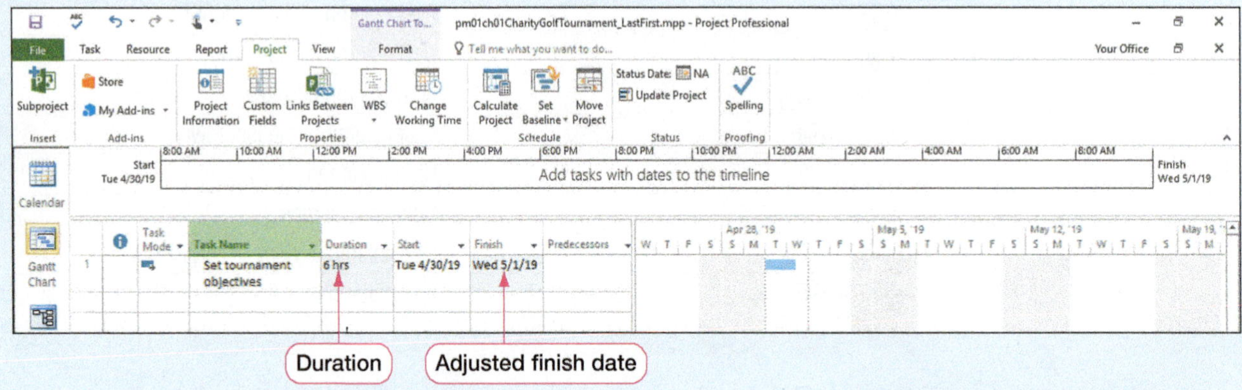

Microsoft Project 2016, Windows 10, Microsoft Corporation

Figure 24 Entry table with task duration

> **SIDE NOTE**
> **Task Information**
> You can also open the Task Information dialog box by double-clicking a task.

e. With **Set tournament objectives** (Task 1) selected, click the **Task** tab, if necessary, and then in the Properties group, click **Information** to open the Task Information dialog box. Explore the various tabs that can contain information about **Set tournament objectives**. Click **Cancel**.

f. Enter the remaining tasks below in the Entry table. Remember you can use abbreviations for the durations.

Task	Task Name	Task Duration
2	Determine project team	4 hours
3	Set tournament date and time	1 day
4	Prepare preliminary budget	6 hours
5	Create tournament website	2 weeks
6	Solicit potential tournament sponsors	1 week
7	Select tournament sponsors	4 hours
8	Solicit celebrity appearances	3 weeks
9	Create volunteer list	4 hours
10	Sign volunteer contracts	1 hour

> **Troubleshooting**
> If the Start or Finish date column displays the date as wrapped text, you may want to widen the column. To widen a column, point to the right side of the column border in the field name. When your pointer turns into a double-pointed arrow, drag to the right until the date displays appropriately. As in Excel, you can also double-click between the columns to automatically widen the column.

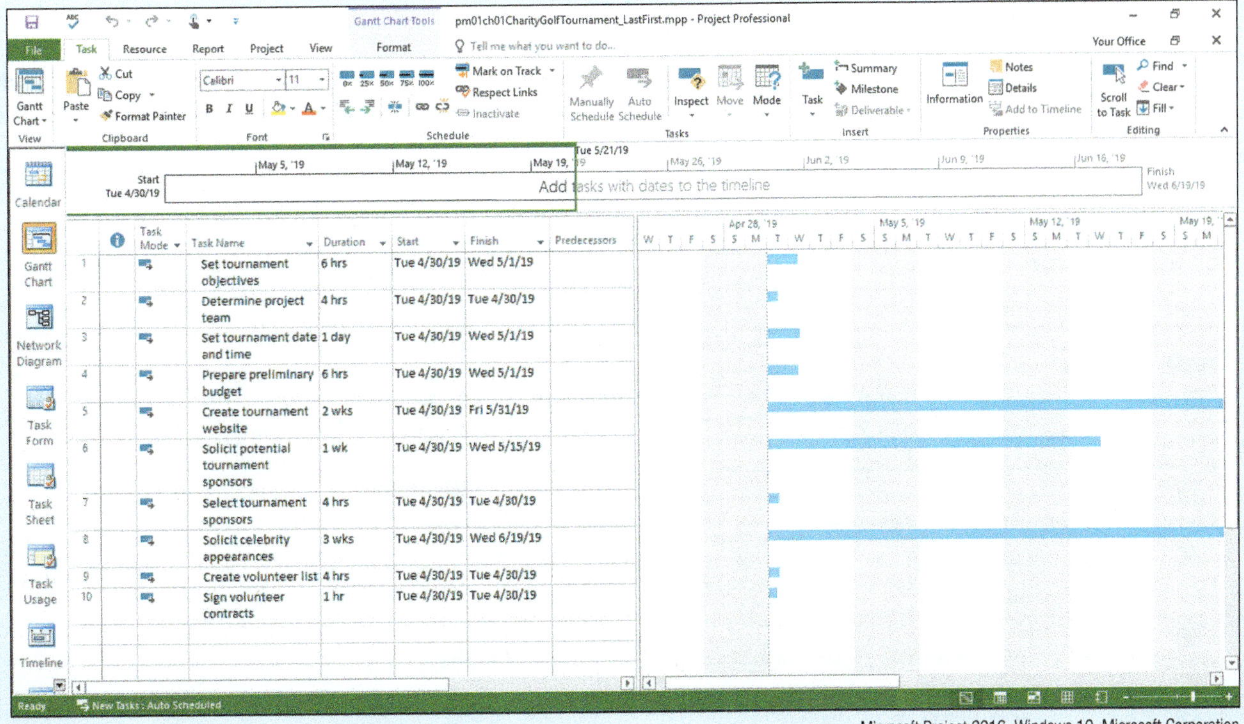

Microsoft Project 2016, Windows 10, Microsoft Corporation

Figure 25 Entry table with tasks added

g. On the Quick Access Toolbar, click the **Spelling** button to check the spelling of the task names.

h. **Save** the project.

> **CONSIDER THIS** | **Task Duration**
>
> Why is a task duration of one day being assigned a calendar duration of two days? The Project calendar for the charity golf tournament was adjusted to a four-hour working day of 8:00 AM to 12:00 PM. Therefore, by entering in a duration of 1d (one day = eight hours), Project scheduled the task to be completed over two calendar days: four available hours on day 1 and four available hours on day 2. Is using the day duration confusing? Consider entering durations in hours instead.

All the tasks are set to start on the project's start date. Project 2016 is scheduling this way because the project is scheduled by Start date and all tasks are scheduled to start *As Soon As Possible*. Project tasks will push ahead in time as you create a more detailed project schedule later in this workshop.

Modify Project Tasks in Project 2016

Project 2016 makes it easy to edit a project plan by adding, deleting, or changing existing tasks. As you are planning your project, you may discover that you need to add an additional task(s) in the middle of your project plan. Project 2016 allows tasks to be inserted by using commands on the ribbon, the shortcut menu, or the keyboard. Inserting a task in the middle of a project plan is similar to adding a row in Excel 2016 because Project 2016 will push every subsequent task down one row and adjust the project accordingly.

Adding and Modifying Project Tasks in the Entry Table

After brainstorming at a team meeting, the charity golf tournament planning team has identified a few additional tasks to be added to the project plan as well as an adjustment to task durations. You will add these tasks.

In this exercise, you will modify a task list.

SIDE NOTE

Adding Tasks in the Entry Table

Similar to Excel 2016, new task rows are added above the active row.

To Modify a Task List

a. Click any cell in task row 4, **Prepare preliminary budget**, and then click the **Task** tab, if necessary. In the Insert group, click the **Task** button to insert a new row. <New Task> appears as the task name.

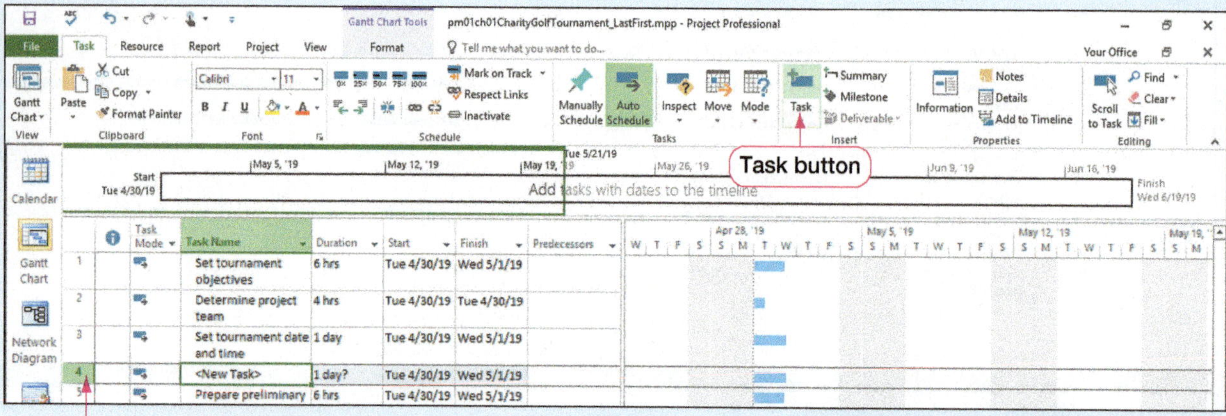

Microsoft Project 2016, Windows 10, Microsoft Corporation

Figure 26 New task row added in Entry table

> **Troubleshooting**
>
> If you selected the Task arrow instead of the Task button, select **Task**.

b. Type **Reserve golf course**, and then press Tab. Type **1h**, and then press Tab. Reserve golf course becomes the new Task 4.

c. With Reserve golf course (Task 4) still selected, press the **Insert** Ins key. A blank row is added above the selected row to create a new task. Notice how a blank row is inserted with this method.

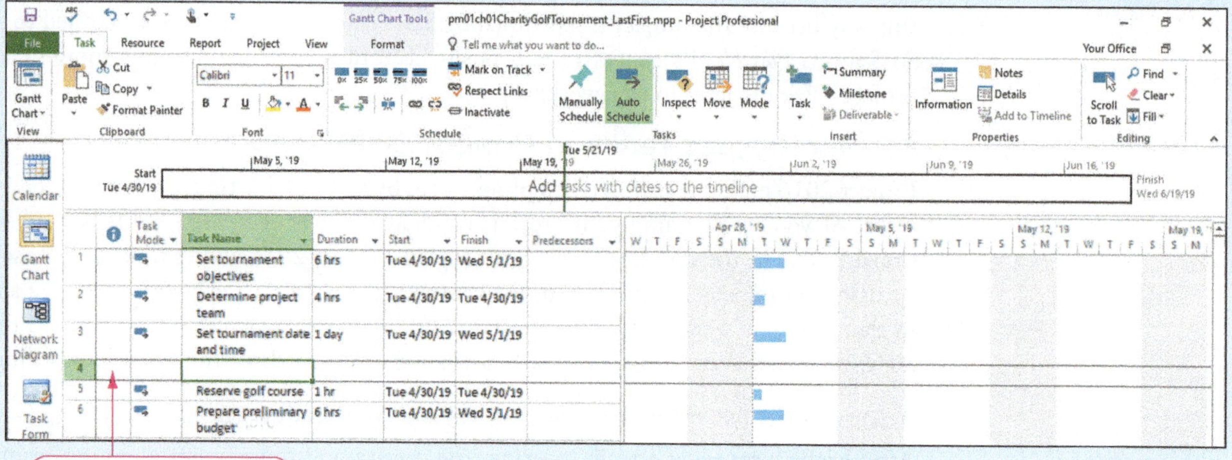

Microsoft Project 2016, Windows 10, Microsoft Corporation

Figure 27 Blank row added in Entry table

Troubleshooting

If your keyboard does not have an Insert key, repeat step a.

SIDE NOTE

Task Changes

When you make changes to a task, Project 2016 will highlight the affected tasks in the Entry table with a light colored background.

d. In the Task Name cell for the new Task 4, type Perform site inspections, and then press Tab. Type 4h, and then press Tab.

e. Click in the Duration column of Task 3, **Set tournament date and time**, and then type 1h to change the duration from 1 day to 1 hour.

f. Select **Solicit potential tournament sponsors** (Task 8), and then on the Task tab, in the Properties group, click **Information**. If necessary, click the General tab. In the upper right-hand corner of the General tab, change the **Duration** from 1 week to 3d.

g. Click the **Notes** tab. Add the note Contact local sporting goods stores for a list of potential sponsors.

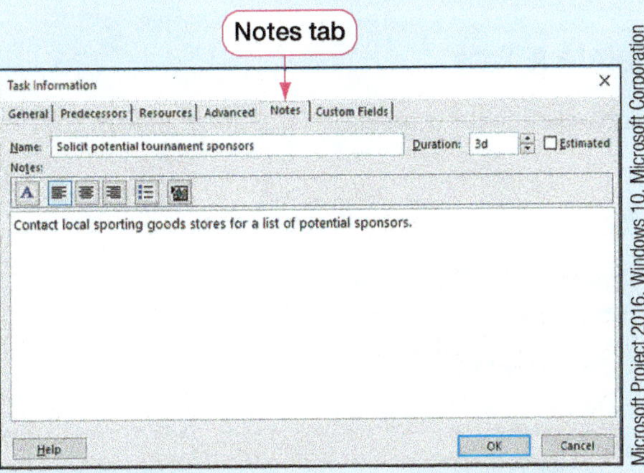

Microsoft Project 2016, Windows 10, Microsoft Corporation

Figure 28 Task Information dialog box Notes tab

SIDE NOTE

Task Note

Double-click the **Note** icon or hover over the Note icon in the Indicators column to display the note.

h. Click **OK**. Notice the **Note indicator** in the Indicators column.

i. Point to the note to see the note text.

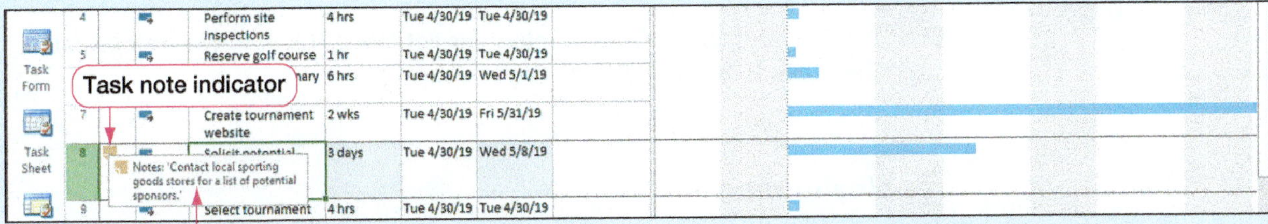

Microsoft Project 2016, Windows 10, Microsoft Corporation

Figure 29 Note indicator in Entry table

j. **Save** the project.

QUICK REFERENCE	Inserting a Task

In the Entry table, click any cell below the row where you wish to insert a task.

- Right-click the row number of the task, and then click Insert Task from the shortcut menu, or
- Click the Task button in the Insert group on the Task tab, or
- Press Insert on the keyboard.

Deleting Project Tasks in the Entry Table

As a project planner, you may decide a project task is no longer needed. As well as inserting tasks, Project 2016 allows for tasks to be deleted. Deleting a task removes an entire task row and moves any subsequent tasks up a row. As with inserting tasks, there are several ways to delete tasks in Project 2016 such as using the ribbon, the shortcut menu, or the keyboard.

Since the project team for this charity golf tournament is already in place, in this exercise, you will delete a task.

PM01.08

To Delete a Task

a. Right-click the row selector for **Determine project team** (Task 2).

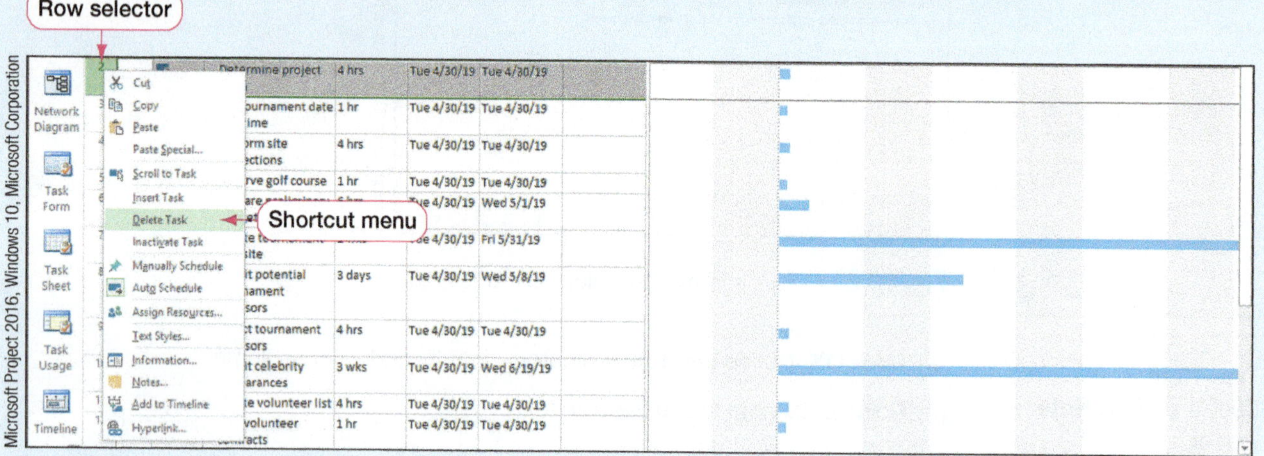

Figure 30 Task shortcut menu

b. Click **Delete Task** from the shortcut menu. The Determine project team task is deleted.

c. Click the row selector for **Create volunteer list** (Task 10). With the task selected, press Del. Task 10 is now deleted.

> **Troubleshooting**
>
> If you press Del on the Task Name cell of a task row, Project 2016 will prompt you to 1) delete the task name or 2) delete the task. To avoid this prompt, select the task row selector, and then press Del.

d. On the Quick Access Toolbar, click **Undo** to undo the deletion of Task 10.

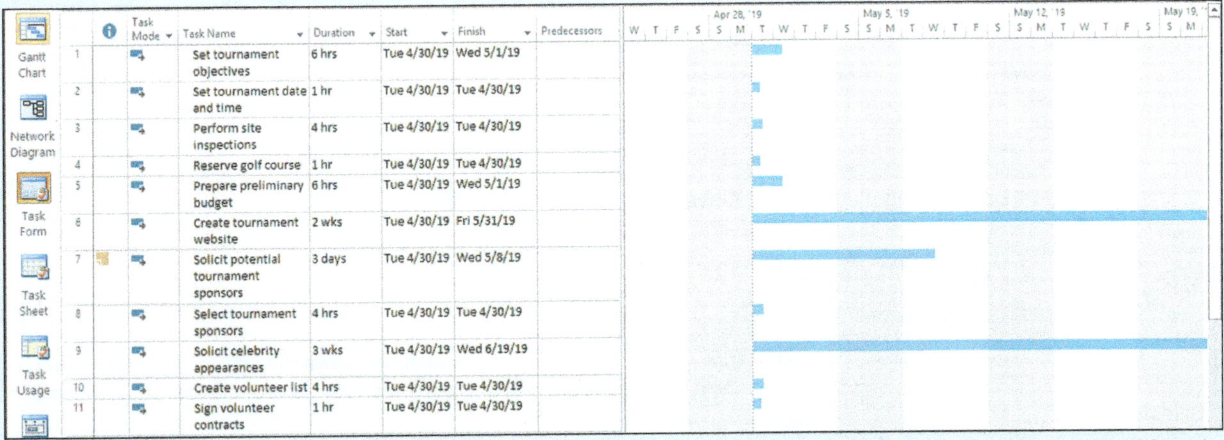

	Task Mode	Task Name	Duration	Start	Finish	Predecessors
1		Set tournament objectives	6 hrs	Tue 4/30/19	Wed 5/1/19	
2		Set tournament date and time	1 hr	Tue 4/30/19	Tue 4/30/19	
3		Perform site inspections	4 hrs	Tue 4/30/19	Tue 4/30/19	
4		Reserve golf course	1 hr	Tue 4/30/19	Tue 4/30/19	
5		Prepare preliminary budget	6 hrs	Tue 4/30/19	Wed 5/1/19	
6		Create tournament website	2 wks	Tue 4/30/19	Fri 5/31/19	
7		Solicit potential tournament sponsors	3 days	Tue 4/30/19	Wed 5/8/19	
8		Select tournament sponsors	4 hrs	Tue 4/30/19	Tue 4/30/19	
9		Solicit celebrity appearances	3 wks	Tue 4/30/19	Wed 6/19/19	
10		Create volunteer list	4 hrs	Tue 4/30/19	Tue 4/30/19	
11		Sign volunteer contracts	1 hr	Tue 4/30/19	Tue 4/30/19	

Microsoft Project 2016, Windows 10, Microsoft Corporation

Figure 31 Entry table with task deleted

e. **Save** the project.

QUICK REFERENCE | **Deleting a Task**

In the Entry table, click any task row you wish to delete.

- Right-click the row number of the task, and then select Delete Task from the shortcut menu, or
- Click the row selector of the task to be deleted, and then press the Delete key on your keyboard, or
- Click any cell of a task you want to be deleted, and then in the Editing group, on the Task tab, click the Clear button to display the menu. Click Entire Row to delete the task.

Moving, Cutting, Copying, and Pasting Project Tasks in the Entry Table

Project planners may decide to reorder tasks or even copy tasks. Moving tasks will simply reorder tasks within the Entry table. If a task is cut, the task will be temporarily deleted and placed on the Project 2016 clipboard. If a task is copied, the task stays in its current location but is also placed on the clipboard to be pasted in another location in the Entry table. Any tasks on the clipboard can be pasted within the Entry table of the project.

After reviewing the project tasks, you have decided it is important to prepare your budget before you perform site inspections. Therefore, you will move Task 5.

In this exercise, you move a task in the Entry table.

PM01.09

To Move a Task

a. Click the row selector for **Prepare preliminary budget** (Task 5) to select the task.

b. Press and hold the row selector again (you will see a four-arrow pointer). Drag the row selector above **Perform site inspections** (Task 3). As you drag Task 5, a dark gray horizontal bar will indicate the position of the task if you were to let go of your mouse.

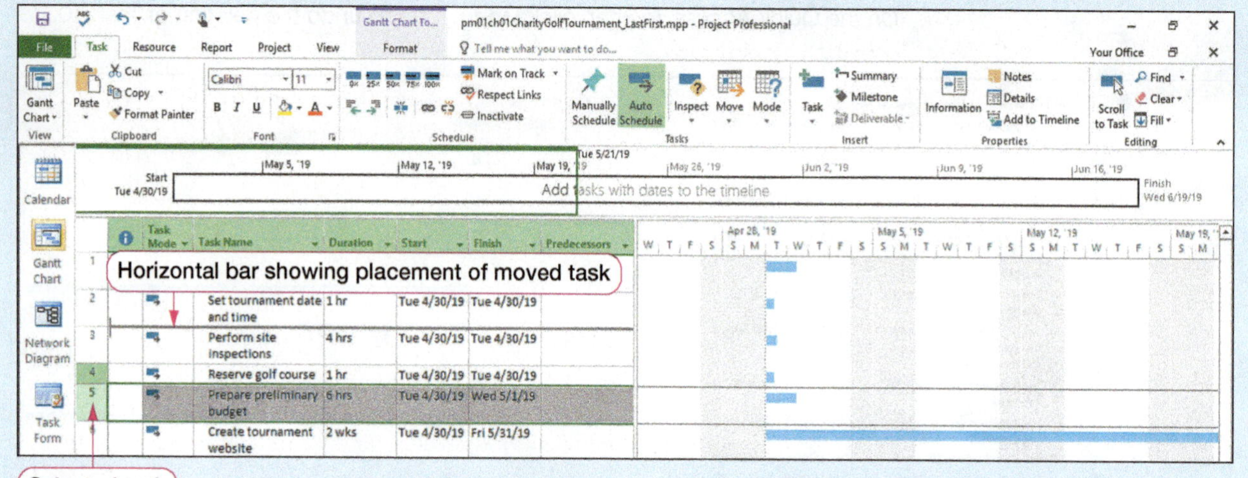

Figure 32 Moving a task in the Entry table

Microsoft Project 2016, Windows 10, Microsoft Corporation

c. Release the mouse button. The **Prepare preliminary budget** task is now Task 3.

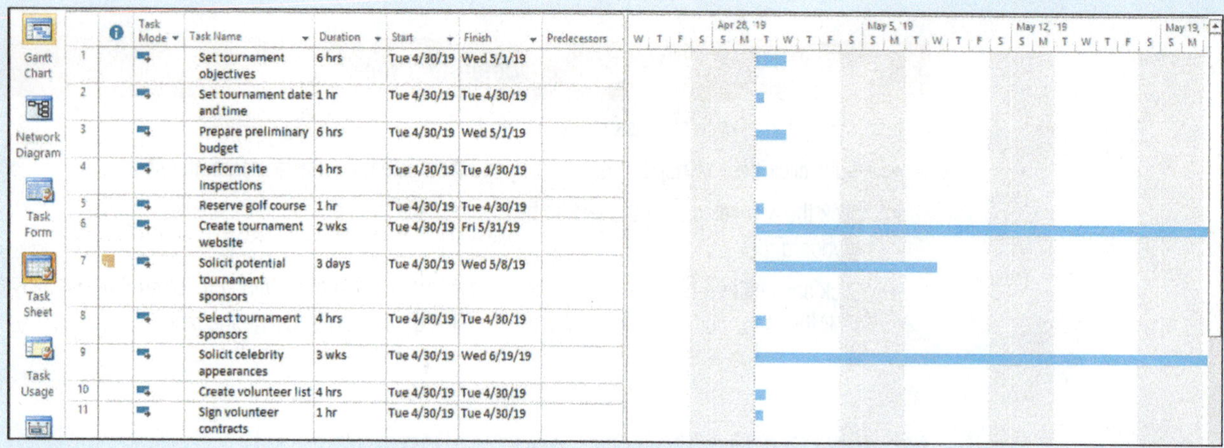

Figure 33 Entry table with task moved

Microsoft Project 2016, Windows 10, Microsoft Corporation

Troubleshooting

If you are having difficulty moving a task, be sure you first click the row selector of a task. Then click the task row selector again and drag the task to the desired location.

d. Right-click the row selector for **Set tournament objectives** (Task 1). Click **Copy** on the shortcut menu. Click in row 12, the first blank row, and then on the Task tab in the Clipboard group, click **Paste**. This creates a copy of the task.

e. Delete the copied task.

> **Troubleshooting**
> When deleting Task 12, be sure to click the row selector for the task.

f. **Save** the project.

Modifying Project Tasks in Calendar View

The Project 2016 software has several views from which to edit or view your project tasks. You can switch from one view to the other using the View Bar, which appears at the left-hand side of the project window. Gantt Chart view displays tasks, task durations, and task dependencies in a Gantt chart with horizontal bars and is the default view in Project 2016. The length of the task bars in the Gantt chart relates to the task detail such as duration and the zoom of the timescale at the top of the Gantt chart.

Calendar view displays tasks as bars on a calendar in a monthly format. Calendar view may be used to see upcoming weekly or monthly tasks. Managers may also choose to print from Calendar view because it gives an overview of the week or month ahead.

Patti Rochelle, the tournament planning manager, has asked you to add additional tasks to the charity golf tournament project plan. You decide to make these additions in the Calendar and Network Diagram views.

In this exercise, you will add and modify tasks in Calendar view.

PM01.10

SIDE NOTE
Alternate Method
You can also switch views by using the Calendar view  on the View Bar.

To Add and Modify Tasks in Calendar View

a. Click **Create volunteer list** (Task 10), and then click the Task tab, if necessary.

b. On the Task tab, in the View group, click the **Gantt Chart** arrow, and then click **Calendar** to switch to Calendar view.

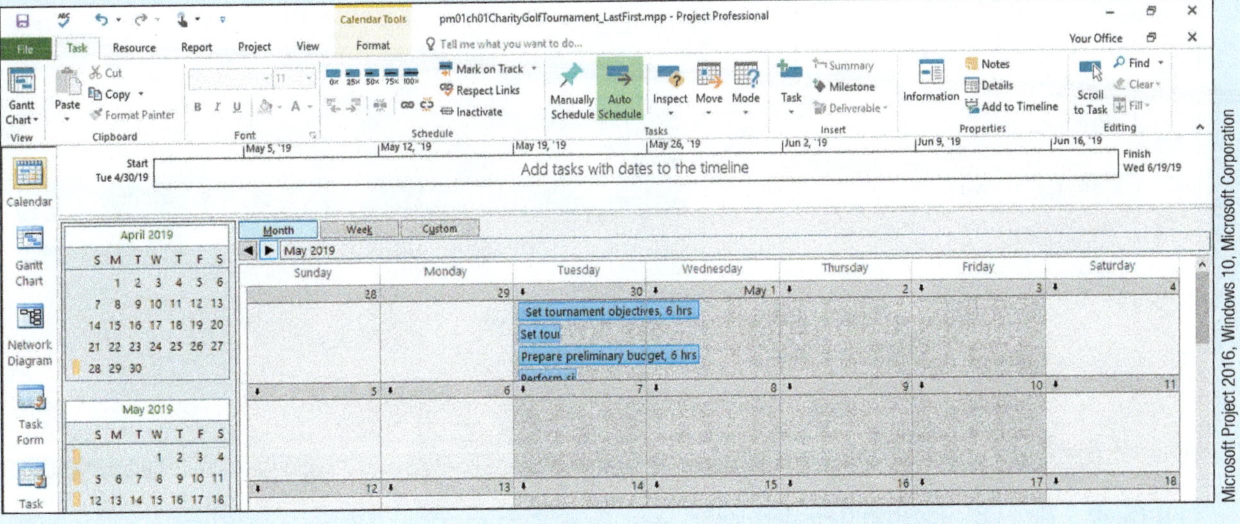

Figure 34 Calendar view

c. In Calendar view, click **Week** to change the calendar to Week view format.

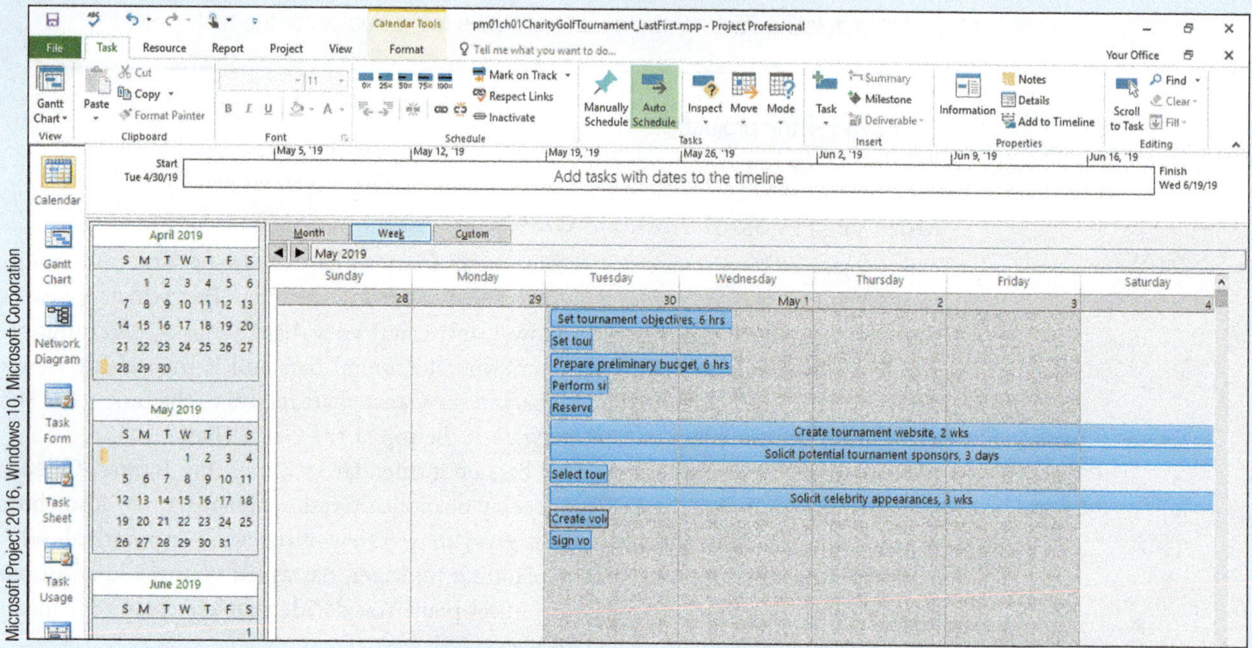

Figure 35 Week view option in Calendar view

d. With Calendar view in the Week format and Task 10 still selected, click the Task tab, if necessary. In the Insert group, click the **Task** button to add a new blank task.

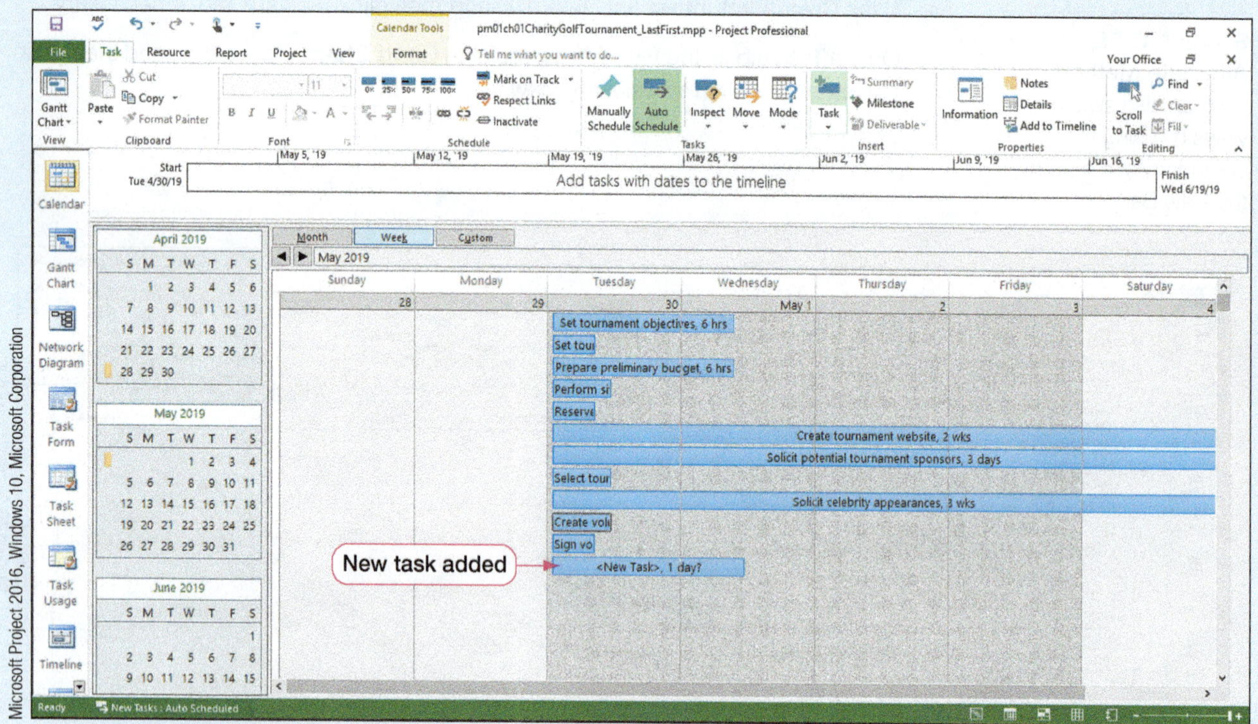

Figure 36 New task added in Calendar view

e. Double-click **<New Task>, 1 day?** on the Calendar to open the Task Information dialog box.

f. On the General tab of the Task Information dialog box, click in the Name box, and then type **Begin online registrations.** Press Tab, and then type **0d** in the Duration box to enter the Milestone task.

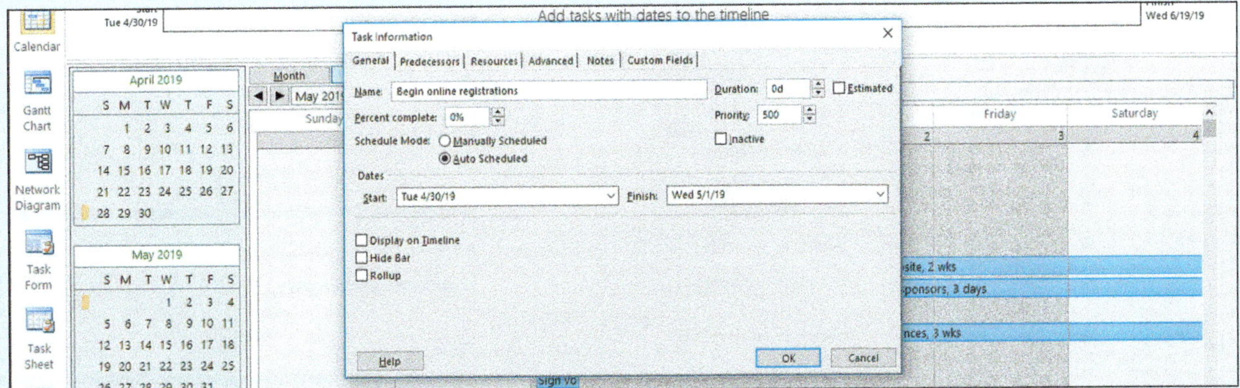

Microsoft Project 2016, Windows 10, Microsoft Corporation

Figure 37 Task Information dialog box

g. Click **OK**.

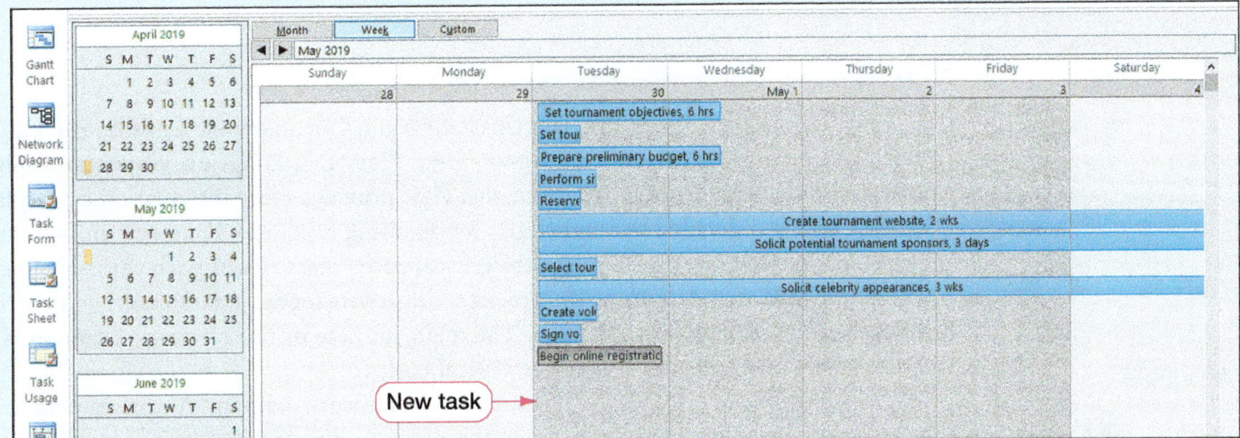

Microsoft Project 2016, Windows 10, Microsoft Corporation

Figure 38 Calendar view with new task added

SIDE NOTE

Milestone Task

Notice the milestone task is identified in the Gantt chart as a diamond.

h. Click **Gantt Chart** on the View Bar on the left-hand side of the Project 2016 window to view the new Task 10 in the Gantt chart.

Troubleshooting

If the View Bar is not visible on the left-hand side of the Project 2016 window, right-click the vertical text GANTT CHART on the left-hand side of the Project 2016 window, and then click View Bar.

i. Click in the **Task Name** cell of Task 10. Click the **Gantt Chart Tools Format** tab. In the Columns group, click **Wrap Text** twice to wrap the text of the new task. Notice the wrapped text of the task names in the Entry table.

j. Click the row selector for **Begin online registrations** (Task 10), and then move the task above **Solicit potential tournament sponsors** (Task 7). Begin online registrations is now Task 7.

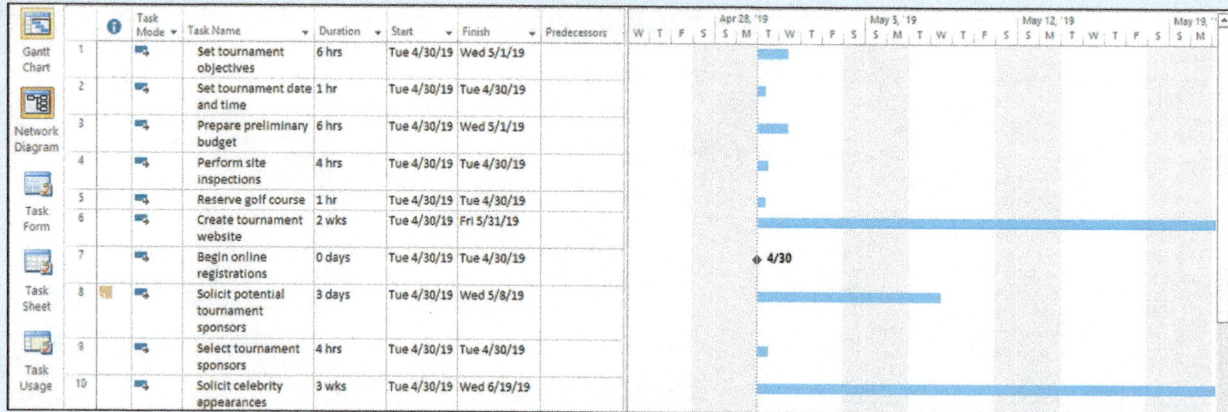

		Task Mode	Task Name	Duration	Start	Finish	Predecessors
1			Set tournament objectives	6 hrs	Tue 4/30/19	Wed 5/1/19	
2			Set tournament date and time	1 hr	Tue 4/30/19	Tue 4/30/19	
3			Prepare preliminary budget	6 hrs	Tue 4/30/19	Wed 5/1/19	
4			Perform site inspections	4 hrs	Tue 4/30/19	Tue 4/30/19	
5			Reserve golf course	1 hr	Tue 4/30/19	Tue 4/30/19	
6			Create tournament website	2 wks	Tue 4/30/19	Fri 5/31/19	
7			Begin online registrations	0 days	Tue 4/30/19	Tue 4/30/19	
8			Solicit potential tournament sponsors	3 days	Tue 4/30/19	Wed 5/8/19	
9			Select tournament sponsors	4 hrs	Tue 4/30/19	Tue 4/30/19	
10			Solicit celebrity appearances	3 wks	Tue 4/30/19	Wed 6/19/19	

Microsoft Project 2016, Windows 10, Microsoft Corporation

Figure 39 Gantt Chart view with new task added and moved

k. **Save** the project.

Modifying Project Tasks in Network Diagram View

Not only can tasks be added in Gantt Chart view and Calendar view, but they can also be added and modified in Network Diagram view. **Network Diagram view** also displays tasks and task dependencies. However, this view provides more information by displaying each task in a detailed box and clearly representing task dependencies with link lines. The Network Diagram also displays the critical path. The **critical path** consists of tasks (or a single task) that determine the project's Finish date (or Start date); tasks on the critical path are considered critical tasks. The main purpose of the Network Diagram is to assist project managers in viewing the critical path.

Critical tasks are displayed in light red on the network diagram. A **critical task** must be completed on time in order to meet the project's Finish date (or Start date). A task becomes critical based on the task dependencies, task durations, and task resource assignments. Project managers must monitor critical tasks to be sure they are being completed on time in order to successfully meet the project schedule. You decide to switch to this view and add another project task.

In this exercise, you will add and modify tasks in Network Diagram view.

SIDE NOTE

Identifying a Critical Task

Task 10 is a critical task because at this point in the planning process, Task 10 has the longest duration.

To Add and Modify Tasks in Network Diagram View

a. With Task 7 still selected, click **Network Diagram** on the View Bar to switch to Network Diagram view.

b. Scroll down the Network Diagram as necessary to view **Begin online registrations** (ID: 7). Note the shape of this task is different from the other tasks with a rectangle shape because Task 7 is a milestone task. Also note the task has a black background because it is the selected task.

c. Scroll down again until you see **Solicit celebrity appearances** (Task 10). Note this task appears in red because it is a critical task.

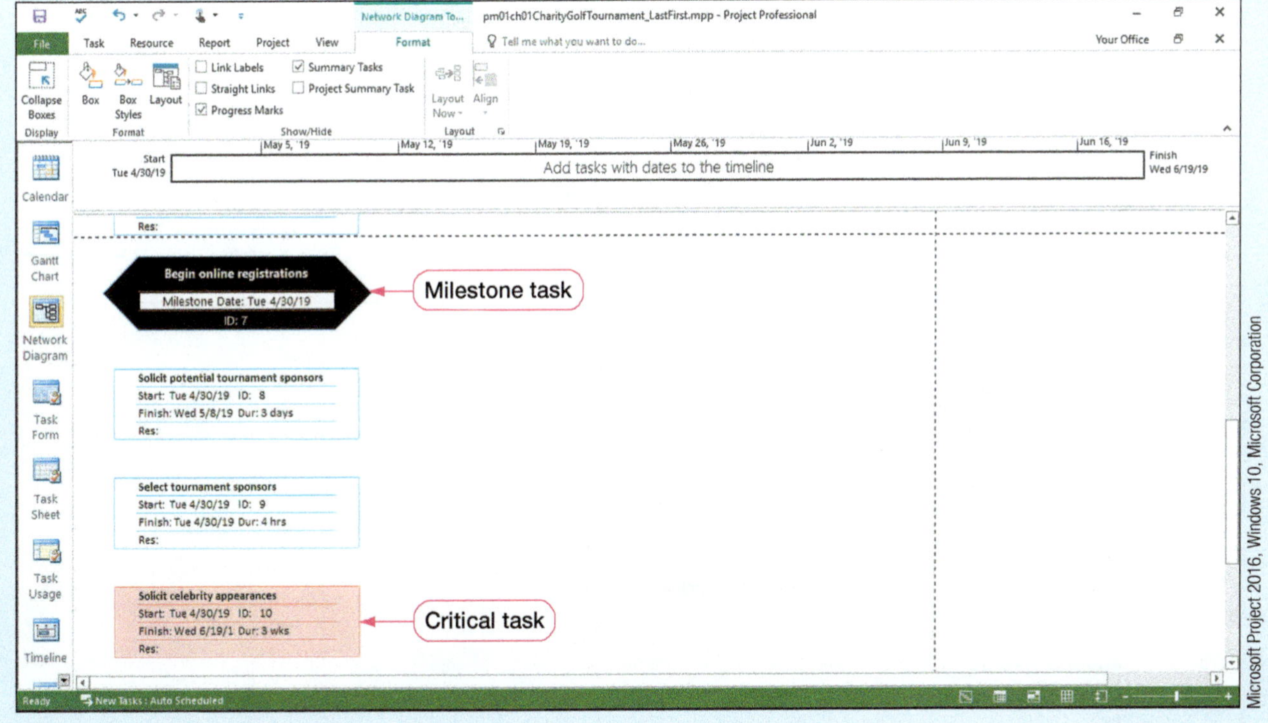

Microsoft Project 2016, Windows 10, Microsoft Corporation

Figure 40 Network Diagram view of tasks

> **SIDE NOTE**
> **Tasks in Network Diagram View**
> A selected task in the Network Diagram will appear with a black background and white text.

d. While still in Network Diagram view, scroll up, and then click **Create tournament website** (Task 6) to select the task.

e. Click the **Task** tab, and then in the Insert group, click **Task** to add a new blank task in Network Diagram view. The new blank task becomes Task 6 with Create tournament website (Task 7) still selected.

f. Double-click the **<New Task>** rectangle to open the Task Information dialog box.

> **SIDE NOTE**
> **Adding a New Task in the Network Diagram**
> You can also add a task in Network Diagram view by clicking in a blank area of the Network Diagram and dragging to draw a small rectangle.

Troubleshooting

If you clicked on the new task's border, the Format Box dialog box will appear. Click Cancel, and then double click inside the task box instead.

g. Click the **General** tab of the Task Information dialog box, add the Name Design tournament logo, and then press Tab.

h. Enter a Duration of 1d, and then click **OK**. The new task has the task name Design tournament logo with a duration of one day.

i. With **Design tournament logo** (Task 6) still selected, click one time in the **Dur:** box, type 2d, and then press Enter to change the duration of the task from one day to two days.

Troubleshooting

If the Task 6 Task Information dialog box opened when attempting to adjust the duration, you double-clicked the task. Close the Task Information dialog box, and then click once to select Task 6.

j. Select **Reserve golf course** (Task 5). Change the duration of Task 5 to 0d to make this task a milestone and change the shape of the task in Network Diagram view.

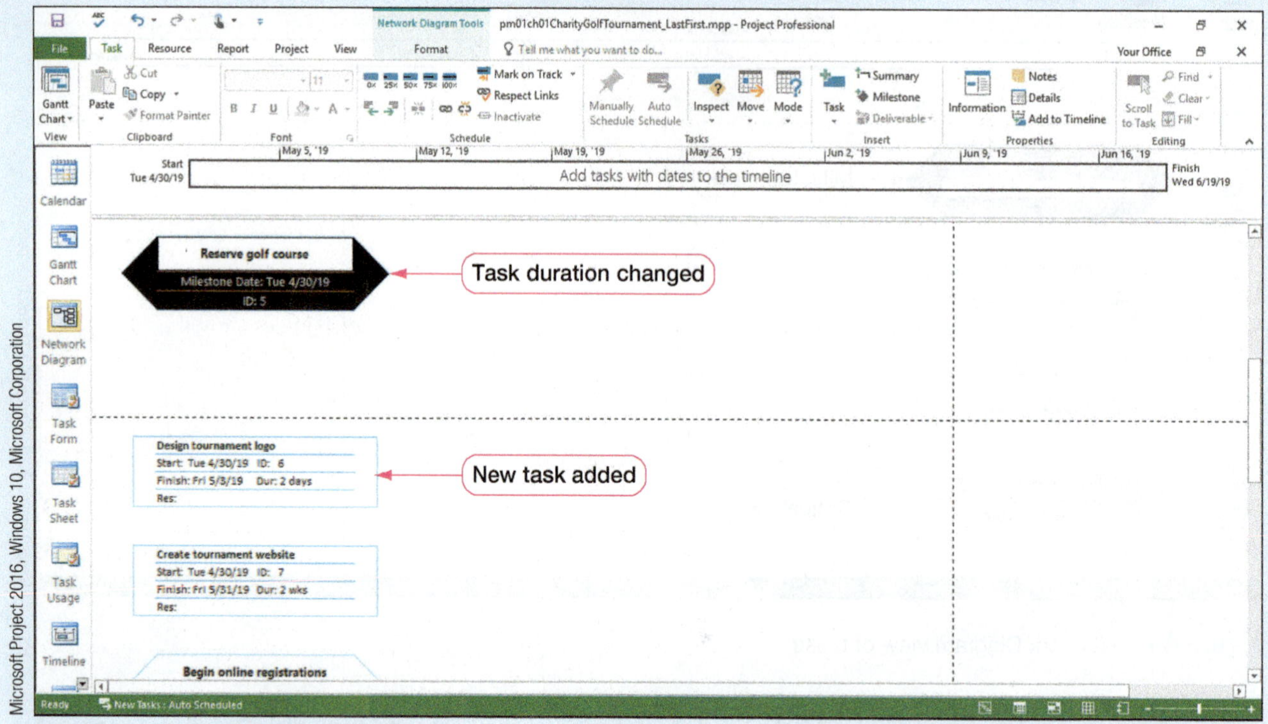

Figure 41 Network Diagram view with task additions and changes

k. Click **Gantt Chart** on the View Bar to return to Gantt Chart view. Note the new tasks and the change in durations.

l. Click **Design tournament logo** (Task 6). Click the **Gantt Chart Tools Format** tab, and then in the Columns group, click **Wrap Text** twice.

m. **Save** the project.

CONSIDER THIS | How Can You Motivate Team Members?

Have you ever been a member of a team? How did your coach motivate you? Did your coach recognize team successes as they occurred? Project successes can be recognized by milestones. Therefore, milestones can help motivate the project team by recognizing project accomplishments.

Create Task Dependencies

When creating a project schedule, if you do not define task dependencies, all tasks will start on the project Start date or finish on the project Finish date. However, in most projects, tasks may be dependent on other tasks. Therefore, Project 2016 allows project planners to create task dependencies.

Task dependencies create predecessor tasks and successor tasks. For example, you could not begin a task of "begin online registrations" without first completing the task of "set tournament date and time." In this case, "set tournament date and time" would be the predecessor task to "begin online registrations" (which then becomes the successor task).

Remember, project managers often use the terms relationship, dependency, or link when referring to how the predecessor or successor tasks are connected.

CONSIDER THIS | Why Create Task Dependencies?

Have you ever baked a cake? If so, then you know you need to purchase the ingredients before mixing them together; mix the ingredients together before pouring them into a pan; prepare the pan before pouring in the ingredients; heat the oven before putting the pan into the oven to bake, etc. Baking a cake is a project during which tasks are completed in a certain order. This order is defined by task dependencies.

There are four types of task dependencies in Project 2016, as shown in Table 4:

Type	Detail	Example
Finish-to-Start (FS)	Default. Task 1 must finish before Task 2 can start.	You must finish selecting the tournament date (Task 1) before beginning online registration (Task 2).
Start-to-Start (SS)	Task 1 must start before Task 2 can start.	As soon as the tournament website goes live (Task 1), you can start accepting online registrations (Task 2).
Start-to-Finish (SF)	Task 1 must start before Task 2 can finish.	You must start working on the tournament website (Task 1) before you can finish promotional materials (Task 2).
Finish-to-Finish (FF)	Task 1 must finish before Task 2 can finish.	You must finish accepting online registrations (Task 1) before you finalize the tournament supply list (Task 2).

Table 4 Task Dependencies

In Project 2016, task dependencies are recorded in the row for the second (successor) task. For example, if you are creating a dependency between "set the tournament date" (Task A) and "begin online registrations" (Task B), you record the dependency in the row for Task B.

Dependencies in the software are also often referred to as task relationships or task links. Project managers often use these terms interchangeably. If you are manually scheduling your project, you can still assign task dependencies. However, if manually scheduling, the task dependencies will not affect the project schedule.

There are several ways to create task dependencies to the default Finish-to-Start relationship:

- Select the tasks to be related in Gantt Chart, Network Diagram, or Calendar view, and then click the Link the Selected Tasks button in the Schedule group on the Task tab as shown in Figure 42.
- Double-click a task in Gantt Chart, Network Diagram, or Calendar view, and then click the Predecessors tab. Enter in the task row(s) of the predecessor task(s), and then click OK.
- In Gantt Chart, Network Diagram, or Calendar view, click the predecessor task and drag to the successor task. Release the mouse and the tasks become linked.
- In Gantt Chart view, click the successor task to select the task. In the Predecessors column, enter the task row(s) of the related task(s), and then press Enter.
- Select the tasks to be related, and then press Ctrl + F2.

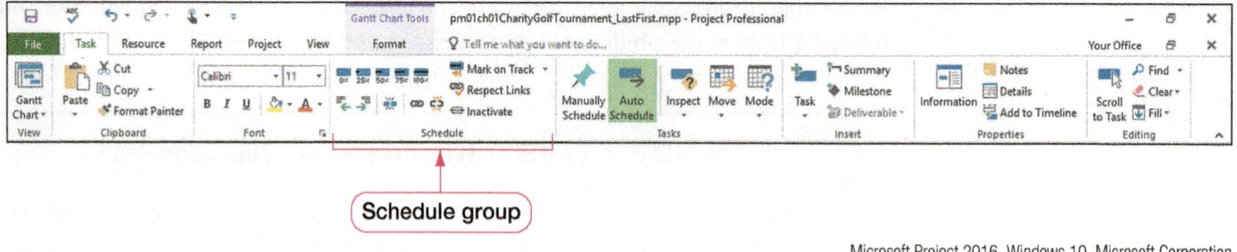

Microsoft Project 2016, Windows 10, Microsoft Corporation

Figure 42 Task tab Schedule group

Adding Task Dependencies

In order to create a more detailed and realistic project plan, you have been asked to create task dependencies for the tournament project tasks.

In this exercise, you will set task dependencies.

SIDE NOTE

Task Relationships

Because the project is scheduled by Start date, the Finish-to-Start relationship between tasks 1 and 2 and the start date of task 2 changes.

To Set Task Dependencies

a. In **Gantt Chart** view, move the split bar between the Gantt chart and the Entry table to the right edge of the Predecessors column by dragging the **split bar** to the right.

b. Click and drag to select the Task Names **Set tournament objectives** (Task 1) and **Set tournament date and time** (Task 2).

c. Click the **Task** tab, and then in the Schedule group, click **Link the Selected Tasks** . Linking Tasks 1 and 2 created a Finish-to-Start relationship. Notice the link line in the Gantt chart as well as the change to the Start date in Task 2. Also notice a "1" was added to the Predecessors column in Row 2.

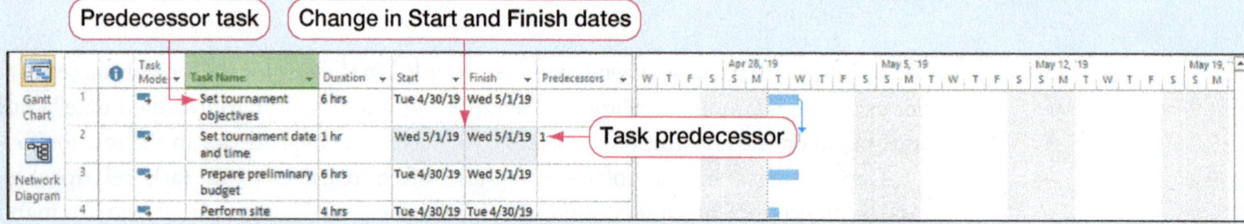

Microsoft Project 2016, Windows 10, Microsoft Corporation

Figure 43 Finish-to-Start relationship between Tasks 1 and 2

d. Click in the **Predecessors** column for **Prepare preliminary budget** (Task 3). Type 2, and then press Enter. Task 2 becomes a predecessor of Task 3.

Troubleshooting

If you cannot see the Predecessor column in the Entry table, click and drag the split bar to the right.

e. In the Gantt chart on the right-hand side of your screen, click and hold the **Prepare preliminary budget** (Task 3) Gantt bar and then drag to the **Perform site inspections** (Task 4) Gantt bar.

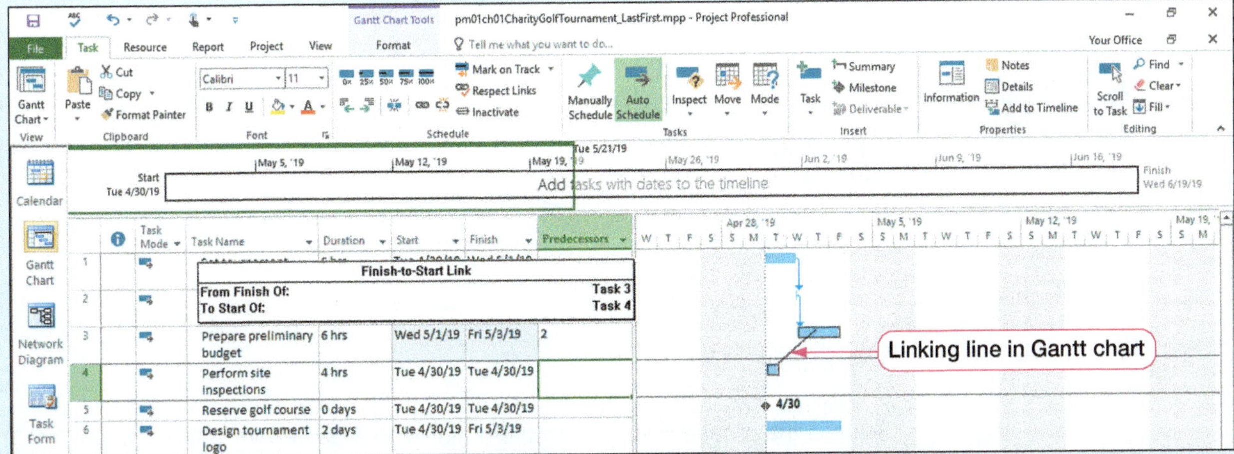

Microsoft Project 2016, Windows 10, Microsoft Corporation

Figure 44 Linking tasks in the Gantt chart

f. Release the mouse button to create a relationship between Tasks 3 and 4.

g. Double-click **Reserve golf course** (Task 5) to open the Task Information dialog box. Click the **Predecessors** tab. Click in the **ID** column of the first row of the Predecessors table. Enter a 4 in the ID column of the first row, and then press Tab to assign the predecessor of Task 4, **Perform site inspections**.

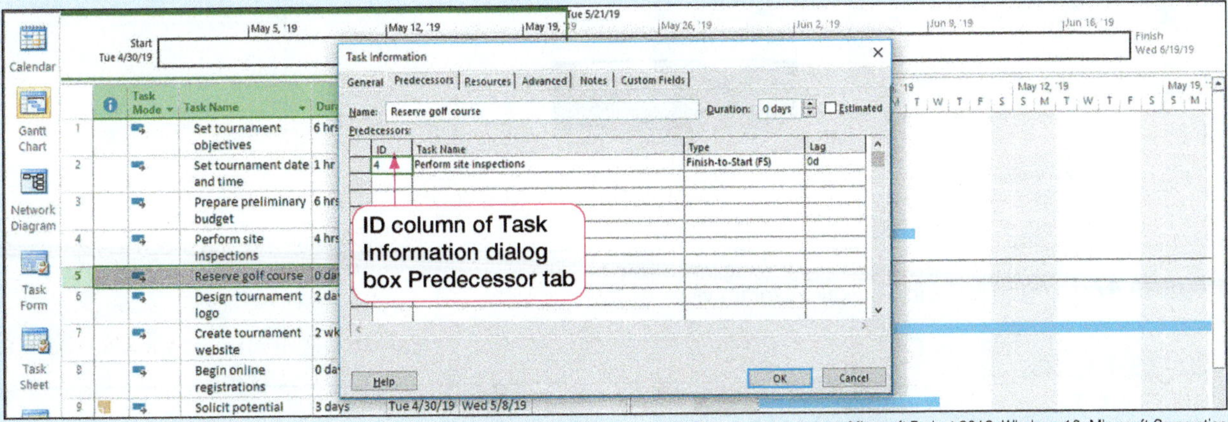

Microsoft Project 2016, Windows 10, Microsoft Corporation

Figure 45 Assigning predecessors in the Task Information dialog box

h. Click **OK**, and then select Task 1, **Set tournament objectives**.

i. On the View Bar, click **Network Diagram**. Click and hold **Set tournament objectives** (Task 1), and then drag to **Design tournament logo** (Task 6).

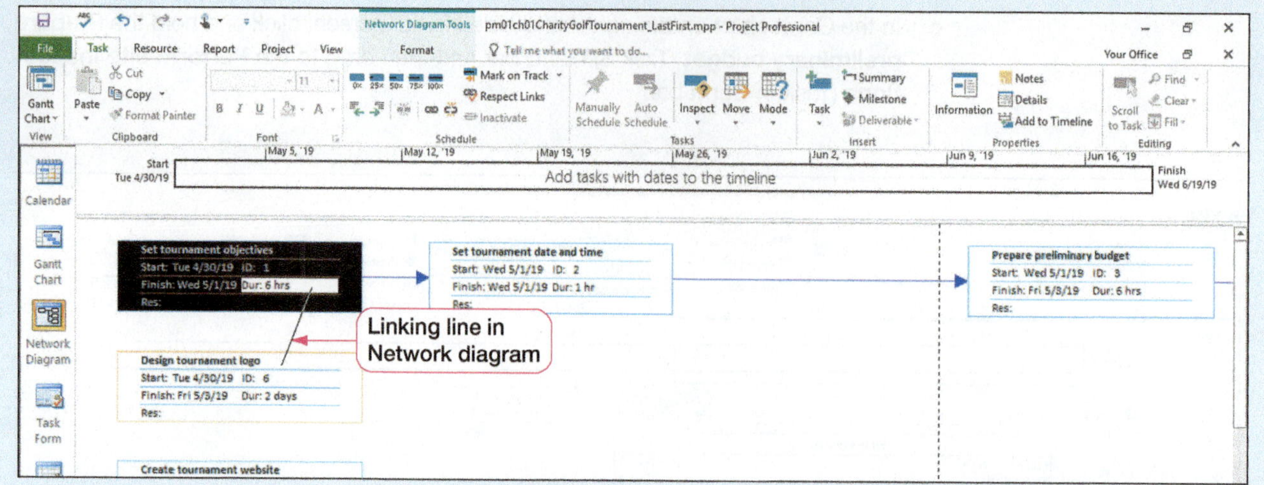

Microsoft Project 2016, Windows 10, Microsoft Corporation

Figure 46 Linking tasks in Network Diagram view

j. Release the mouse button to create a Finish-to-Start relationship between Task 1 and Task 6.

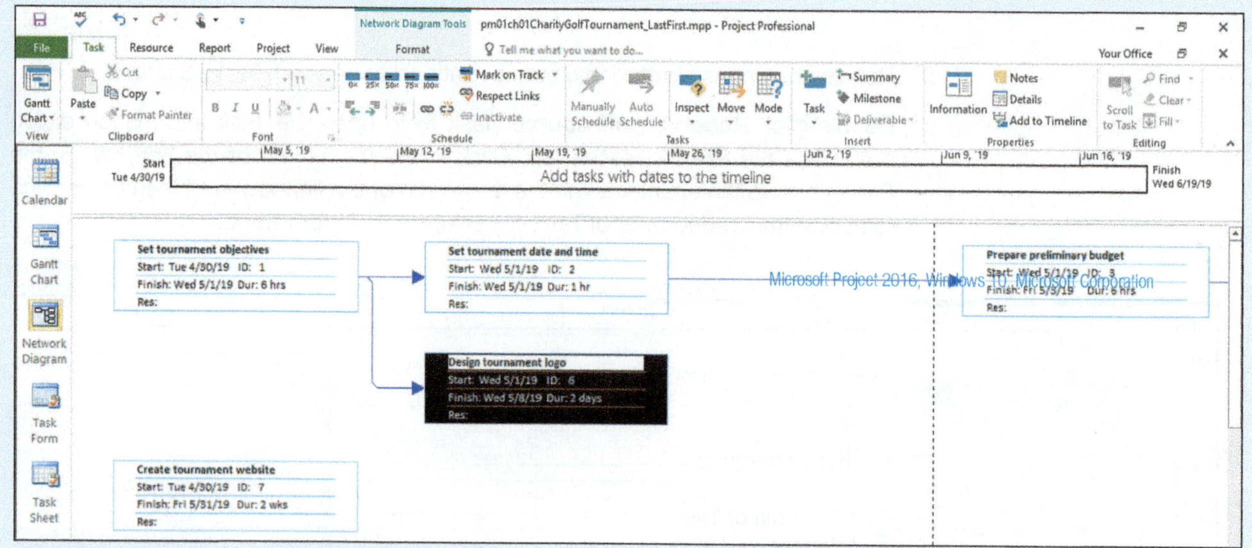

Microsoft Project 2016, Windows 10, Microsoft Corporation

Figure 47 Linked tasks in Network Diagram view

SIDE NOTE

Linking Tasks

When linking tasks in the Gantt chart, you will see the Link the Selected Tasks symbol as you drag from one task box to the next.

Troubleshooting

If you do not see the tasks in Network Diagram view you desire, you may need to scroll to the left or right to view the tasks. You can also click the Zoom button in the Zoom group on the View tab, and then select from the Zoom In or Zoom Out options.

SIDE NOTE

Scrolling to Task

To view a task from the Entry table that is not visible in the Gantt chart, right-click the task, and then click Scroll to Task.

k. Click and hold **Prepare preliminary budget** (Task 3) and drag to **Design tournament logo** (Task 6). Tasks 3 and 6 now have a Finish-to-Start relationship.

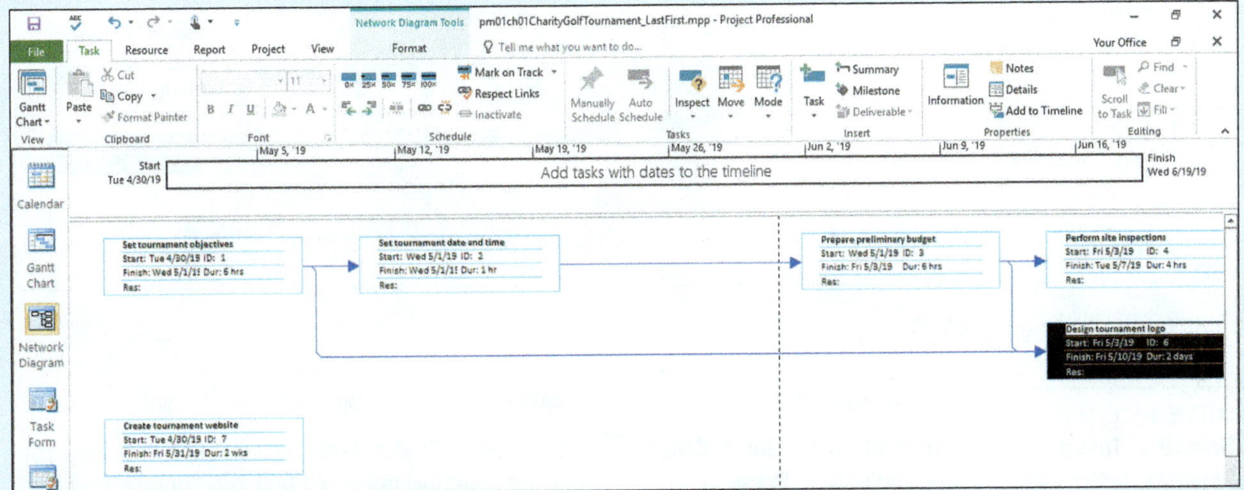

Microsoft Project 2016, Windows 10, Microsoft Corporation

Figure 48 Network Diagram view with tasks linked

SIDE NOTE

Dragging to Link Tasks

If you selected Task 7 and dragged to Task 6, the relationship would have a different result than selecting Task 6 and dragging to Task 7.

l. Click **Calendar view** in the View Bar. Click and hold **Design tournament logo** (Task 6), and then drag to **Create tournament website** (Task 7).

Troubleshooting

If you do not see the tasks you are looking for in Calendar view, be sure your Calendar is showing the correct month in which your project tasks are scheduled. You may need to change the Calendar to Week view and expand the Week view and scroll to the week of May 1, 2019.

Microsoft Project 2016, Windows 10, Microsoft Corporation

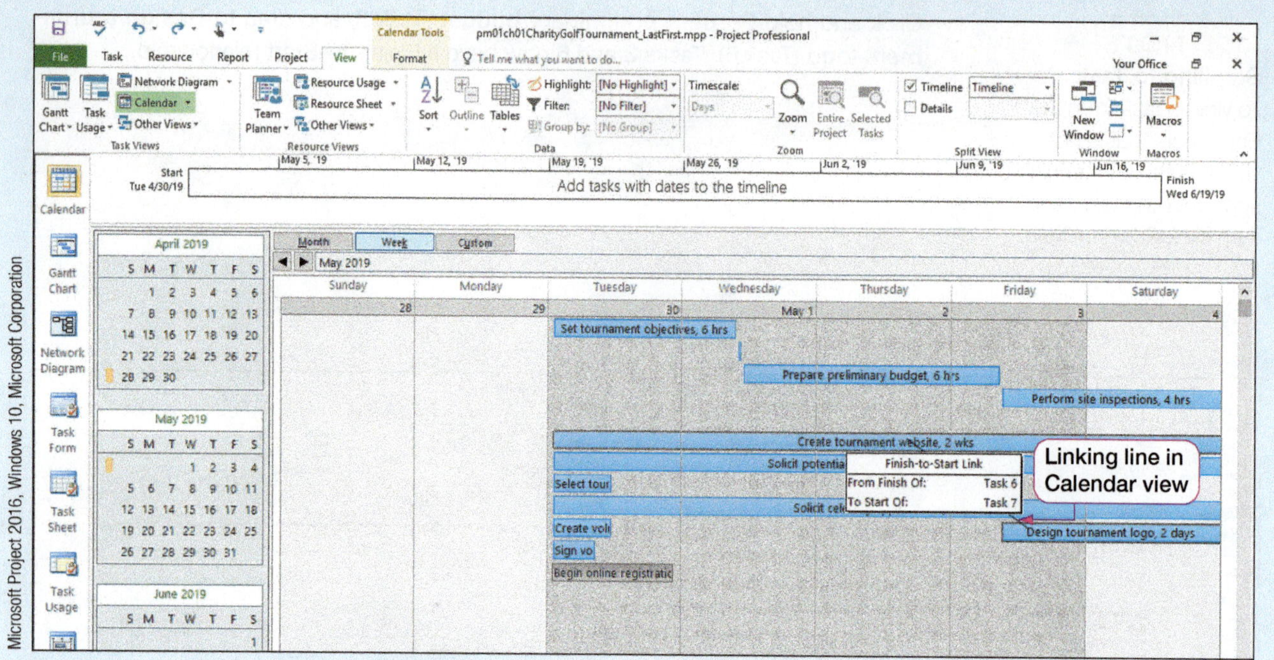

Figure 49 Linking tasks in Calendar view

> **SIDE NOTE**
>
> **Selecting Tasks**
>
> When you select more than one row in an Entry table, the selected tasks will be shaded.

m. Release the mouse button to create a relationship between Tasks 6 and 7.

n. Return to **Gantt Chart** view. Select **Tasks 7-13** by selecting the task row selectors. Press Ctrl + F2 to link the selected tasks. All task relationships are now defined.

Microsoft Project 2016, Windows 10, Microsoft Corporation

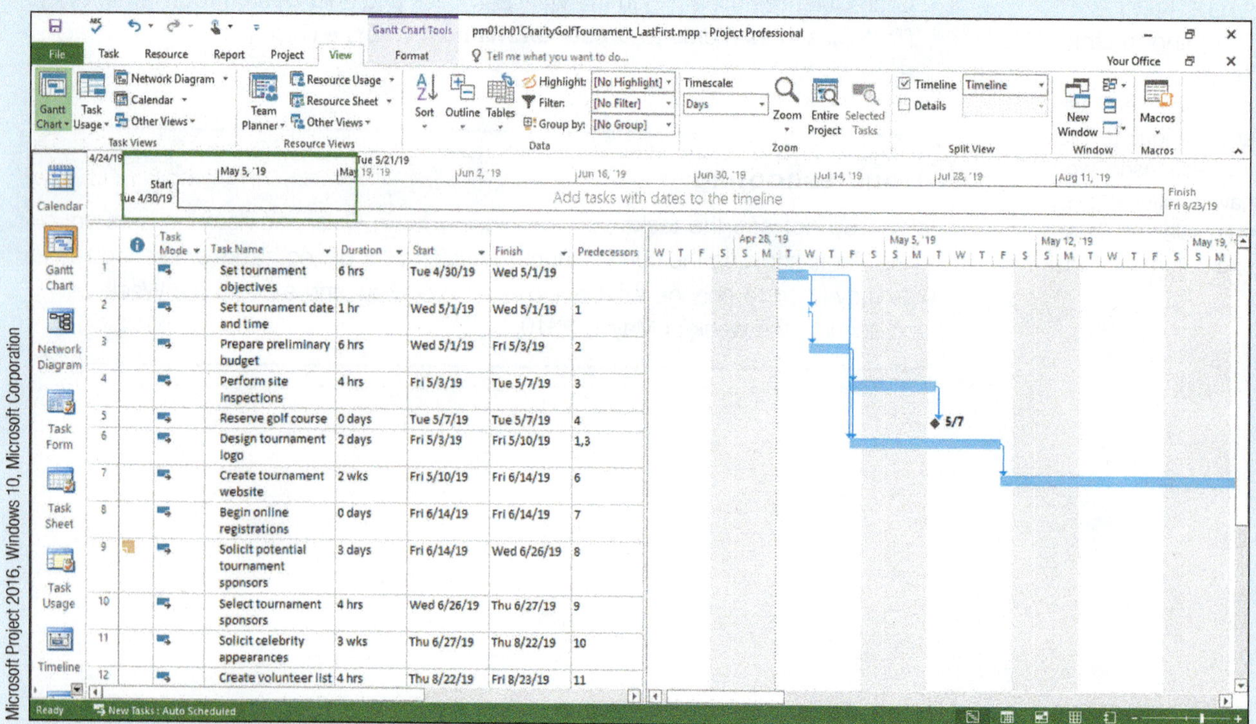

Figure 50 Gantt Chart view with task relationships defined

o. Click **Save**.

Modify Task Dependencies and Task Constraints

Although setting task relationships and task constraints is an important part of the planning process, it is equally important for project managers to evaluate the task relationships and constraints to be sure the results are logical. Therefore, Project 2016 allows project managers to modify, add, or delete task relationships and task constraints throughout the planning process. Task constraints can be modified by using the Task Information dialog box Advanced tab.

Task relationships can be added, deleted, or modified in the following ways:

- Using the Predecessors column of Gantt Chart view
- Using the Task Information dialog box Predecessors tab
- Double-clicking the link line in Gantt Chart and Network Diagram views and using the Task Dependency dialog box

Although a project may be set to Auto Scheduled, ultimately the project manager of the project has control over the scheduling of tasks. For example, a project manager can add, delete, or change task relationships to adjust the project schedule. A project manager can also add task constraints such as constraint deadlines, constraint types, and/or constraint dates to further control how tasks are being scheduled.

Modifying Dependencies and Constraints

After reviewing the project schedule, you want to make a few adjustments to the way the tasks are being scheduled. You will add a deadline to a task to ensure the task is completed on or before a certain date. You will also change a task's constraint type and change a task relationship.

In this exercise, you will modify task dependencies and task constraints.

PM01.13

SIDE NOTE

Task Constraints

Changing the constraint from As Late As Possible to As Soon As Possible allows the task to begin once its predecessor tasks are complete.

To Modify Task Dependencies and Task Constraints

a. Double-click **Reserve golf course** (Task 5), and then click the **Advanced** tab in the Task Information dialog box.

b. Click in the **Deadline** box, and then type 5/20/2019. Click **OK**. Note that the Green arrow indicator on the Gantt chart indicates the task must finish by this date.

	Task Mode	Task Name	Duration	Start	Finish	Predecessors
1		Set tournament objectives	6 hrs	Tue 4/30/19	Wed 5/1/19	
2		Set tournament date and time	1 hr	Wed 5/1/19	Wed 5/1/19	1
3		Prepare preliminary budget	6 hrs	Wed 5/1/19	Fri 5/3/19	2
4		Perform site inspections	4 hrs	Fri 5/3/19	Tue 5/7/19	3
5		Reserve golf course	0 days	Tue 5/7/19	Tue 5/7/19	4
6		Design tournament logo	2 days	Fri 5/3/19	Fri 5/10/19	1,3
7		Create tournament website	2 wks	Fri 5/10/19	Fri 6/14/19	6
8		Begin online registrations	0 days	Fri 6/14/19	Fri 6/14/19	7

Deadline task constraint

Figure 51 Modified task constraint

c. Select **Create volunteer list** (Task 12). If necessary, right-click the task, and then click **Scroll to Task** to view the task and its predecessor in the Gantt chart.

d. Press Ins to add a blank task row. Type Schedule celebrity appearances for the task name. Press Tab, type 1w, and then press Tab. Press Tab two more times, type 11 in the Predecessor column, and then press Enter.

e. Select **Create tournament website** (Task 7). Right-click the task, and then click **Scroll to Task** to view the task and its predecessor in the Gantt chart.

f. In the Gantt chart, double-click the **link line** between Tasks 6 and 7 to open the Task Dependency dialog box.

SIDE NOTE
Changing Dependencies
You can also type in a task dependency in the Predecessor column such as 6SS.

Troubleshooting

If you have difficulty determining which link line is between Tasks 6 and 7, zoom in on the Gantt chart.

g. In the Task Dependency dialog box, click the **Type** arrow. Click **Start-to-Start**.

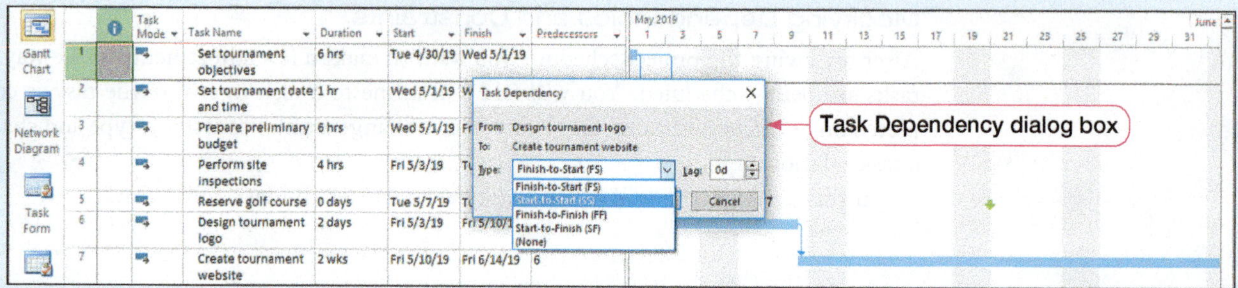

Microsoft Project 2016, Windows 10, Microsoft Corporation

Figure 52 Task Dependency dialog box

h. Click **OK**.

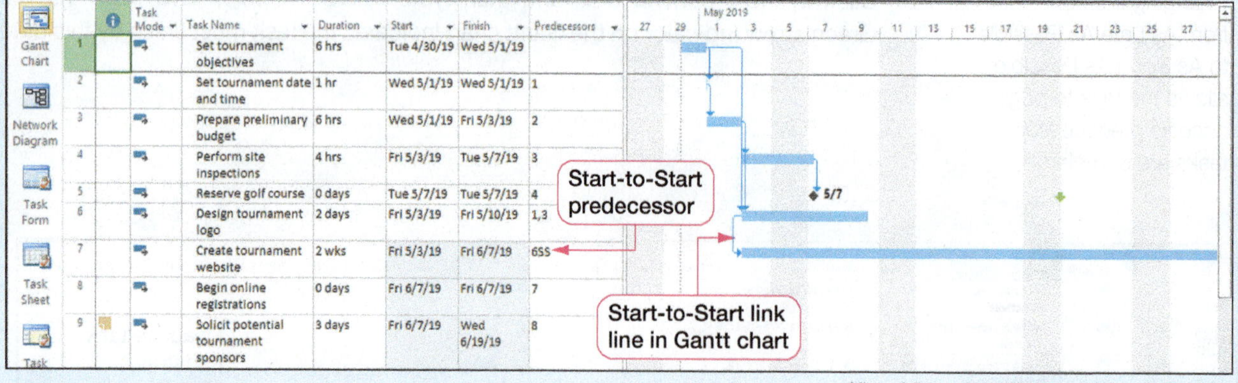

Microsoft Project 2016, Windows 10, Microsoft Corporation

Figure 53 Start-to-Start task dependency set

i. Select **Sign volunteer contracts** (Task 14). Press F2 on the keyboard to enter Edit mode. Select the word "Sign" and then type Mail to rename the task "Mail volunteer contracts." Press Enter to accept the change.

j. Double-click **Begin online registrations** (Task 8). Click the **Advanced** tab.

k. Click the **Constraint type** arrow, and then select **Start No Earlier Than**. In the Constraint date box, type 6/21/19. Click **OK**. Notice how this constraint changed the scheduled finish date of the project. Also, note the Constraint indicator in the Indicators column.

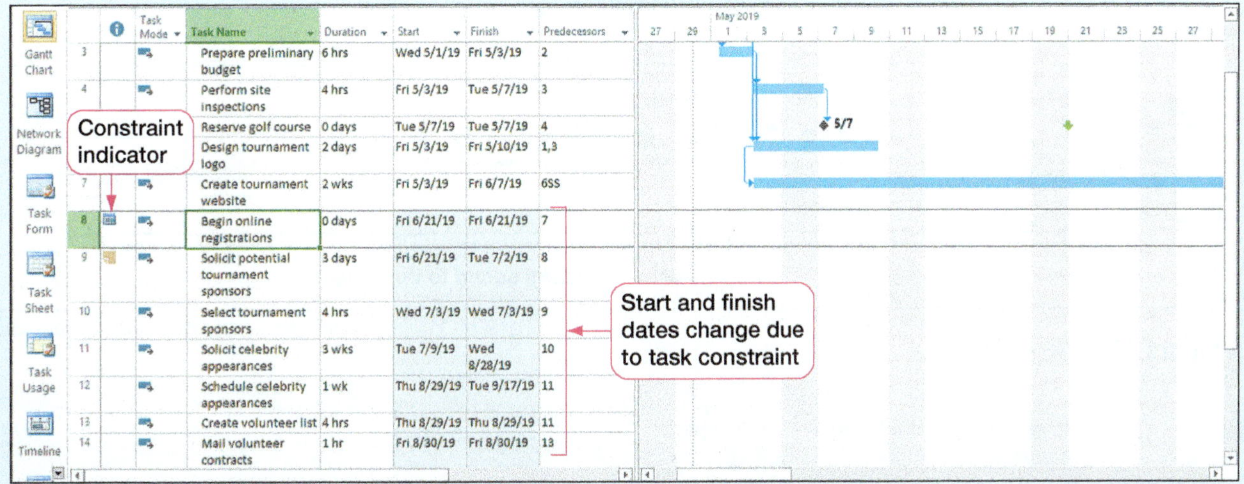

Microsoft Project 2016, Windows 10, Microsoft Corporation

Figure 54 Constraint indicator

l. **Save** the project.

If a project is scheduled by Start date, another way to modify task dependencies is to create lag time or lead time. **Lag time** moves a successor task forward in time so the Start dates between the tasks become further apart. **Lead time** moves a successor task back in time so the two tasks overlap and the Start date between the tasks gets closer. Lead time is the opposite of lag time and is sometimes referred to as negative lag. Lag time will likely extend the length of the project.

REAL WORLD ADVICE **Using Lag Time in a Project**

In projects, some tasks can be assigned to begin past the task's original assigned start date by adding a lag time. For example, a task "website goes live" may have a successor task of "analyze website traffic" with a Start-to-Start relationship. Although you can start analyzing website traffic at the start of the website going live, it makes sense to wait a week or two before you begin analyzing data. In this case, you would add lag time to the dependency. Adding lag time to tasks on the critical path will increase the overall project's duration. Lag time can be added by:

1. Double-clicking the link line between tasks in the Gantt chart or the Network Diagram.
2. In the Task Dependency dialog box, entering a duration in number or percentage format.

Adding Tasks to the Timeline

A timeline is used to display tasks, such as milestone tasks, in a simple compact format. The timeline can be used to display a summary of project plans. Timelines can also be shared with other Microsoft applications such as Microsoft PowerPoint 2016.

In this exercise, you will add tasks to the Timeline.

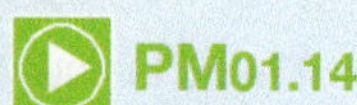

To Add Tasks to the Timeline

a. Click **Reserve golf course** (Task 5), and then on the Task tab, in the Properties group, click **Add to Timeline**.

b. Click **Begin online registrations** (Task 8), and then on the Task tab, in the Properties group, click **Add to Timeline**.

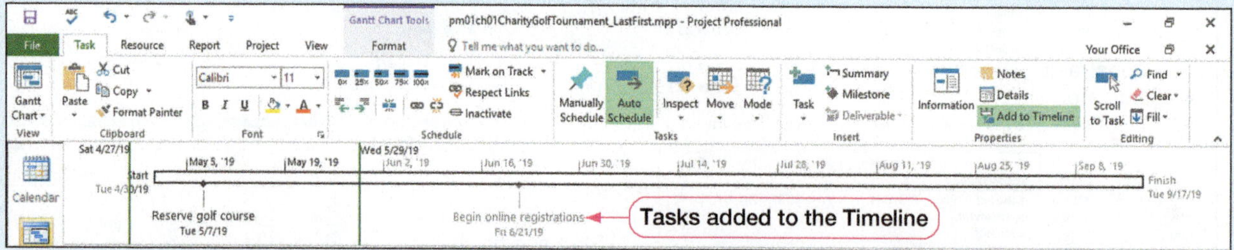

Microsoft Project 2016, Windows 10, Microsoft Corporation

Figure 55 Project Timeline

c. **Save** the project.

Deleting Task Dependencies

After linking tasks and setting task dependencies, you may decide a dependency is no longer needed or was created in error. Project 2016 allows you to not only modify task dependencies but also delete task dependencies.

You realize the scheduling of these tasks does not work with your project plan, so you explore ways of adjusting how these tasks are scheduled.

In this exercise, you will modify task dependencies and task constraints.

To Delete a Task Dependency

a. Double-click **Mail volunteer contracts** (Task 14).

b. On the Task Information dialog box, click the **Advanced** tab.

c. Type a Constraint date of 9/17/2019, and then click **OK**.

d. On the Task tab, in the Schedule group, click **Unlink Tasks**. Note the task Start date did not change because a Constraint date has been set on the task.

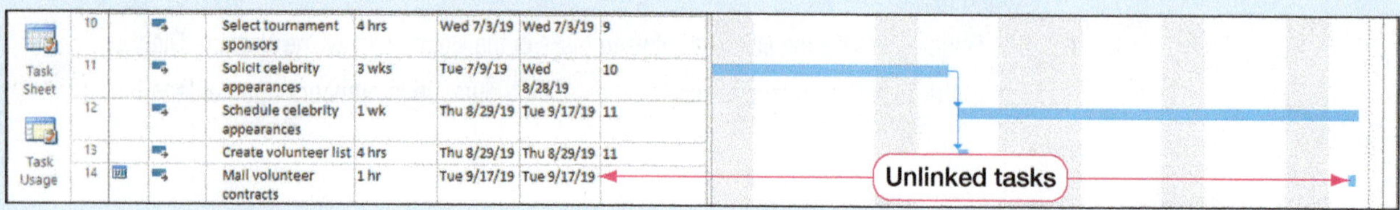

Microsoft Project 2016, Windows 10, Microsoft Corporation

Figure 56 Gantt Chart view with unlinked task

e. **Save** the project.

Prepare Project for Printing Project Views

Various views can be printed in Project 2016. Prior to printing, it is important to set up the project view to the appropriate zoom, include any header or footer information, and be sure all printing options are set the way you desire. Printing options are found on the File tab in Backstage view. **Backstage view** is where you manage your project file and perform tasks such as saving, printing, and setting project options. In Backstage view, you can preview each page layout before printing. You can also view the status of your project and make related project changes in Backstage view. Backstage view displays in full screen to allow for more window space to work with relevant features.

When printing in Gantt Chart view, the printout will appear as it looks on your screen. For example, if you only want to print the Task Name column and the Gantt chart, move the split bar to the right edge of the Task Name column with a left click and drag before printing. If the split bar is in the middle of a column, Project will not print that column. The default is for a legend to appear in the bottom portion of each page in Gantt Chart view.

When printing in Network Diagram view, you may want to zoom in to view fewer tasks or zoom out to view more tasks. When printing from Calendar view, you should decide if you want to print a month calendar or a week calendar. If neither option fits your needs, you can customize a Calendar Print option.

A header or footer can be added to all views in Project 2016. However, adding a header in Gantt Chart view does not add a header to Calendar view. If you desire a header on Calendar view or Network Diagram view, you will need to add one in each view by clicking on the Page Setup link in the Backstage view Print option.

Preparing to Print in Gantt Chart View

You want to print the Gantt chart to show the team the charity golf tournament project plan you have started. Before printing, you will prepare your project views by adding your name to the header in the Gantt Chart view.

In this exercise, you will prepare to print in Gantt Chart view.

To Prepare for Printing in Gantt Chart View

a. Drag the **split bar** between the Entry table and the Gantt chart to the right edge of the Finish date column in Gantt Chart view.

> **Troubleshooting**
>
> If your screen does not display a column you want to print when you are in Backstage view, make sure the entire column is visible in Gantt Chart view. Project will not print a column if the split bar is even slightly covering the column.

b. Click the **File** tab, and then click **Print**. Your project will appear in the Preview pane on the right side of the screen.

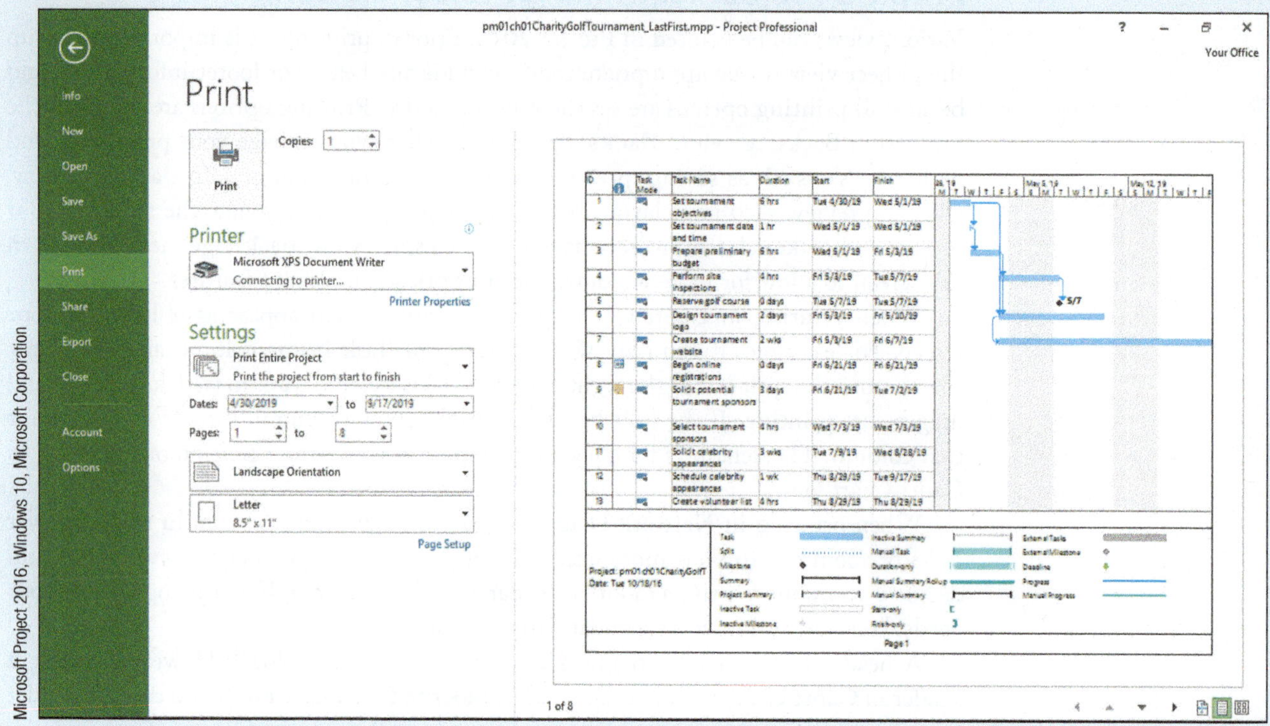

Figure 57 Gantt Chart in Preview pane

Troubleshooting

The printer displayed in the Printer list is determined by your installation and may be different than the printer shown in Figure 57.

c. Click in the Preview pane on the right-hand side of the Project 2016 window. The preview will zoom so you can see more detail.

d. Click the **Multiple Pages** button in the lower, right-hand corner of the Preview pane to view all pages of Gantt Chart view.

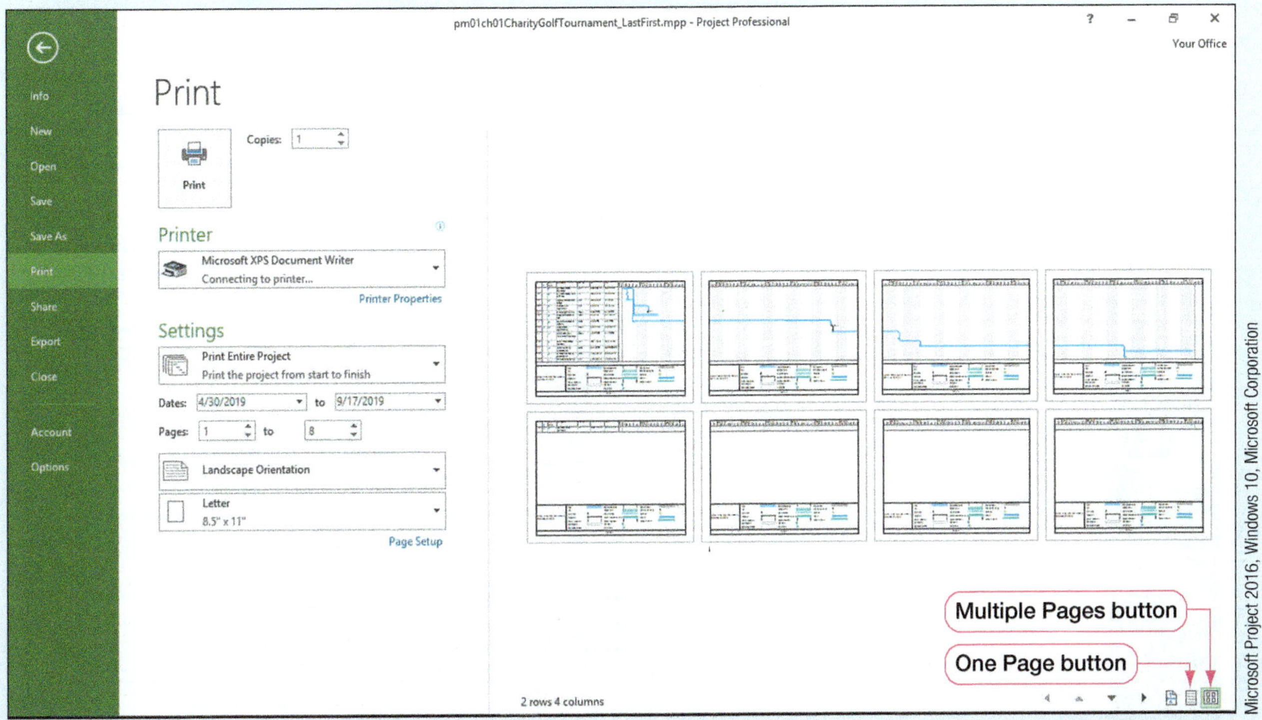

Figure 58 Preview pane navigation buttons

e. Click the **Page Setup** link. The Page Setup dialog box will open.

f. Click the **Header** tab. Click the **Right** tab, and then type your first and last name.

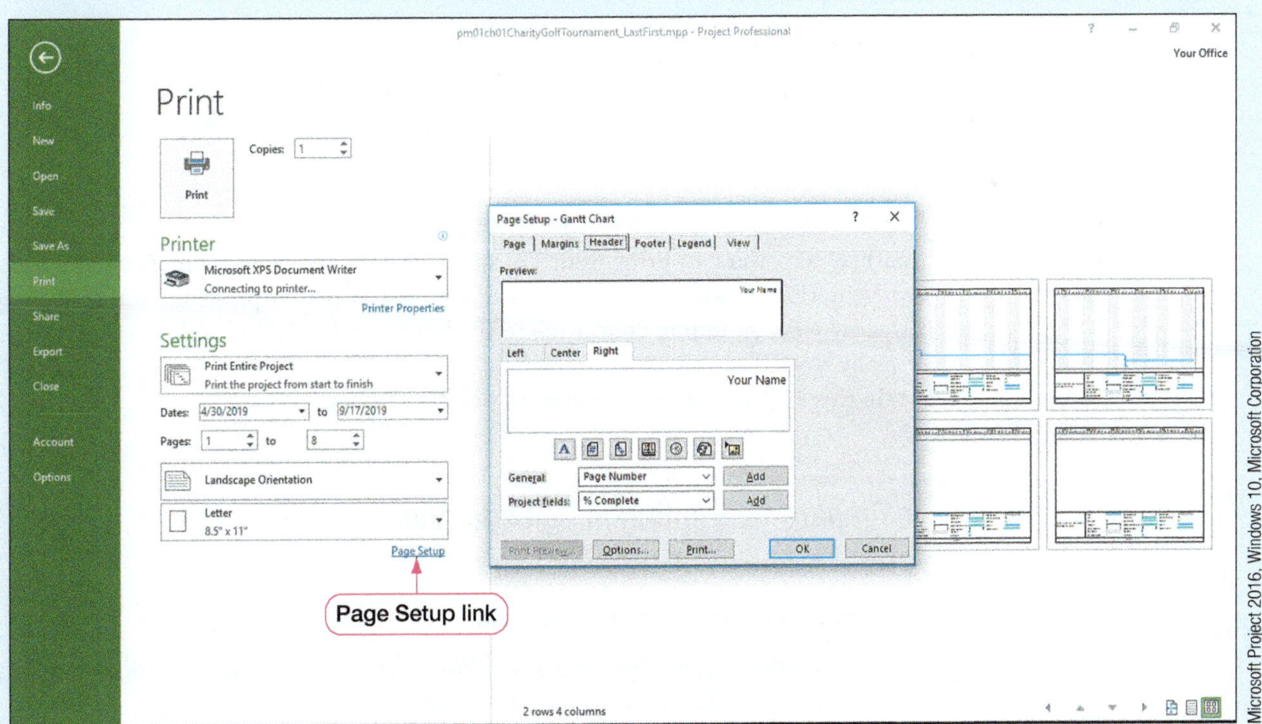

Figure 59 Page Setup dialog box

g. Click **OK**.

h. Click the **One Page** button in the lower right-hand corner of the Preview pane to view one page of the Gantt chart along with your change to the header.

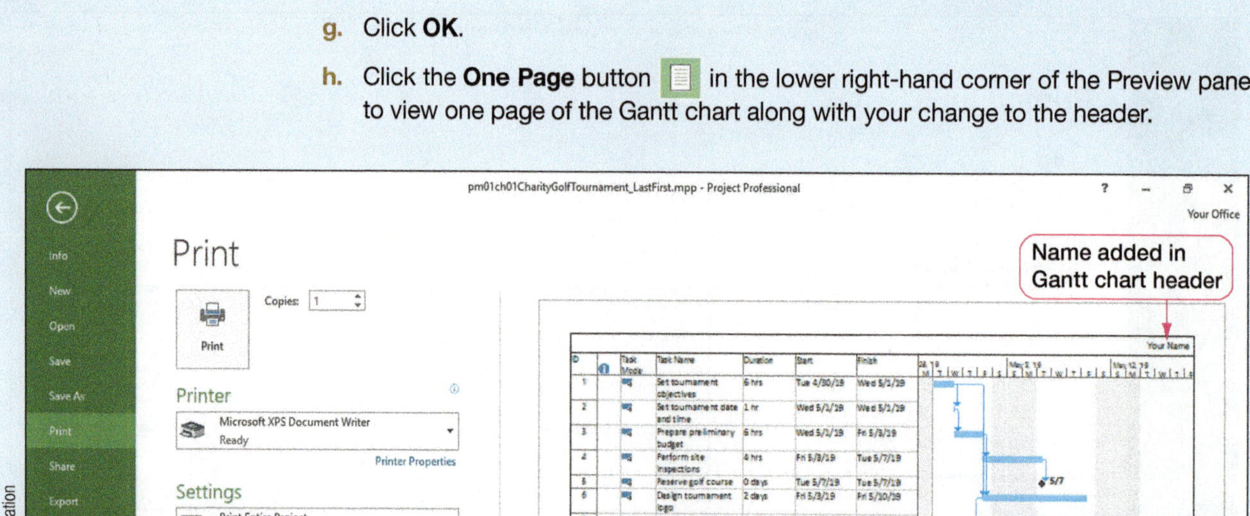

Microsoft Project 2016, Windows 10, Microsoft Corporation

Figure 60 Preview pane with header added

i. Click **Back**, and then **Save** the project.

Preparing to Print in Calendar View

You may also want to print from Calendar view to give your team members a visual representation of what will happen week to week. Before printing, you will prepare Calendar view by adding your name to the header and setting up the Calendar to print week by week.

In this exercise, you will prepare to print in Calendar view.

PM01.17

To Prepare for Printing in Calendar View

a. Click **Calendar** on the View Bar.

b. Click the **File** tab, and then click **Print**.

c. Click the **Page Setup** link, and then click the **Header** tab. Click the **Right** tab, and then type your first and last name. Click **OK**.

d. To view the project tasks, click the **list arrow** for the starting date.

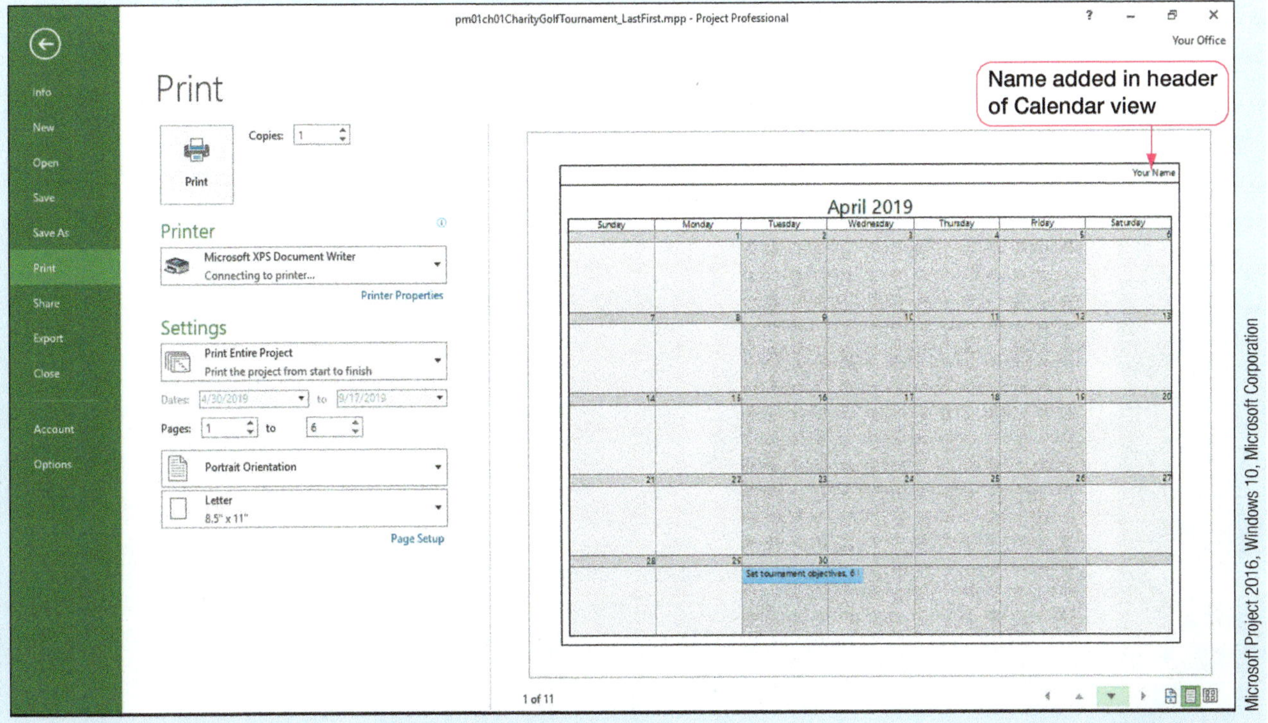

Figure 61 Preview pane with header added in Calendar view

e. Click **5/20/2019**.

Troubleshooting

If you only see the month of April, use the view buttons in the lower right-hand corner of the preview window to scroll to the month of May in the preview pane.

f. Click **Back**.

g. **Save** the project.

Preparing to Print in Network Diagram View

One of your team members has asked for a printout of the project's task to be in a graphical format, not in Calendar or Gantt Chart format. Therefore, you decide to print the project tasks in Network Diagram view.

In this exercise, you prepare the Network Diagram view to print.

To Prepare for Printing in Network Diagram View

a. On the View Bar, click **Network Diagram** view.

b. Click the **File** tab, and then click **Print**.

c. Click the **Page Setup** link, and then click the **Header** tab. Click the **Right** tab, and then type your first and last name. Click **OK**.

d. Click the **Landscape Orientation** arrow, and then click **Portrait Orientation**.

e. Use the **Page Navigation** buttons to scroll through the pages that will print. Note the shape of the milestone tasks in the Network Diagram.

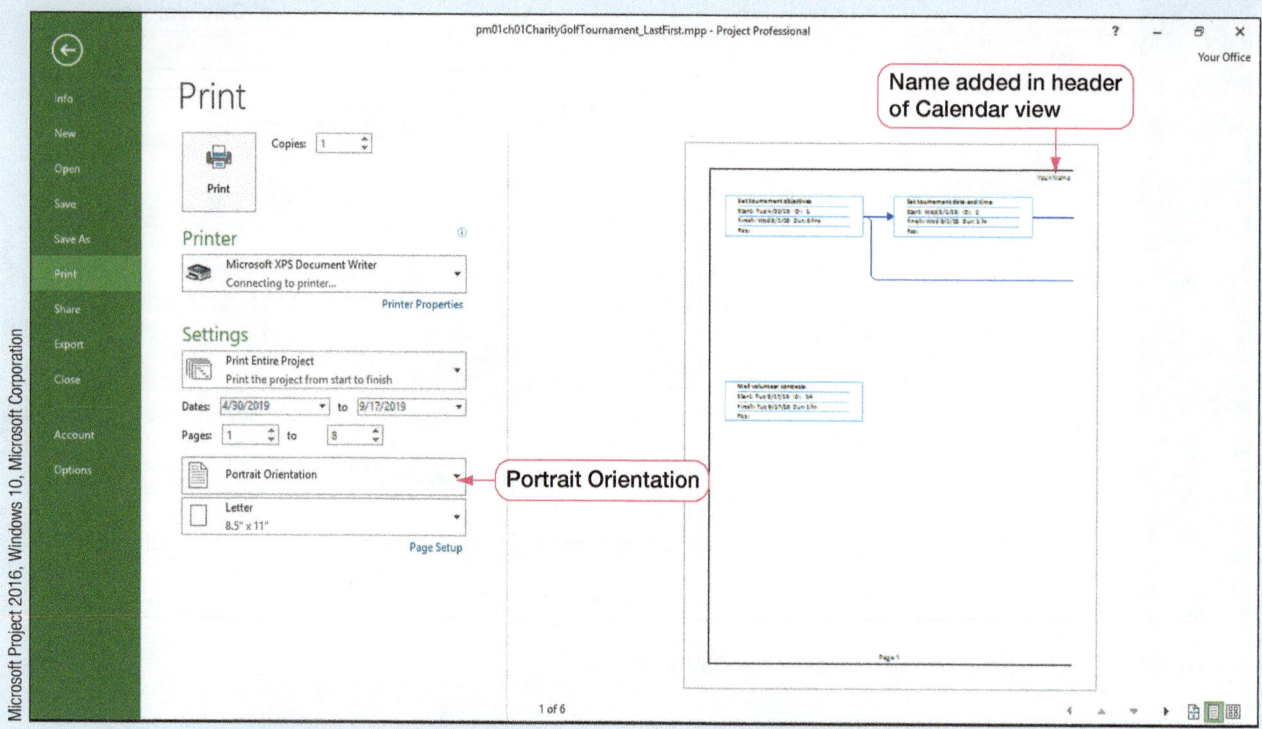

Microsoft Project 2016, Windows 10, Microsoft Corporation

Figure 62 Preview pane with header added in Network Diagram view Portrait and Orientation

f. Click **Back**.

g. **Save** the project, exit Project 2016, and then submit your file as directed by your instructor.

Concept Check

1. Explain the following terms to someone new to Project 2016 software:
   a. Predecessor task
   b. Successor task
   c. Constraint
   d. Milestone
2. What is the purpose of a Gantt chart?
3. Describe the components of the Project Information dialog box.
4. Why is it important for a project's base calendar to accurately reflect the available working time of a project?
5. Describe the difference between a Manually Scheduled and an Auto Scheduled project.
6. List the task durations and task duration abbreviations in Project.
7. How can a Note be applied to a task? When would a Note be applied to a task?
8. Describe at least three ways you can add task dependencies.
9. Describe at least three ways you can change a task dependency between tasks.
10. How do you add your name to the header of the Gantt chart?

Key Terms

Visual Summary

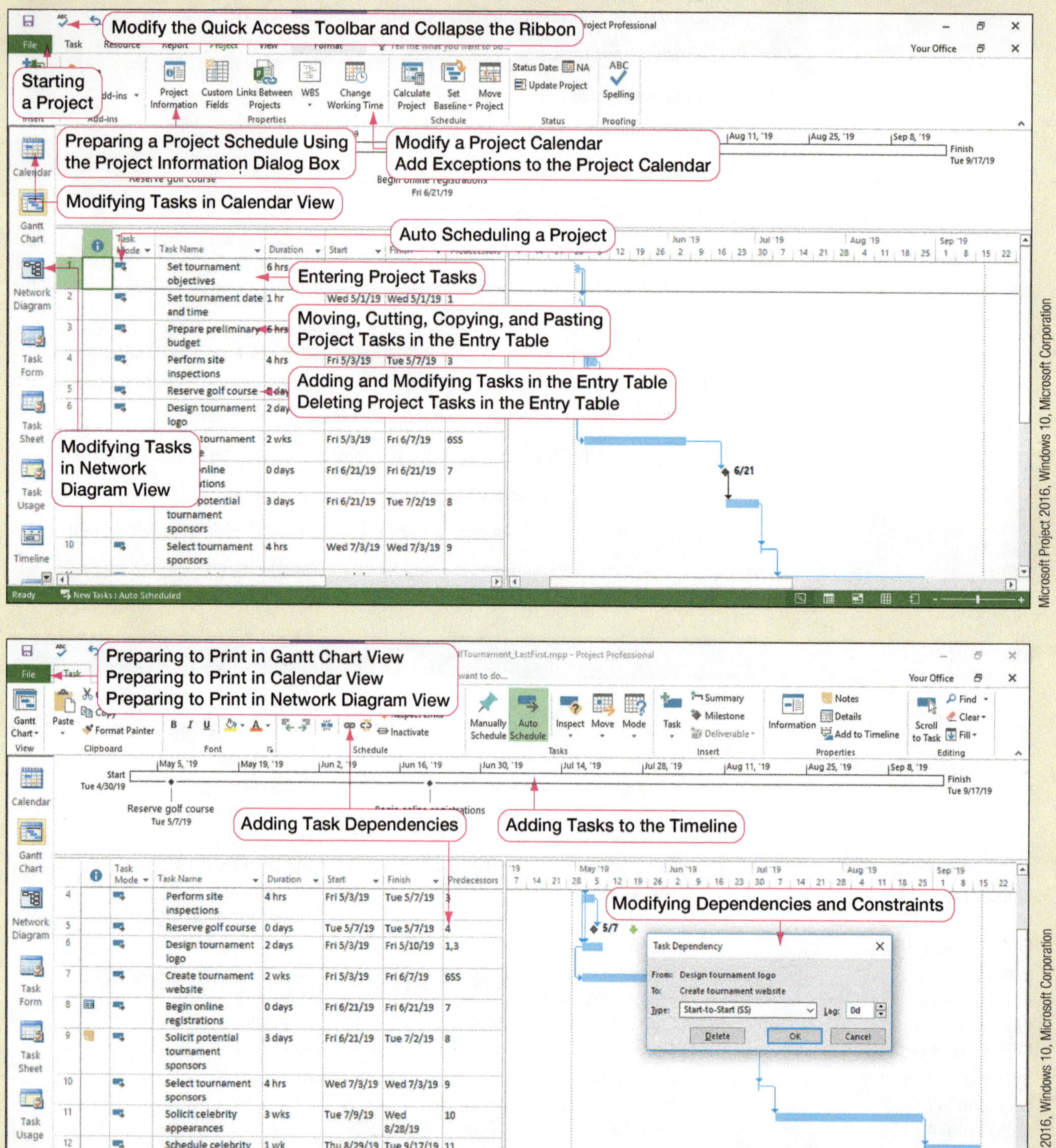

Figure 63

Practice

Student data file needed:

No data file needed

You will save your file as:

pm01ch01BloodDrive_LastFirst.mpp

Organizing a Blood Drive at Your Community College

Information Technology

You have been asked by the student senate to be the project lead of a blood drive at your school to promote a cause that saves millions of lives each year. To demonstrate your project management skills, you decide to use Project 2016 to set up the plan for the blood drive. The senate would like to hold the blood drive in October. They note that the campus will be closed on September 27, 2019. You decide to use Project 2016 to help determine a date for the blood drive. You are available to work on the planning of this project Wednesday through Friday, 8:00 AM to 12:00 PM.

a. Open a **Blank Project**. Click the **File** tab, and then click **Save**. Click **Browse**, and then navigate to the location where you are saving your files. Click in the **File** name box, type pm01ch01BloodDrive_LastFirst.mpp using your last and first name, and then click **Save**.

b. Click the **Project** tab, and then in the Properties group, click **Project Information.** Set the Start date to August 29, 2019. Click **OK**.

c. On the Project tab, in the Properties group, click **Change Working Time**. Click the **Work Weeks** tab, and then click **Details**. Select **Monday** and **Tuesday**. Click **Set days to nonworking time**.

d. Click **Wednesday**, press and hold Shift, and then click **Friday**. Click **Set day(s) to these specific working times**. Select row 2 in the specific working times grid. Press Del to clear the 1:00 PM to 5:00 PM working times. Click **OK**.

e. Click the **Exceptions** tab in the Change Working Time dialog box. Enter the exception name College closed for inservice, and then press Tab. Click in the Start column in row 1. Change the start date in row 1 to September 27, 2019, and then press Tab. Click **OK**.

f. Click the **Task** tab. In the Tasks group, select the Mode arrow, and then click **Auto Schedule**.

g. Be sure the View Bar is showing on the left-hand side of your screen. (Hint: If the View Bar is not showing, right-click GANTT CHART on the left-hand side of your screen, and then click View Bar from the shortcut menu.)

h. If necessary, add the **Timeline** below the ribbon. (Hint: If the Timeline is not showing, click the **View** tab, and then in the Split View group, click Timeline.)

i. Enter the following tasks and durations into the Entry table:

	TASK NAME	DURATION
1	Select blood drive campus location	4h
2	Set blood drive goal	1h
3	Form a recruitment team	2d
4	Divide team roles and duties	2h
5	Plan promotional strategies	4h
6	Publicize the blood drive	1d
7	Schedule appointments	2w
8	Check site arrangements	4h
9	Get visitor parking passes	2h
10	Email appointment reminder messages	4h
11	Post directional arrows and posters around campus	1h

j. On the Quick Access Toolbar, click the Spelling button to check the spelling of the task names.

k. Click **Publicize the blood drive** (Task 6). Press Ins to add a blank task. With the new blank task selected, add the task name Create promotional materials. Assign this task a duration of 5 hours.

l. Click the row selector of **Get visitor parking passes** (Task 10). While holding the mouse, drag Task 10 after Email appointment reminder messages (Task 11). Release the mouse. Get visitor parking passes is now moved to become Task 11.

m. Click **Publicize the blood drive** (Task 7). Click the **Task** tab, if necessary, and then in the Insert group, click **Task** to add a new task. Enter the task name Contact local businesses, and then add the duration of 6 hours. Task 7 is now Contact local businesses.

n. Double-click **Contact local businesses** (Task 7) to open the Task Information dialog box. Click the **Notes** tab. Type Contact the webmaster to place blood drive info on college website. Click **OK**.

o. Click the **File** tab, and then click **Print**. Click the **Page Setup** link, and then click the **Header** tab. Click the **Right** tab, and then type your first and last name. Click **OK**.

p. Click the **Back** button to exit Backstage view and return to Gantt Chart view.

Click **Network Diagram** on the View Bar. Click **Post directional arrows and posters around campus** (Task 13). Click the **Task** tab, if necessary, and then in the Insert group, click **Task** to add a new task in Network Diagram view.

q. Double-click the new task, and then type the task name Blood drive begins. Type a duration to 0 days to make this task a milestone task. Click **OK**. Note the shape of the Milestone task in the Network Diagram view.

r. With Blood drive begins (Task 13) selected, in the Properties group of the Task tab, click **Add to Timeline.** The milestone is now added to the Timeline.

s. Click **Gantt Chart** on the View Bar to switch to Gantt Chart view.

t. Move **Blood drive begins** (Task 13) after **Post directional arrows and posters around campus** (Task 14) to make it the final project task.

u. Select **Tasks 1-14**. Click Ctrl + F2 to link all the tasks.

v. Select **Schedule appointments** (Task 9), and then change the duration from 2 weeks to 20h.

w. Change the relationship to a **Start-to-Start** relationship between Schedule appointments (Task 9) and Check site arrangements (Task 10).

x. Click **Email appointment reminder messages** (Task 11). On the Task tab, in the Properties group, click the **Information** button to open the Task Information dialog box. Click the **Advanced** tab. Add the Constraint date October 9, 2019.

y. Select the task names. Click the **Format** tab. In the Columns group, click **Wrap Text** twice

z. Save your **pm01ch01BloodDrive_LastFirst** project file, exit Project 2016, and then submit your file as directed by your instructor.

Problem Solve

Student data file needed:

 No data file needed

You will save your file as:

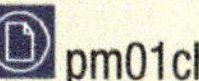 pm01ch01JobSearchPortfolio_LastFirst.mpp

Planning Your Job Search Portfolio

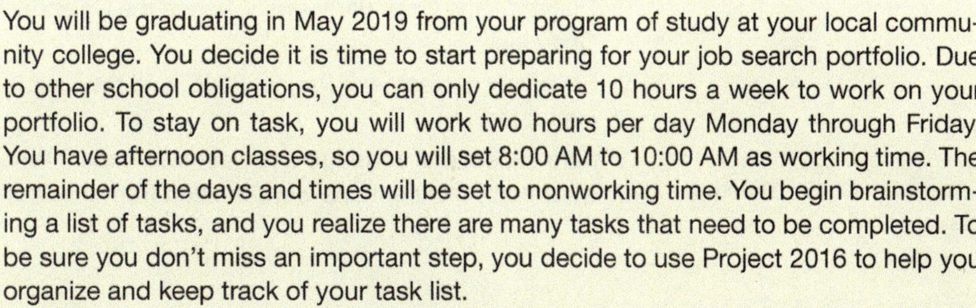

Sales & Marketing

You will be graduating in May 2019 from your program of study at your local community college. You decide it is time to start preparing for your job search portfolio. Due to other school obligations, you can only dedicate 10 hours a week to work on your portfolio. To stay on task, you will work two hours per day Monday through Friday. You have afternoon classes, so you will set 8:00 AM to 10:00 AM as working time. The remainder of the days and times will be set to nonworking time. You begin brainstorming a list of tasks, and you realize there are many tasks that need to be completed. To be sure you don't miss an important step, you decide to use Project 2016 to help you organize and keep track of your task list.

a. Open a blank Project 2016 file, and then save it as pm01ch01JobSearchPortfolio_LastFirst.mpp in the location where you store your files.

b. Since you are just starting your portfolio, you will leave the default schedule of Project Start Date. Set the Start date to February 1, 2019.

c. Change the project calendar to set working time to Monday through Friday, 8:00 AM to 10:00 AM. The remainder of the days and times will be set to nonworking time.

d. Add the exception Spring Break to set March 11–15, 2019, as nonworking days.

e. Set the project to Auto Scheduled so the task dates are calculated by Project 2016.

f. Enter in the following tasks:

	TASK	DURATION
1	Purchase portfolio supplies	2 h
2	Get an unofficial transcript	4 h
3	Identify references	1 w
4	Write resume	6 h
5	Create a resume in PDF format	2 h
6	Write a cover letter	3 h
7	Conduct online job search	5 d
8	Gather work examples for portfolio	10 h
9	Conduct a mock interview	3 h
10	Send resumes to potential employers	2 h
11	Compile portfolio	4 h

g. Select **Create a resume in PDF format** (Task 5). Add a note to Task 5 Use a PDF resume for online applications.

h. With Task 5 still selected, in a Project 2016 view of your choice, add a new task Edit resume with a duration of 2 hours. The Edit resume task becomes Task 5.

i. Move Write a cover letter (Task 7) after Conduct online job search (Task 8). The Write a cover letter task becomes Task 8.

j. Add the task note Contact Career Resource Center. to Gather work examples for portfolio (Task 9). Click **OK**.

k. Change the duration of Identify references (Task 3) to 8 hours.

l. In Gantt Chart view, move the split bar to the right edge of the Predecessors column. Link Tasks 1–12 in the order they appear in the Entry table.
m. If the Timeline is showing, remove it from Gantt Chart view.
n. Hide the View Bar.
o. Hide the Task Mode column. (Hint: Right-click the Task Mode column.)
p. Add your first and last name as a header on the right tab of Gantt Chart, Network Diagram, and Calendar views. Change the Calendar view to Week. Return to Gantt Chart view.
q. Save your project, exit Project 2016, and then submit your file as directed by your instructor.

Critical Thinking Why are exceptions added to a project's calendar? What could be the result to a project's schedule if exceptions were omitted from the Project calendar?

Perform 1: Perform in Your Life

Student data file needed:

 No data file needed

You will save your file as:

Preparing a Business Plan

You have decided to start a virtual assistant business in which you work from your home offering office-related assistance and software solutions to local businesses. In order to secure funding for your business, you must prepare a detailed business plan. You decide to use Project 2016 to help organize the details of preparing your business plan. Your goal is to have the business plan completed by July 1, 2019. Based on your knowledge of preparing a Project 2016 file, you will:

a. Determine if you will set your project to schedule by Start date or by Finish date. As directed by your instructor, explain why you chose Start date or Finish date.
b. Adjust the Standard calendar for a work week maximum of 20 hours of working time. Any combination of days and hours is acceptable. Add a minimum of one exception to the calendar.
c. As directed by your instructor, explain the adjustments made to the calendar and detail any exceptions to the calendar.
d. Determine whether you want your project to be Auto Scheduled or Manually Scheduled. As directed by your instructor, explain how you set Project 2016 to schedule your project and why you chose that method.
e. Research preparing a business plan. There is more than one way to prepare a business plan. (Hint: Open Excel 2016, and in the Search box, type business plan.) You will use Project 2016 to enter a list of tasks you would need to complete to prepare your virtual assistant business plan. You must list a minimum of ten key tasks to preparing a business plan. For example, Step 1 (Task 1) may be "Define business vision."
f. After identifying a minimum of ten key steps to preparing a business plan, determine task durations based on your research and/or knowledge of preparing a business plan. Take into consideration your time available to work on the tasks as well.
g. Create appropriate task relationships (dependencies) for the project tasks. Assign a relationship other than Finish-to-Start to at least one task. As directed by your instructor, explain why you selected the task relationships for the project tasks.

h. Add at least one task constraint. As directed by your instructor, explain why you added the constraint and how it affects the project plan.

i. Add your first and last name as a header in Gantt Chart, Network Diagram, and Calendar views. Save your project as pm01ch01BusinessPlan_LastFirst.mpp in the location where you store your files.

j. Exit Project 2016, and then submit your file as directed by your instructor.

Microsoft Project 2016

Chapter 2 | CREATING A DETAILED PROJECT PLAN

OBJECTIVES

1. Identify the critical path p. 60
2. Create a Work Breakdown Structure p. 62
3. Create and assign project resources p. 70
4. Change task durations by adding resources p. 76
5. View resource assignments in the Team Planner view p. 83
6. Enhance a project schedule with elapsed duration and recurring tasks p. 84
7. Share project information p. 88
8. Copy and paste project information to other applications p. 91
9. Share project information with Microsoft Excel p. 96
10. Use and create Project templates p. 108

Prepare Case

MyITLab®

Painted Paradise Golf Resort—First Annual Charity Golf Tournament

The Painted Paradise Golf Resort will be holding its first annual charity golf tournament to raise money for the purchase of textbooks to be donated to the elementary schools in Santa Fe, New Mexico. Patti Rochelle, the project manager of this event, has assigned you to start an initial list of project tasks using Microsoft Project 2016 to organize this event. She has looked over your list of tasks and made a few adjustments. Now Patti is asking you to develop a more detailed project plan by creating a Work Breakdown Structure for this project and assigning resources to individual tasks.

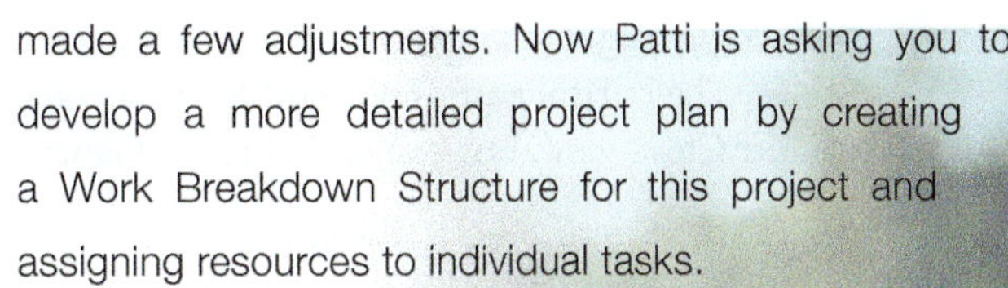

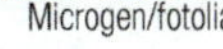

Microgen/fotolia

Student data files needed for this workshop:

pm01ch02CharityGolfTournament.mpp

pm01ch02CharityGolfTournamentTasks.xlsx

You will save your files as:

pm01ch02CharityGolfTournament_LastFirst.mpp

pm01ch02CharityGolfTournament_LastFirst.docx

pm01ch02CharityGolfTournament_LastFirst.xlsx

pm01ch02CharityGolfTournamentGanttChart_LastFirst.docx

pm01ch02CharityGolfTournamentTimeline_LastFirst.docx

pm01ch02CharityGolfTournamentExport_LastFirst.xlsx

pm01ch02SimpleProjectPlan_LastFirst.mpp

pm01ch02EventTemplate_LastFirst.mpt

pm01ch02EventTemplate_LastFirst.mpp

Detailing a Project Plan

Project managers may choose to use Microsoft Project 2016 to assist them in planning and achieving project success. Project 2016 can provide project managers with an orderly way of creating a project schedule. To determine a project's schedule, project managers must adjust a project's calendar to reflect available working time, determine a project's scheduling method of automatic or manual, identify the project's tasks, define task relationships, and set task resources. Once this has been accomplished, project managers will have an idea of when the project should start or when the project should finish. However, project managers should not rely on the software to make all the scheduling decisions for a project. After all, Project 2016 is an application used to assist project managers in meeting the project goal, but it should not be the decision-making authority on the project plan.

Identify the Critical Path

Project managers create a project plan by setting task dependencies (relationships). By setting task dependencies, Project 2016 will create the critical path. The critical path consists of tasks that must be completed on time in order for a project to stay on track and come to a successful completion.

Creating task dependencies changes the start and finish dates of tasks. Creating task dependencies also creates the project's critical path. The critical path consists of tasks (or a single task) that determine the project's finish date (or start date). It is a list of tasks that must be completed on time for the project to meet the project timeline. Tasks on the critical path are critical tasks. Critical tasks do not have slack. **Slack** is the time a task can be delayed from its scheduled start date without delaying the project.

The best way to view the critical path is in Network Diagram view. In Network Diagram view, the critical path is represented by red task boxes and red link lines. This view can help project managers analyze the critical path and critical tasks and make informed project decisions. The critical path is not visible in Calendar view. By default, it is also not displayed in Gantt Chart view, but you can add it to Gantt Chart view if desired.

Identifying the Critical Path

You want to view your project's critical path so you are aware of which tasks are critical tasks and therefore must be completed on time. You want to view the project's critical path in both the Network Diagram and Gantt Chart views.

In this exercise, you will view the critical path.

 PM02.00

SIDE NOTE
Project Calendar
It is important to review a project's calendar to understand how Project is scheduling tasks.

SIDE NOTE
Noncritical Tasks
Tasks not displayed in red are noncritical tasks. Project determines the critical path by task relationships and task constraints.

To View the Critical Path

a. Open **Microsoft Project 2016**. Click **Open Other Projects.** Navigate to the location of your student data files and browse for **pm01ch02CharityGolfTournament.mpp**, and then click **Open**.

b. Click the **File** tab, and then click **Save As**. Click **This PC**, and then if necessary click **Browse** and navigate to the location where you are storing your files. Click in the File name box and type pm01ch02CharityGolfTournament_LastFirst, using your last and first name. Click **Save**.

c. Click the **Project** tab. In the Properties group, click **Change Working Time** to view the project's calendar. Note the working days, nonworking days, and calendar exceptions. Click **OK**.

d. Click **Network Diagram** view from the View Bar. Scroll through Network Diagram view to view the project's tasks. The tasks in red are critical tasks. The tasks that do not appear in red are considered noncritical tasks.

Troubleshooting

If the View Bar is not visible on the left-hand side of the Project window, as shown in Figure 1, right-click the vertical text GANTT CHART on the left-hand side of the Project window, and then click View Bar.

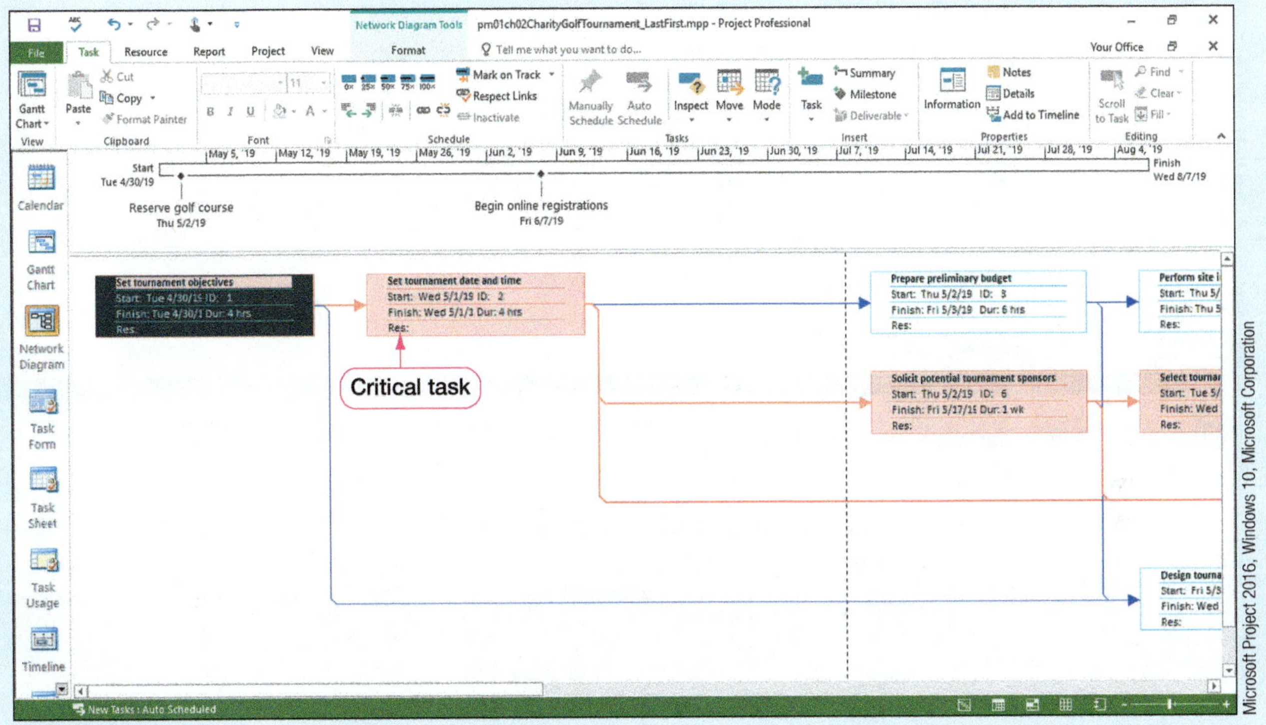

Figure 1 Critical path in Network Diagram view

Troubleshooting

If you do not see the same number of tasks on your screen, you can use the Zoom Slider in the lower right corner of the Project window to adjust the zoom in all Project views.

e. Return to **Gantt Chart** view, and then click the **Gantt Chart Tools Format** tab.

f. In the Bar Styles group, click the **Critical Tasks** check box to add the critical path to Gantt Chart view. Notice the critical path on the Gantt chart.

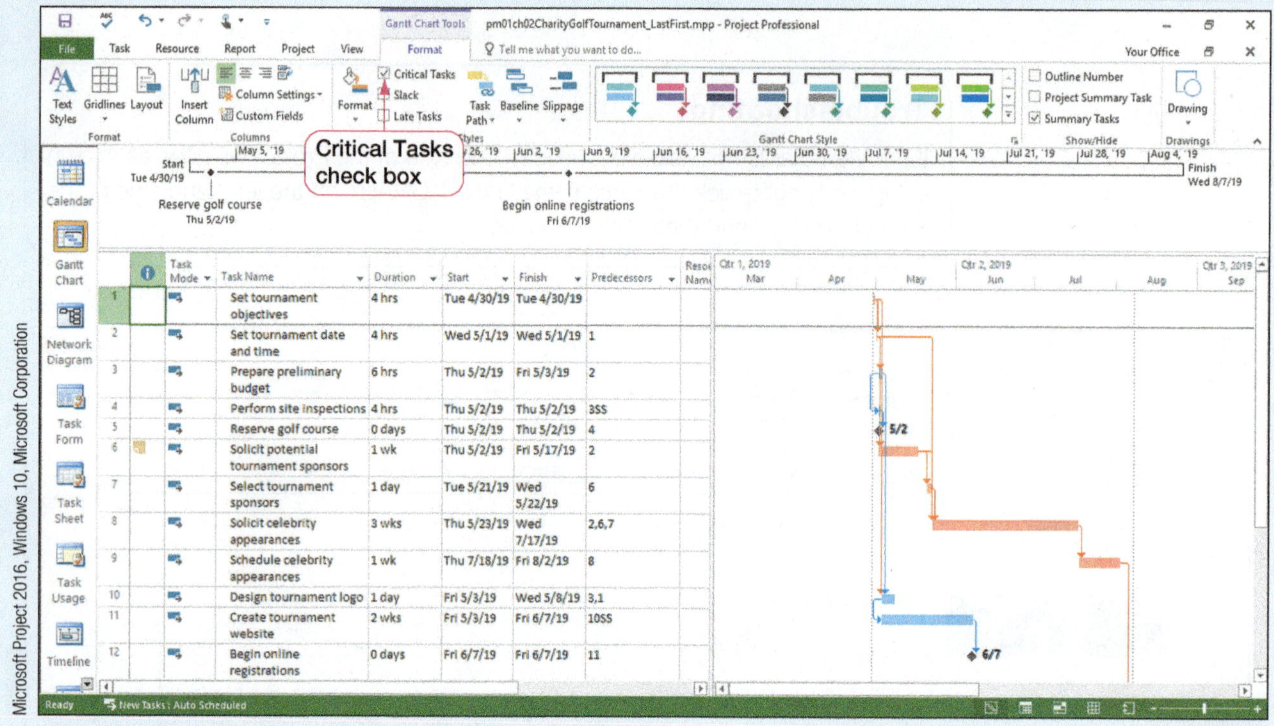

Figure 2 Gantt Chart view with critical path

g. Click the **Critical Tasks** check box again to remove the critical path from the Gantt chart.

h. **Save** the project.

REAL WORLD ADVICE Adjusting the Critical Path

Entering tasks, defining task relationships, assigning project resources, and adjusting the project calendar all affect how Project determines the critical path. However, project managers still have control over the project's critical path and should be the final decision makers of the project plan. If Project predicts a project's finish date (or a project's start date) that is later than what you had in mind, you can shorten the critical path by doing the following:

- Changing task relationships (for example, change Finish-to-Start relationship to a Start-to-Start relationship)
- Adding additional resource assignments to tasks
- Removing task relationships
- Adjusting task durations
- Adjusting the available working time in the project calendar
- Creating a task calendar

Create a Work Breakdown Structure

An important step to project planning success is to organize the project tasks in a logical way. A method of organizing tasks in a hierarchical structure is by creating a Work Breakdown Structure. A **Work Breakdown Structure (WBS)** creates a project plan structure in which project tasks are identified, task relationships are defined, and task resources are assigned. When creating a WBS, a project manager will define the main goals of the scope of a project and then identify the tasks that must go into completing these goals.

A WBS is often created in a top-down structure, similar to a detailed outline, where the main goals are defined and then supporting tasks to complete these goals are identified. Figure 3 shows an example of a WBS for the Charity Golf Tournament project. In this example, the project is broken down into four main goals of tournament initiation, sponsorship, promotion, and events. Under the main goals are the tasks that need to be completed to meet the project goal.

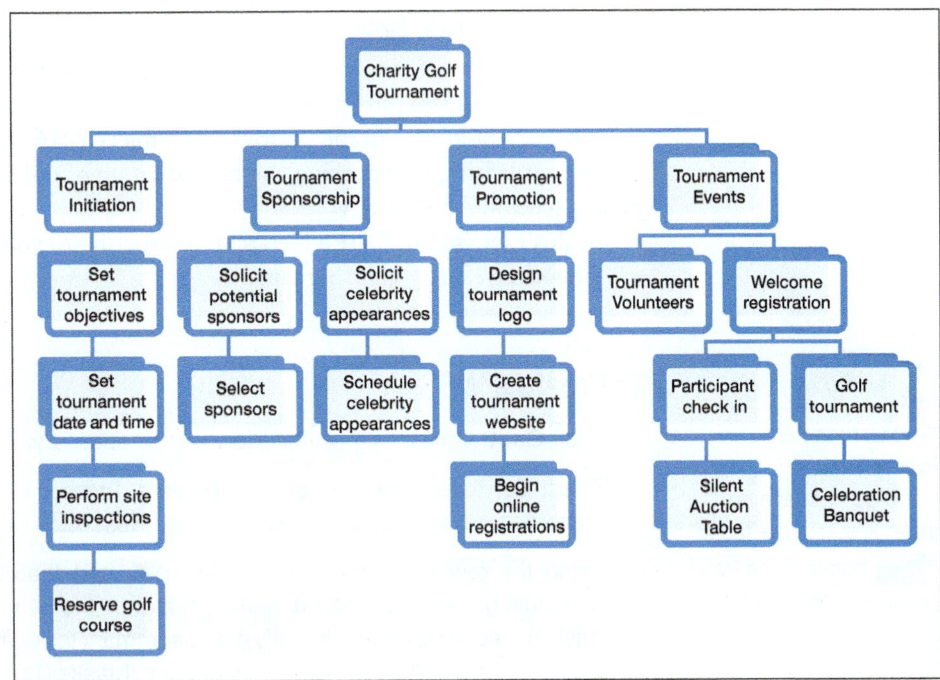

Figure 3 WBS example

Projects may also be broken into phases in which each phase is a main heading or goal in a WBS, and the steps to complete each phase are the individual tasks. If you recall, the phases of the project management planning process are initiation, planning, executing, monitoring, and closing. It is common for project managers to plan a project by these phases. Some managers, however, may choose phases that are more specific to their project plan.

In order to create a Work Breakdown Structure in Project 2016, you must identify the main project goals or phases of the project. The main goals are like main headings in an outline. These main headings or goals are called summary tasks in the Project software. **Summary tasks** are tasks listed in bold in the Entry table and are groups of tasks that logically belong together. In Figure 3 above, an example of a summary task is Tournament Promotion. Summary tasks are not tasks that are to be completed; rather, they are headings for grouped tasks. Related tasks that further define the summary tasks are called **subtasks**.

To create summary tasks, you can indent and outdent tasks or use the Summary button in the Insert group on the Task tab. **Indenting** a task moves a task to the right in the Entry table and makes it a lower level task in a WBS, such as a task that needs to be completed to achieve the main goal. **Outdenting** a task moves a task to the left in the Entry table and makes it a higher level task in a WBS, such as a main goal. As shown in Figure 4, indenting and outdenting tasks can be done in the Schedule group on the Task tab.

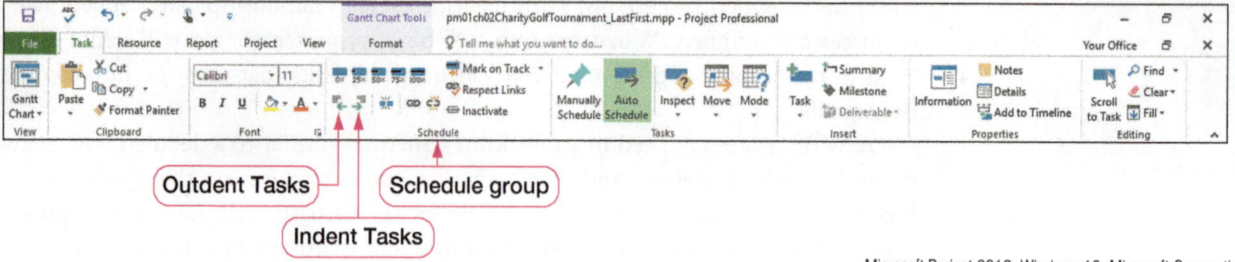

Microsoft Project 2016, Windows 10, Microsoft Corporation

Figure 4 Task tab Schedule group

Creating a Work Breakdown Structure

You can add new tasks to create summary tasks as well. Once a new task is added and given a main goal title, the related tasks would be indented to make the newly added task the summary task. Due to the flexibility of Project 2016, you can change the level of any task by outdenting or indenting the task or group of tasks. Project 2016 will adjust the project schedule accordingly.

In this exercise, to create a hierarchical structure to your project plan, you will create a WBS for the charity golf tournament.

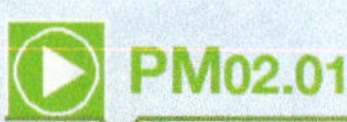

SIDE NOTE

Insert Task

If you do not have an Insert key, use the Task button in the Insert group on the Task tab.

SIDE NOTE

Summary Tasks

Do not adjust the duration of a summary task; it is determined by subtasks. To adjust summary task durations, adjust subtask durations or relationships.

To Create a WBS

a. Click **Gantt Chart** on the View Bar if necessary.

b. Select **Set tournament objectives** (Task 1). Press Ins to insert a new blank task. Enter the task name Tournament Initiation. Press Tab but do not set a task duration.

c. Using the row selectors, select **Tasks 2–5**, and then click the **Task** tab. In the Schedule group, click **Indent Task**. Notice the new task, Tournament Initiation (Task 1), becomes bold to identify it as a summary task. The duration of the summary task is determined by the durations of the subtasks (Tasks 2–5).

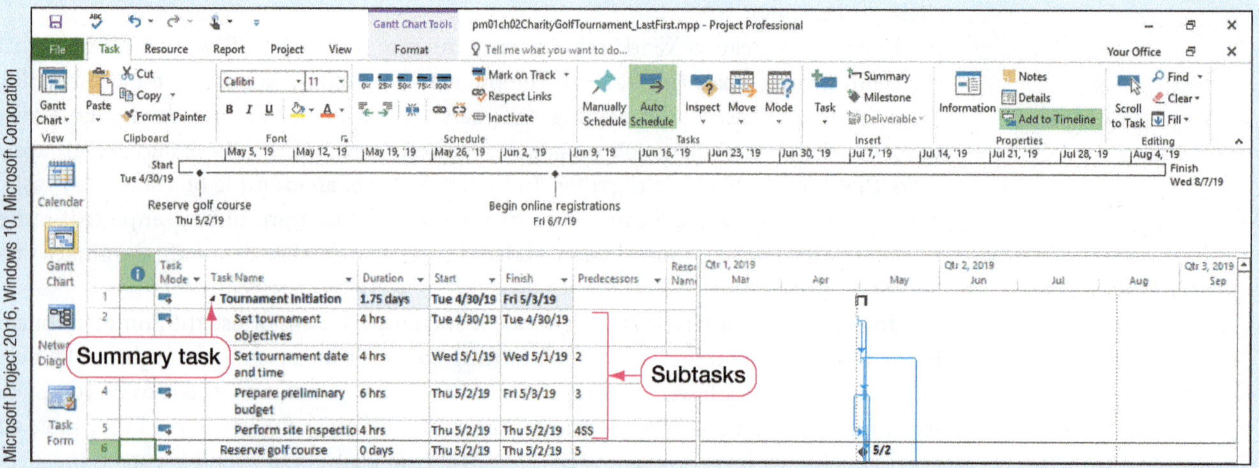

Microsoft Project 2016, Windows 10, Microsoft Corporation

Figure 5 Summary task and subtasks

d. Select **Reserve golf course** (Task 6). Press Alt + Shift + → to indent Task 6. Task 6 is now a subtask of Tournament Initiation.

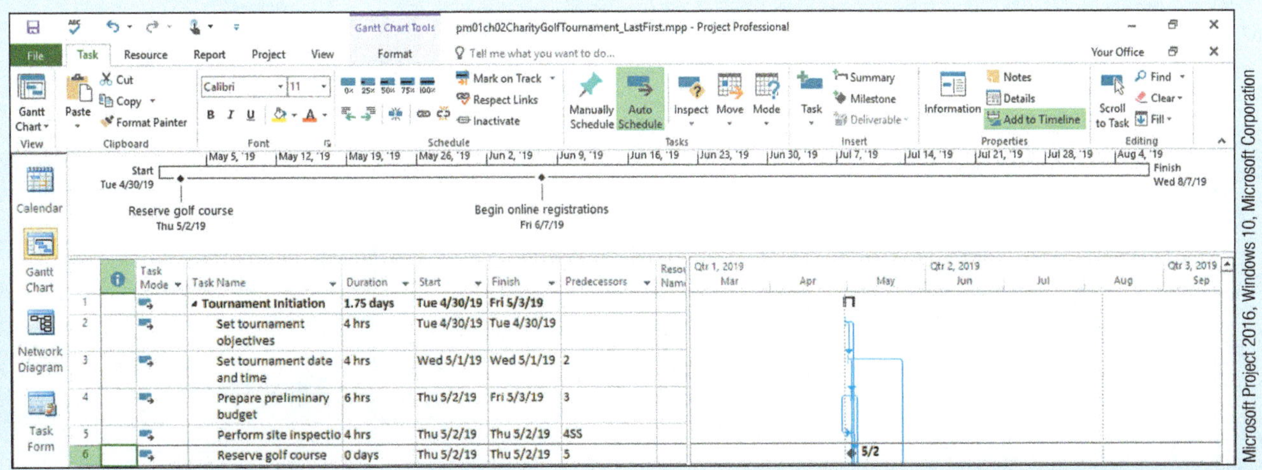
Microsoft Project 2016, Windows 10, Microsoft Corporation

Figure 6 Task 6 as a subtask.

e. Select **Solicit potential tournament sponsors** (Task 7).

f. On the Task tab, in the Insert group, click **Task** to insert a new blank task.

g. Type the task name Tournament Promotion, and then press Tab but do not add a duration. Notice Tournament Promotion (Task 7) becomes a subtask of Tournament Initiation (Task 1).

h. On the Task tab, in the Schedule group, click **Outdent Task** to promote Tournament Promotion (Task 7).

i. Select **Tasks 8–11**, and then in the Schedule group, click **Indent Task** to make Tasks 8–11 subtasks of Tournament Promotion (Task 7).

j. If necessary, select the task names for Tasks 1–11, click the **Gantt Chart Tools Format** tab, and then in the Columns group, click **Wrap Text** twice.

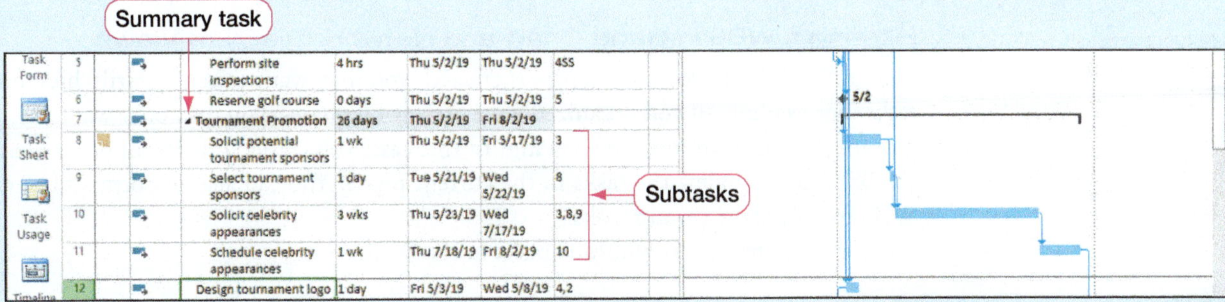

Microsoft Project 2016, Windows 10, Microsoft Corporation

Figure 7 Tournament Promotion summary task and subtasks

k. Select Task 12 through Task 14. Click the **Task** tab, if necessary, and then in the Insert group, click **Summary** to insert a summary task. Type the summary task name Tournament Website, and then press Tab.

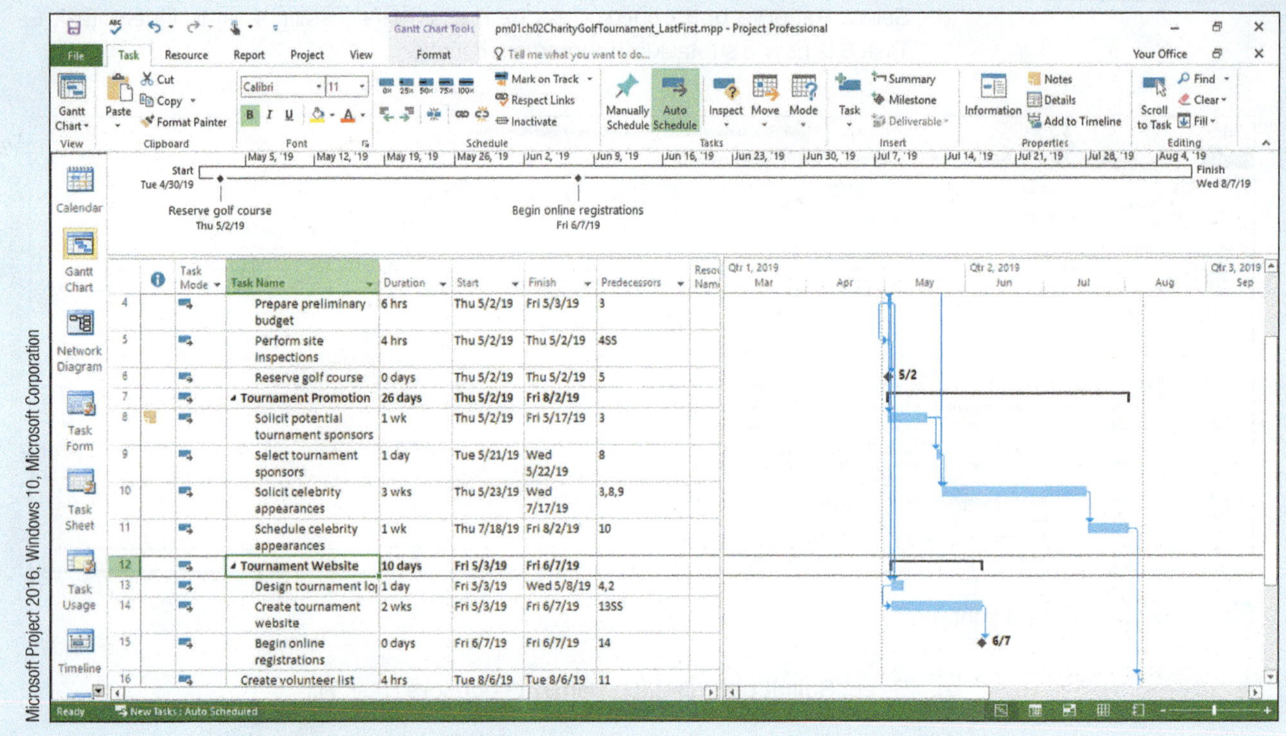

Figure 8 Project Work Breakdown Structure

l. **Save**  the project.

> **CONSIDER THIS** | **Why Create a Work Breakdown Structure?**
>
> Have you ever written a report or a research paper? Did you create an outline to keep track of large amounts of information or to show a logical ordering of information before you actually started writing your paper? An outline for a written report is similar to a Work Breakdown Structure for a project plan.

Filtering a WBS in Gantt Chart and Network Diagram Views

Once a Work Breakdown Structure is created, you may want to temporarily hide project tasks. For example, if you organized your project by phases, you may only want the phase you are currently working in showing. In this case, you could collapse all other phases of the WBS to only view the tasks in the current phase. You can also perform a filter of the WBS to only show certain tasks.

In this exercise, you will hide tasks in the WBS.

To Hide Tasks in a WBS

a. Click **Tournament Promotion** (Task 7). Click the **Collapse arrow** ◢ in the left-hand side of the Task Name cell. The subtasks of Tournament Promotion (Task 7) are now hidden.

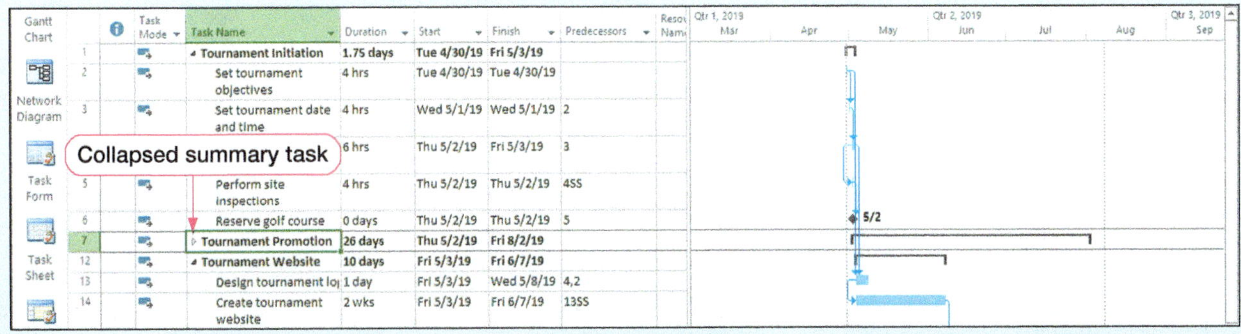

Microsoft Project 2016, Windows 10, Microsoft Corporation

Figure 9 Work Breakdown Structure with summary task collapsed

b. Click the **Expand arrow** on the left-hand side of the Task Name cell for Tournament Promotion (Task 7). The Tournament Promotion subtasks reappear.

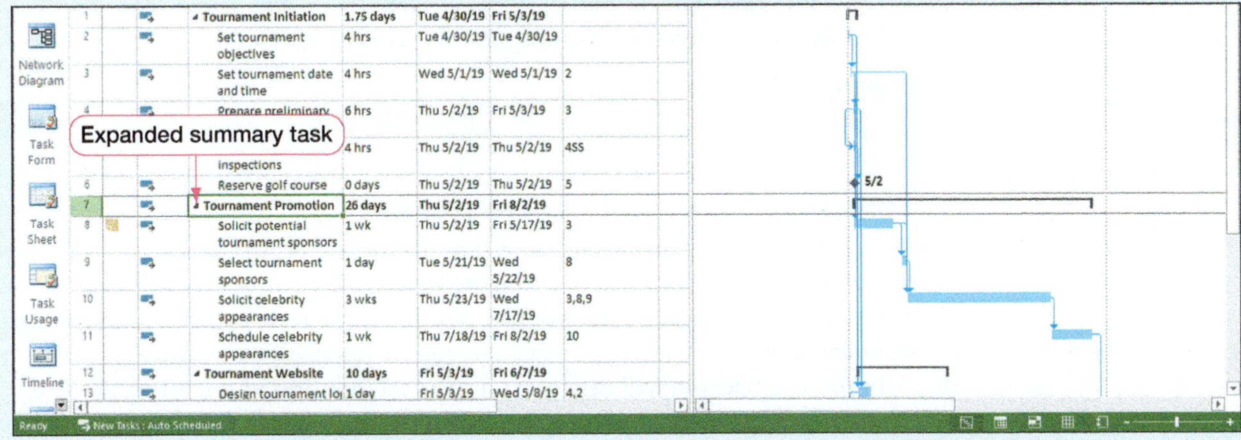

Microsoft Project 2016, Windows 10, Microsoft Corporation

Figure 10 Work Breakdown Structure with summary task expanded

c. To filter Gantt Chart view, select the **View** tab. In the Data group, click the **Filter** arrow, and then click **Summary Tasks**. Gantt Chart view is now filtered to show only summary tasks.

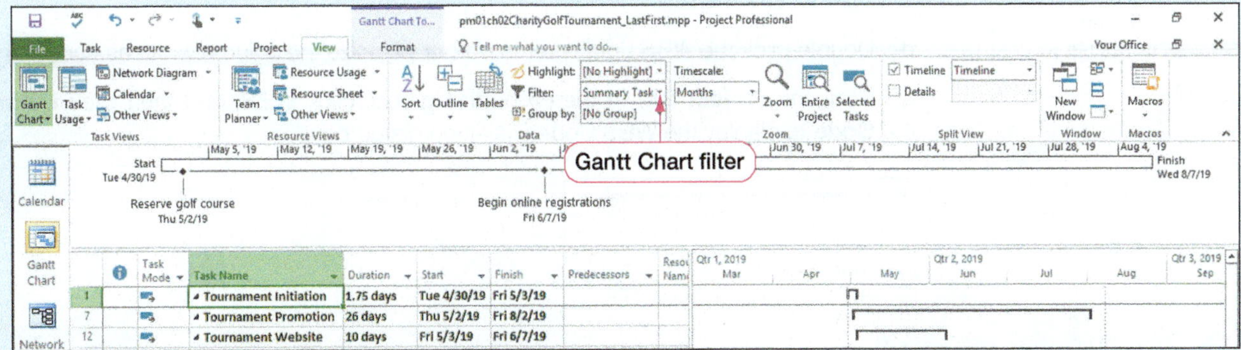

Microsoft Project 2016, Windows 10, Microsoft Corporation

Figure 11 Filtered Gantt Chart

d. Click the **Task** tab. Select the summary tasks by highlighting the row selectors.

e. In the Properties group, click **Add to Timeline** to add the summary tasks to the Timeline.

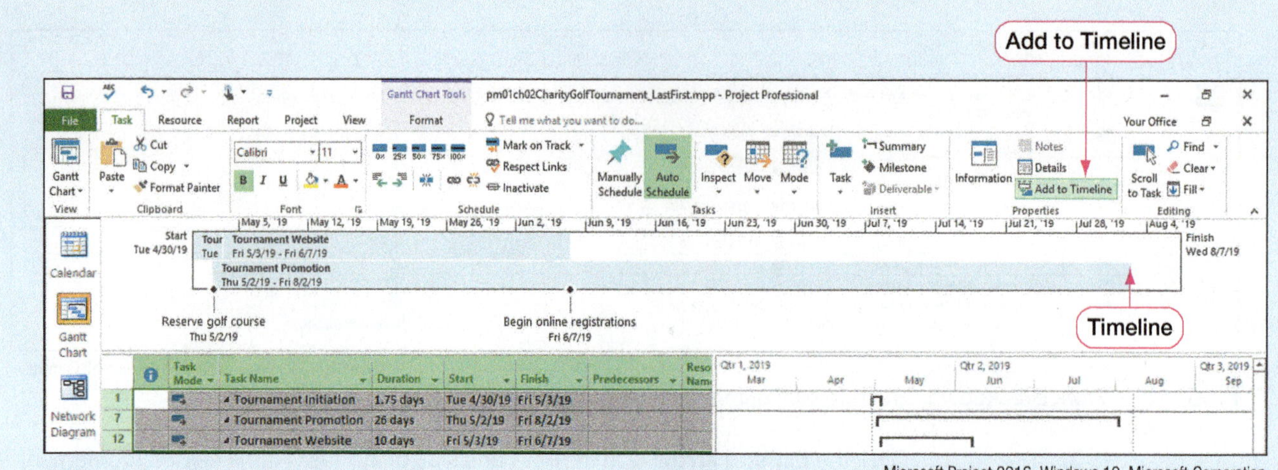

Microsoft Project 2016, Windows 10, Microsoft Corporation

Figure 12 Summary tasks added to Timeline

f. Click the **View** tab. In the Data group, click the **Filter** arrow, and then click **[No Filter]**. All summary tasks and subtasks are now visible.

g. **Save** the project.

Displaying WBS Code in the Entry Table

When you create a WBS by including summary tasks, Project can assign a WBS code for each task. If you want to refer to tasks by a WBS code, which will give you more definition than using the task row, you can define the code and then add the code to the Entry table.

In this exercise, you will define and display a Work Breakdown Structure code.

SIDE NOTE

Alternate Method

You can also point to the right edge of a column title and then click and drag to the left or right to adjust the column width.

To Define and Display a WBS Code

a. Click the **Task** tab, and then right-click the **Task Mode** column. Click **Hide Column**.

b. Right-click the **Task Name** column, and then click **Insert Column**.

c. Type w, and then click **WBS**.

d. Double-click the **WBS** right column border to resize the column width as necessary.

e. Click the **Project** tab. In the Properties group, click **WBS**, and then click **Define Code** to display the WBS Code Definition dialog box.

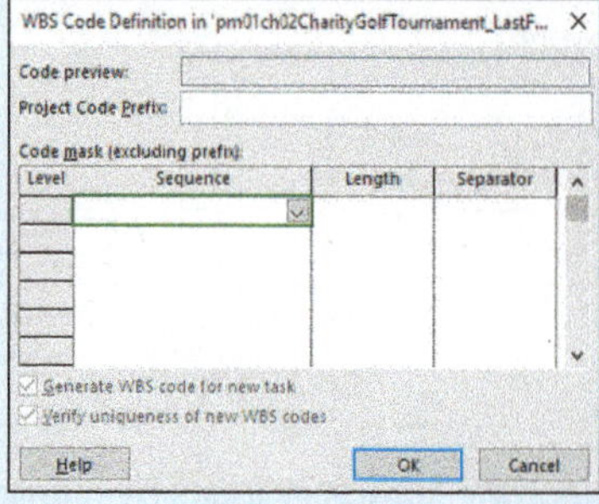

Figure 13 WBS Code Definition dialog box

f. To define the WBS code, in the first row of the table of the dialog box, click the **Sequence** list arrow, and then select **Uppercase Letters (ordered)**. Click in the second row, and then click **Numbers (ordered)**. Click in the third row, and then click **Lowercase Letters (ordered)**.

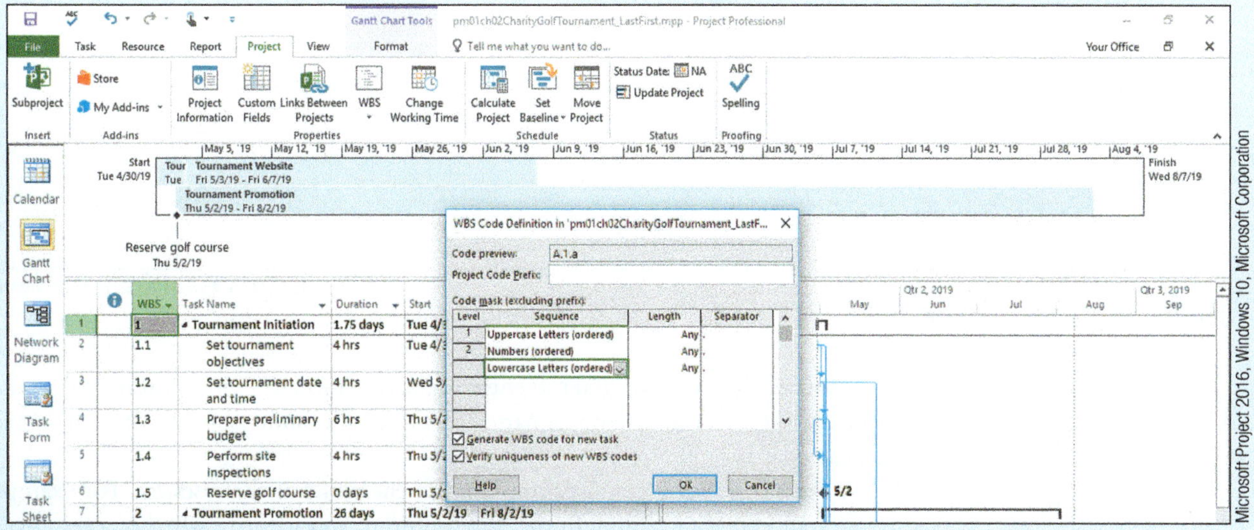

Microsoft Project 2016, Windows 10, Microsoft Corporation

Figure 14 WBS Code Definition dialog box with code defined

g. Click **OK**.

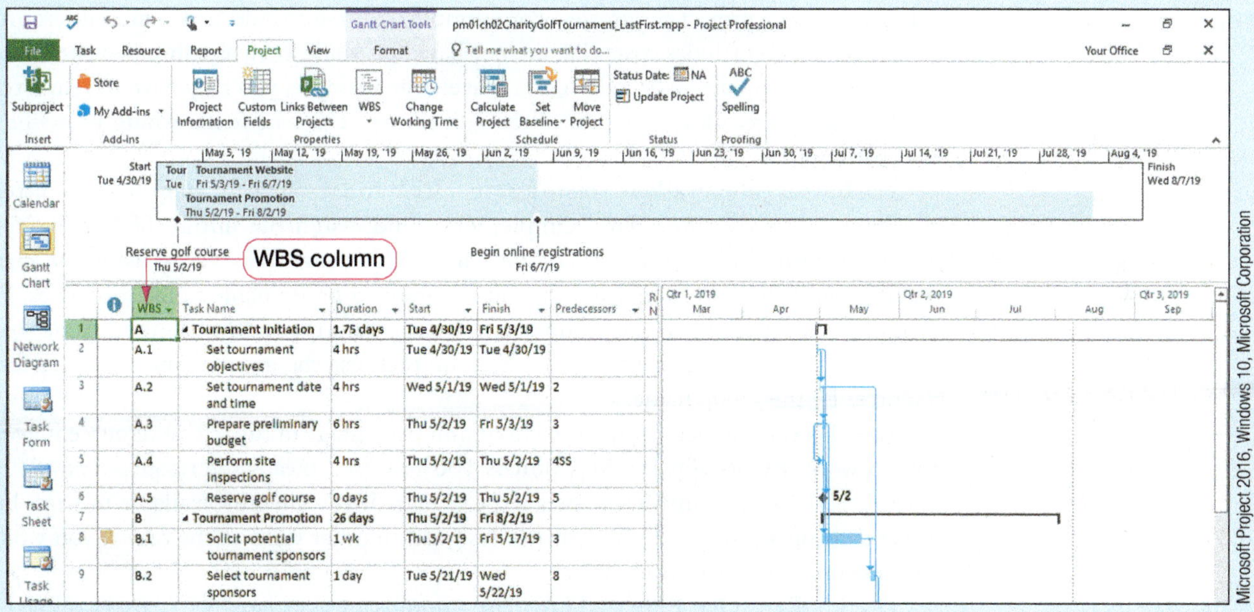

Microsoft Project 2016, Windows 10, Microsoft Corporation

Figure 15 Gantt Chart view with WBS column added

h. **Save** the project.

Create and Assign Project Resources

One of the main advantages of using project planning software such as Project 2016 is the ability to assign and track resources. Resources are the people, materials, or costs needed to complete project tasks. When you add resources in Project 2016, you are making them available to assign them to project tasks. Resources can be added in many views in Project 2016. However, the most common way of adding resources is by using Resource Sheet view, as shown in Figure 16.

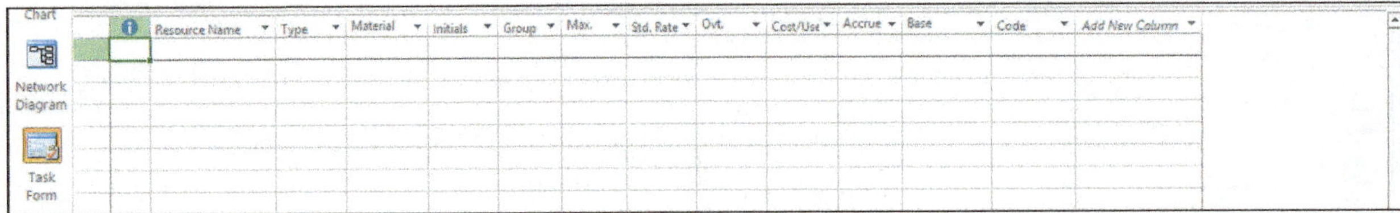

Microsoft Project 2016, Windows 10, Microsoft Corporation

Figure 16 Resource Sheet view

In **Resource Sheet view**, you can enter resource information in columns and rows to include information such as resource name, resource type, and resource cost, and you can assign a calendar to a resource.

In the Resource Name column, you identify the name of the resource. For example, a resource could be Your Name. In the Type column, you identify whether a resource is a work, material, or cost resource. A **work resource** is the person and equipment that needs to be used to complete a project task. For example, a chef hired to prepare the meal for the golf charity tournament is a resource; the equipment rented to prepare the meal is also a work resource. A **material resource** is a consumable resource such as supplies that gets used up as a project progresses. For example, golf tees would be a material resource. A **cost resource** includes costs that are not based on work, such as equipment needed to complete a task or airfare or lodging for travel. For example, you may have to rent a tent for the staging area off the first tee of the golf course. The tent rental would be assigned as a cost resource.

The Initials column allows you to assign initials to a resource for identification instead of a longer resource name. For example, you could assign the initials of YN for Your Name and then display the initials in the Gantt chart to save space versus using the entire resource name. In the Group column, you can assign a group name to like resources. For example, you could assign the group name "Caddy" and then add this group name to all resources that are tournament caddies. You can then use the group name to sort or filter resources by the group name.

The Max column determines the maximum percentage of capacity a resource is available to work. By default, the Max unit is 100%, which means the resource is available to work 100% of the time when assigned to a task. If you are only available to work half of the time on a project because you are assigned to other tasks at the resort, you would assign yourself a Max unit of 50%.

The Std. Rate, Ovt. Rate, and Cost/Use columns are associated with costs assigned to a resource. A cost is an expense associated with completing a task. Variable costs are costs that change based on amount used. For example, labor (work resource) is a variable cost because the amount earned may vary from person to person. Fixed costs can be related to resources but do not vary with use. For example, a fixed cost would be a one-time fee for renting an outdoor tent.

The Accrue column determines how costs will be applied to a task. Start means the cost would be paid at the start of the project. End means the cost would be paid at the end of the project. Prorated is the default, and if assigned, costs would be accrued as the resource was working on the project task(s).

The Base column determines which calendar your resource will be assigned. From this calendar assignment, Project will determine working time and nonworking time of a resource. The Standard calendar is the default base calendar.

QUICK REFERENCE	Creating a Resource Calendar

To create a resource calendar, select the resource and then:

1. Click the Resource tab.
2. Click Information in the Properties group.
3. On the General tab of the Resource Information dialog box, click Change Working Time.
4. Click the Work Weeks tab, and then click Details.
5. In the Details dialog box, select the Working times or Nonworking times button. Edit the From and To times as necessary. Click OK in the three dialog boxes to accept the change to the resource calendar.

The availability of the selected resource will now reflect the resource calendar.

Creating Project Resources

To keep track of who will help you complete the charity golf tournament project tasks, you have decided to add project team members into the Resource Sheet. You will add the project team members in Resource Sheet view and then assign resources to your project tasks. Since all project team members' tasks are part of their general job duties, you will not assign a resource cost to the tasks.

In this exercise, you will create project resources.

To Create Project Resources

a. Click the **Task** tab. In the View group, click the **Gantt Chart** arrow.

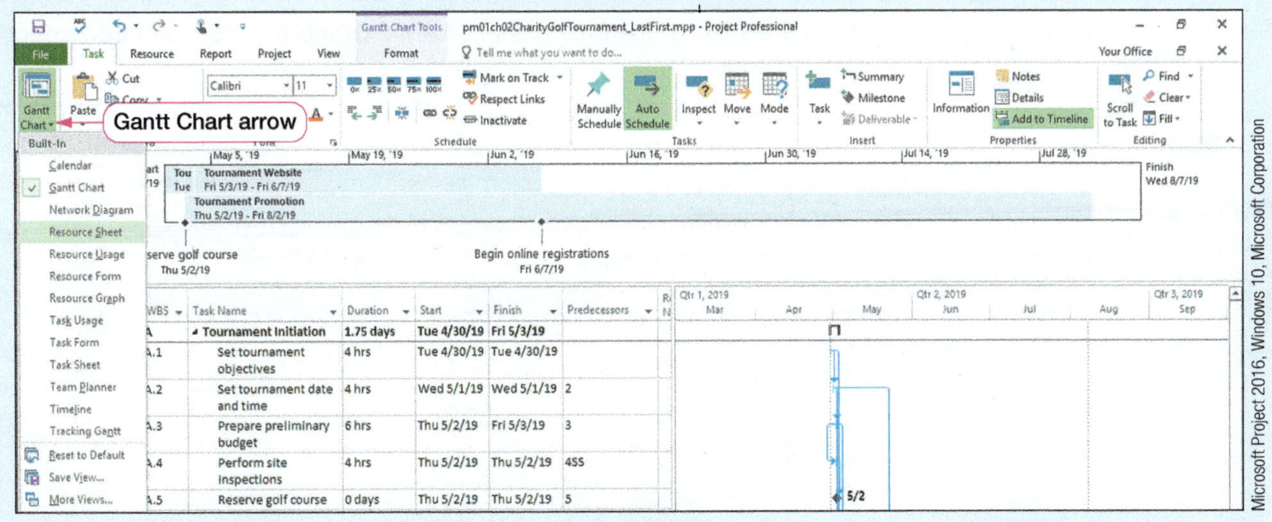

Figure 17 Resource Sheet selection

b. Click **Resource Sheet** to open the Resource Sheet. In the first row of the Resource Sheet table, in the Resource Name column, enter your **first and last name.** Press Tab to assign the Type **Work** to the resource. Press Tab two more times,

SIDE NOTE

Grouping Resources

Grouping resources can assist project managers in understanding resource allocations.

and then add **your initials** in the Initials column. Press Tab, and then enter the title **Events** in the Group column.

c. Add the resources into the indicated columns as follows:

Resource Name	Type	Initials	Group
Patti Rochelle	Work	PR	Events
Lesa Martin	Work	LM	Events
Thomas Vance	Work	TV	Events
Rosalinda Hill	Work	RH	Events
Barry Cheney	Work	BC	Golf
John Schilling	Work	JS	Golf
Jorge Cruz	Work	JC	Golf
Robin Sanchez	Work	RS	Chef

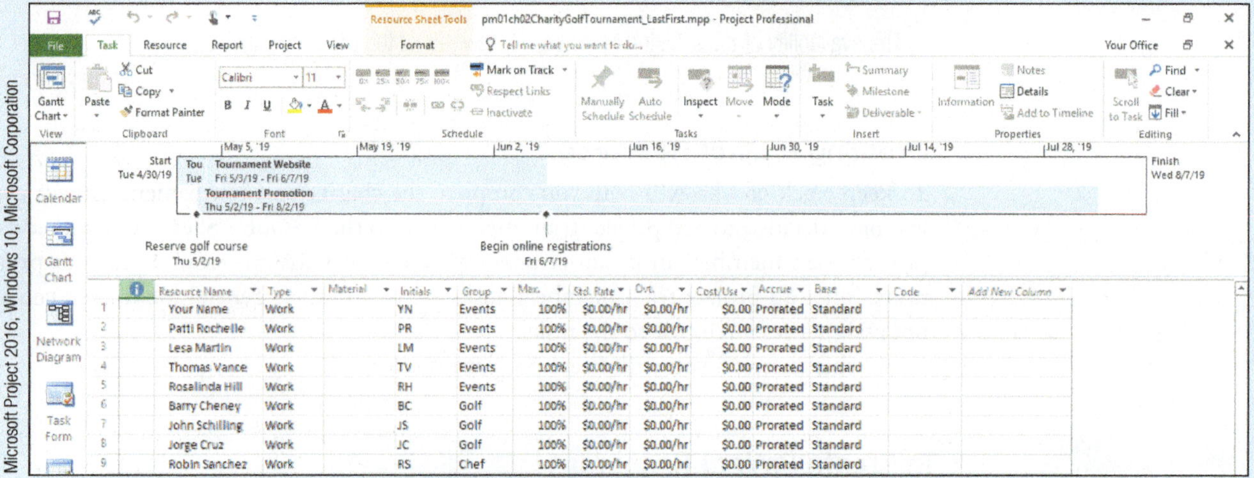

Figure 18 Resource Sheet view with resources added

d. Click the **View** tab. In the Data group, click the **Group by** arrow, and then select **Resource Group**.

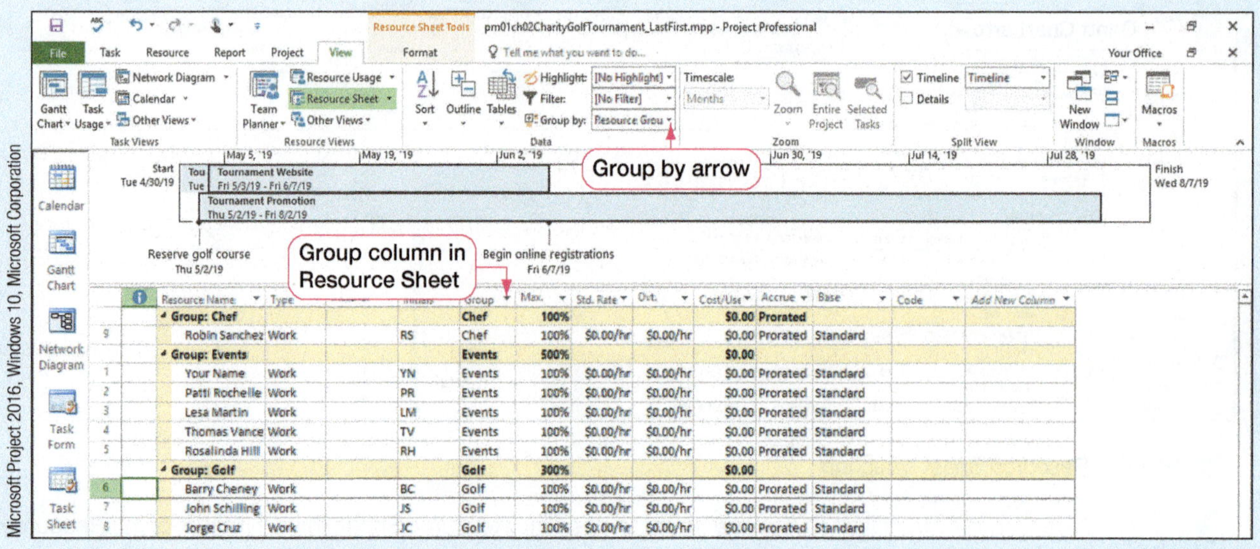

Figure 19 Resource Sheet with grouped resources

e. **Save** the project.

You can also add a new resource using the Task Information dialog box. In the Task Information dialog box, select the Resources tab, select the first blank row in the Resource Name column, add a resource name and accompanying information, and then click OK.

REAL WORLD ADVICE | **Resource Calendars**

If you have ever been assigned to a team project, it is likely your teammate's availability differed from your availability. With this in mind, Project 2016 gives you the ability to create individual resource calendars that can be specifically designed for an individual resource. You can create a resource calendar in the Resource Information dialog box in the Properties group on the Resource tab. Once a resource calendar is created, it would be applied to a specific resource using the Resource Information dialog box. To open the Resource Information dialog box, click Information in the Properties group on the Resource tab.

Assigning Project Resources

Once resources are created, they must be assigned to tasks. Assigning a resource to a task means the resource is responsible for completing or overseeing the task. Project 2016 will assign the resource work, and therefore, the resource would be unavailable to complete other tasks at the same time. There are various ways of assigning project resources to tasks:

- The Assign Resources dialog box
- A cell in the Resource Names column arrow of the Entry table in Gantt Chart view
- The Resources tab in the Task Information dialog box
- The Task Work Form in Details view

The Assign Resources dialog box, used to assign resources to tasks, will remain open even when you click outside of the dialog box to select tasks in the Entry table. You can also create new resources in the Assign Resources dialog box. If you double-click a resource in the dialog box, it will open the Resource Information dialog box.

Now that you have created your project resources, you want to assign those resources to the project tasks. You will assign resources from the Assign Resources dialog box, the Resource Names column in the Entry table, and the Task Information dialog box.

In this exercise, you will assign project resources.

To Assign Project Resources

a. Click **Gantt Chart** on the View Bar, and then drag the **split bar** (vertical bar between Entry table and Gantt Chart) to the right edge of the Resource Names column.

b. Click the **Resource** tab, and then in the Assignments group, click **Assign Resources** to open the Assign Resources dialog box.

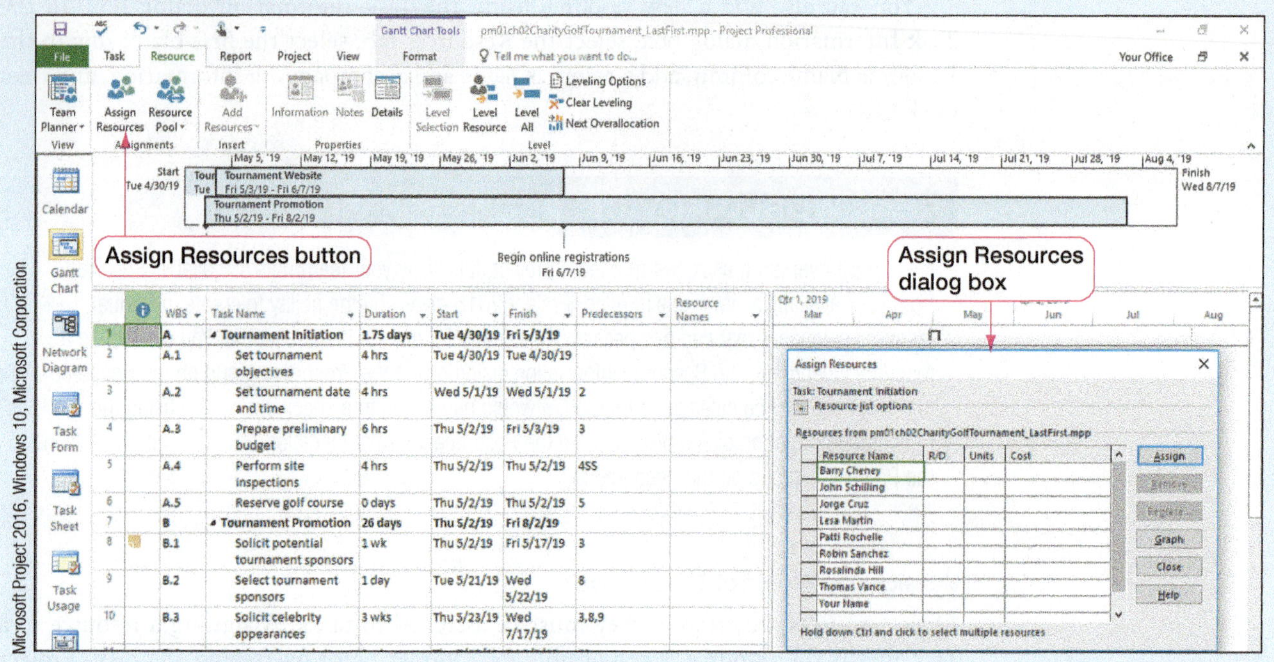

Figure 20 Assign Resources dialog box

SIDE NOTE

Resource Names in Gantt Chart

When you assign resources to tasks, notice the resource name will appear next to the Gantt bar in the Gantt chart.

c. With the Assign Resources dialog box still open, select **Set tournament objectives** (Task 2) in the Entry table. Click **Patti Rochelle** in the Assign Resources dialog box, and then click **Assign**.

d. Select **Set tournament date and time** (Task 3). Click **Patti Rochelle** in the Assign Resources dialog box, if necessary, and then click **Assign**.

e. Select **Prepare preliminary budget** (Task 4). Again, click **Patti Rochelle** in the Assign Resources dialog box, if necessary, and then click **Assign**.

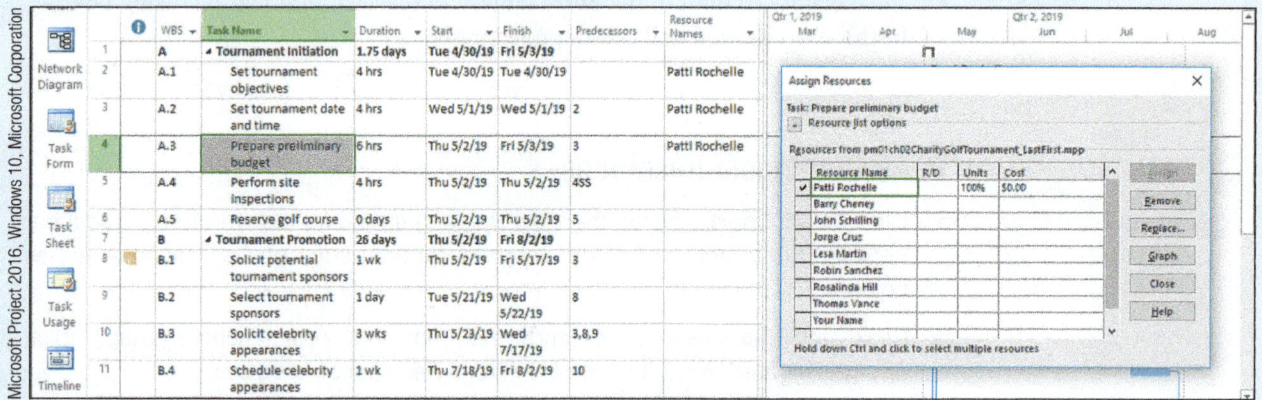

Figure 21 Resources assigned to tasks

> **SIDE NOTE**
> **Alternate Method**
> If you are assigning the same resource to consecutive tasks, you can select the consecutive tasks and then use the Assign Resources dialog box to assign the resource to all the selected tasks at one time.

f. Use the same procedure you used in step e to make the following assignments.

Task 5	Perform site inspections	Your Name
Task 6	Reserve golf course	Your Name

g. Click **Close** in the Assign Resources dialog box.

	WBS	Task Name	Duration	Start	Finish	Predecessors	Resource Names
1	A	Tournament Initiation	1.75 days	Tue 4/30/19	Fri 5/3/19		
2	A.1	Set tournament objectives	4 hrs	Tue 4/30/19	Tue 4/30/19		Patti Rochelle
3	A.2	Set tournament date and time	4 hrs	Wed 5/1/19	Wed 5/1/19	2	Patti Rochelle
4	A.3	Prepare preliminary budget	6 hrs	Thu 5/2/19	Fri 5/3/19	3	Patti Rochelle
5	A.4	Perform site inspections	4 hrs	Thu 5/2/19	Thu 5/2/19	4SS	Your Name
6	A.5	Reserve golf course	0 days	Thu 5/2/19	Thu 5/2/19	5	Your Name
7	B	Tournament Promotion	26 days	Thu 5/2/19	Fri 8/2/19		
8	B.1	Solicit potential tournament sponsors	1 wk	Thu 5/2/19	Fri 5/17/19	3	
9	B.2	Select tournament sponsors	1 day	Tue 5/21/19	Wed 5/22/19	8	

Microsoft Project 2016, Windows 10, Microsoft Corporation

Figure 22 Gantt chart with resource assignments

h. Click **Solicit potential tournament sponsors** (Task 8) in the Resource Names cell. On the right-hand side of the cell, click the **arrow**, and then select the check box for **Lesa Martin**.

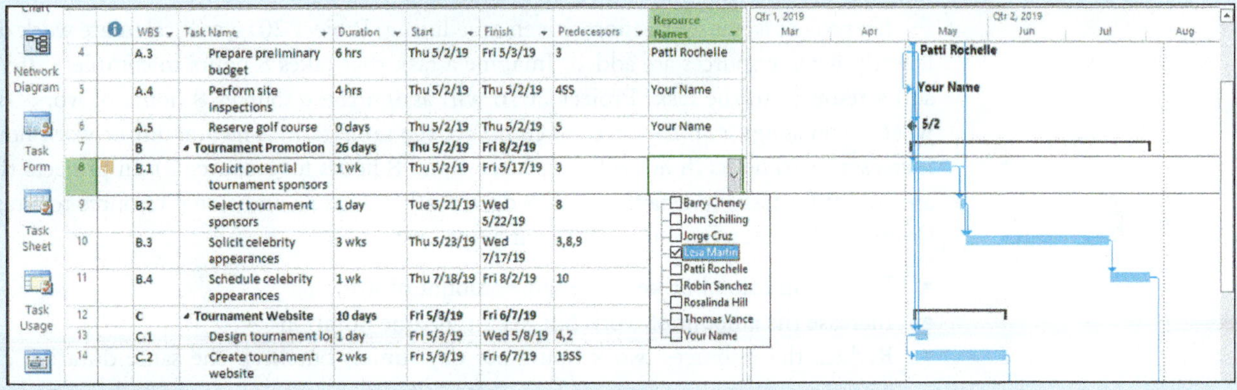

	WBS	Task Name	Duration	Start	Finish	Predecessors	Resource Names
4	A.3	Prepare preliminary budget	6 hrs	Thu 5/2/19	Fri 5/3/19	3	Patti Rochelle
5	A.4	Perform site inspections	4 hrs	Thu 5/2/19	Thu 5/2/19	4SS	Your Name
6	A.5	Reserve golf course	0 days	Thu 5/2/19	Thu 5/2/19	5	Your Name
7	B	Tournament Promotion	26 days	Thu 5/2/19	Fri 8/2/19		
8	B.1	Solicit potential tournament sponsors	1 wk	Thu 5/2/19	Fri 5/17/19	3	
9	B.2	Select tournament sponsors	1 day	Tue 5/21/19	Wed 5/22/19	8	
10	B.3	Solicit celebrity appearances	3 wks	Thu 5/23/19	Wed 7/17/19	3,8,9	
11	B.4	Schedule celebrity appearances	1 wk	Thu 7/18/19	Fri 8/2/19	10	
12	C	Tournament Website	10 days	Fri 5/3/19	Fri 6/7/19		
13	C.1	Design tournament lo	1 day	Fri 5/3/19	Wed 5/8/19	4,2	
14	C.2	Create tournament website	2 wks	Fri 5/3/19	Fri 6/7/19	13SS	

Microsoft Project 2016, Windows 10, Microsoft Corporation

Figure 23 Assigning resources using the Resources Names column

i. Press Enter to assign Lesa Martin to the task.

j. Click **Select tournament sponsors** (Task 9) in the Resource Names cell. Click the **arrow**, and then select the check box for **Patti Rochelle**. Press Enter to assign Patti Rochelle to the task.

k. **Save** the project.

Change Task Durations by Adding Resources

Task durations may change when resources are added. Therefore, you must understand how work is calculated in Project 2016. How Project 2016 calculates the duration of a task depends on whether the task is effort driven or fixed duration. **Effort driven scheduling** is a method of scheduling in Project 2016 in which the duration of a task is shortened as resources are added or lengthened as resources are removed from a task; however, the amount of effort (work) necessary to complete a task remains unchanged. In other words, the more effort assigned to a task (units), the shorter the duration will be (even though the total work does not change). When you remove a resource from an effort driven task, Project 2016 will lengthen the duration of the task. With effort driven scheduling, Project 2016 calculates work using the following formula: W=D*U {Work (W)=Duration (D)*Units (U)}.

Imagine a task that takes 8 hours to complete. If you add a resource to the task, Project 2016 will assign that resource 8 hours of work. But what if you assign two resources to complete the same task? The amount of work hours stays the same (8 hours); however, the calendar time needed to complete the task (duration) will shorten the duration by 4 hours because the two resources (units) will be working together to get the task done faster. This scenario is based on the assumption that the task is effort driven.

- W=D*U or D=W/U
- 8=4*2 or 4=8/2

There is an exception to this rule, however. If you assign multiple resources to a task at the same time, Project 2016 will not change the duration even if a task is set to effort driven.

Effort driven scheduling is typically not a default setting in Project 2016. To turn on effort driven scheduling when starting a project, on the File tab, click Options, and then click Schedule. Individual tasks can also be set to effort driven scheduling by using the Task Information dialog box for each task. For example, in an effort driven project schedule, you may want to change one task to non-effort driven because the duration of a task may actually stay the same even if additional resources are added.

If a project is not set to effort driven scheduling, Project 2016 will calculate work differently when resources are added. Imagine a task that takes 8 hours to complete. If you add a resource to the task, Project 2016 will assign the resources 8 hours of work. But what if you assign two resources to complete the same task? The amount of work hours increases to 16 hours (8 hours for resource 1 and 8 hours for resource 2). In projects that are not set for tasks to default to effort driven, if you add an additional resource to a task, Project 2016 will offer you the following options:

- Reduce duration but keep the same amount of work
- Increase the amount of work but keep the same duration
- Reduce the resources' work hours per day (units) but keep the same duration and work (For example, assign each resource 50% of the task work not to be completed consecutively.)

To understand these choices, refer to Table 1, which is based on a task with an 8-hour duration using W=D*U (U1=first resource, U2=second resource).

8-Hour Task Duration	W	D	U1	U2
Reduce duration but keep the same amount of work (effort driven)	8h	4h	4h	4h
Increase the amount of work but keep the same duration (work consecutively)	16h	8h	8h	8h
Reduce the hours resources work per day (units) but keep the same duration and work (work separately)	8h	8h	4h	4h

Table 1 Calculating task work for effort driven tasks

When a resource is assigned to more work than available working hours, the resource will be **overallocated**. Project managers know that overallocating resources may lead to project failure because the work will likely not get done in the time it was scheduled. Therefore, Project provides a leveling tool. **Leveling** is a process of correcting overallocated resources to ensure no resource is assigned more hours than available work hours.

REAL WORLD ADVICE | **Leveling of Resources**

If a project's team members are assigned more work than they have time for, not only may they have poor performance or burnout, but it is also likely they won't be able to finish all the work assigned. If work doesn't get done on time, the project may not meet the schedule deadline and may also go over budget. Project managers may choose to manually level resources by changing resource assignments, removing resource assignments, shortening task durations, adjusting the work of a resource on a task, or adding additional resource assignments to tasks. Project managers may also decide to allow Project to level the resources using Project's leveling tools on the Resource tab.

Another way of leveling a project is by adding additional resources to a project to be sure the project is still completed on time. Adding additional resources to the project is called **crashing**. A project manager may also decide to crash a project to complete tasks faster than predicted to shorten the project's duration. Crashing a project may help to level a project or complete a project faster but may also cause the project to go over budget.

CONSIDER THIS | **What Would You Do?**

Have you ever fallen behind on studying for a test? If so, what did you do, pull an all-nighter? What if your project has fallen behind schedule? Or what if you want to finish the project earlier than predicted to get a jump on the competition? Project managers may decide to add additional resources to the project, knowing this will likely increase the project's budget.

Setting Your Project to Effort Driven

For the golf charity tournament, you believe your tasks will take less time to complete (duration) if you add additional resources to your tasks. Therefore, you want to set your project to schedule all tasks as effort driven unless otherwise specified.

In this exercise, you will set new project tasks to effort driven.

 PM02.06

SIDE NOTE
Effort Driven Tasks
Making new tasks effort driven does not change existing tasks to effort driven.

To Set New Project Tasks to Effort Driven

a. Click the **File** tab, and then click **Options**.

b. In the Project Options dialog box, click **Schedule** in the left pane.

c. Scroll down until you see the **Scheduling options for this project** section. If necessary, click to select the **New tasks are effort driven** check box to set all new tasks as effort driven tasks.

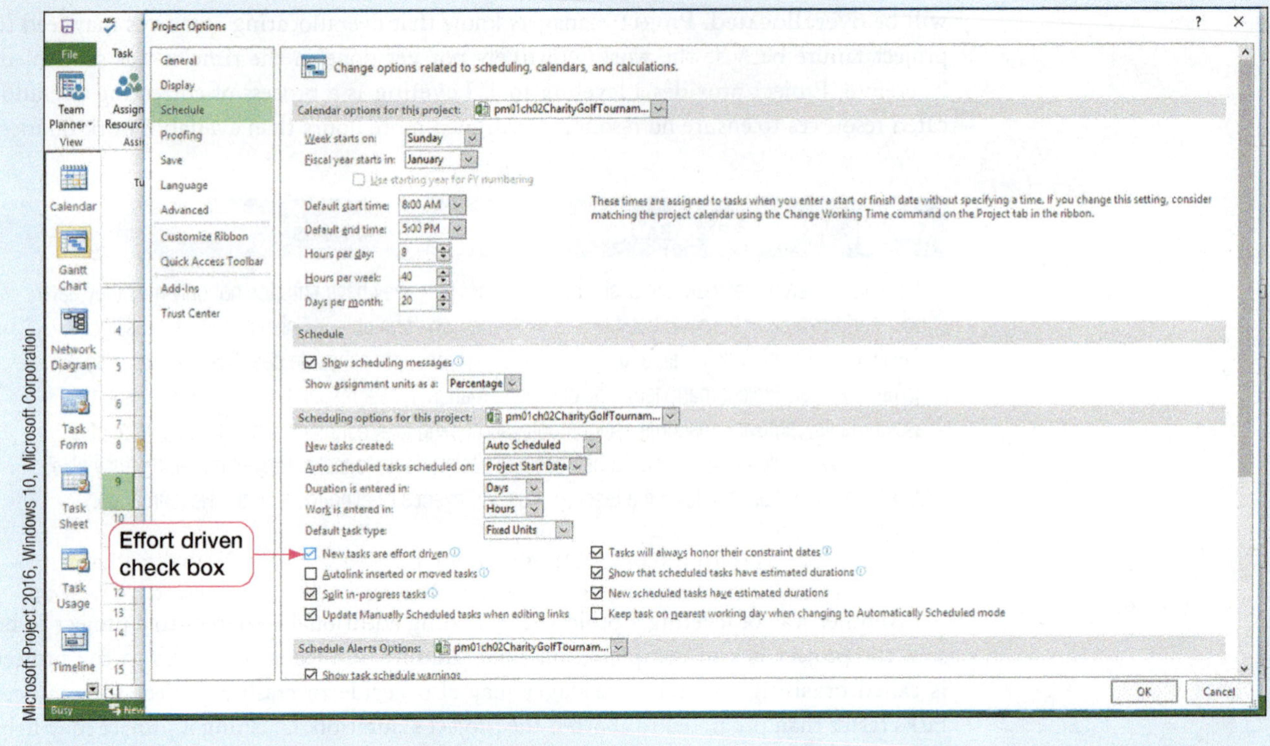

Figure 24 Project Options scheduling dialog box

d. Click **OK**.

e. **Save** the project.

Changing Task Durations with Resource Assignments

Now that new project tasks will be scheduled as effort driven, you will continue resource assignments for the remaining project tasks.

In this exercise, you will change task durations by adding resources.

To Change Task Durations by Adding Resources

a. Click **Gantt Chart** if necessary, and then click **Design tournament logo** (Task 13). Assign **Rosalinda Hill** to Task 13.

b. Double-click **Create tournament website** (Task 14) to open the Task Information dialog box. Click the **Resources** tab. Notice the duration on this task is two weeks (80 hours).

c. Click the first cell under the Resource Name heading, and then click the **Resource Name** arrow. Click **Thomas Vance** to add him as a resource to this task, and then click **OK**. Thomas is now assigned 80 hours of work on Create tournament website (Task 14).

d. In the Resource Names column of **Create tournament website** (Task 14), click the **Resource Names** arrow to also select Rosalinda Hill. Click **Rosalinda Hill**, and then press Enter.

e. Project will give an informational warning symbol in the upper left corner of the Resource Names cell. Click on the **warning symbol** to reveal the three selections for assigning the additional resource.

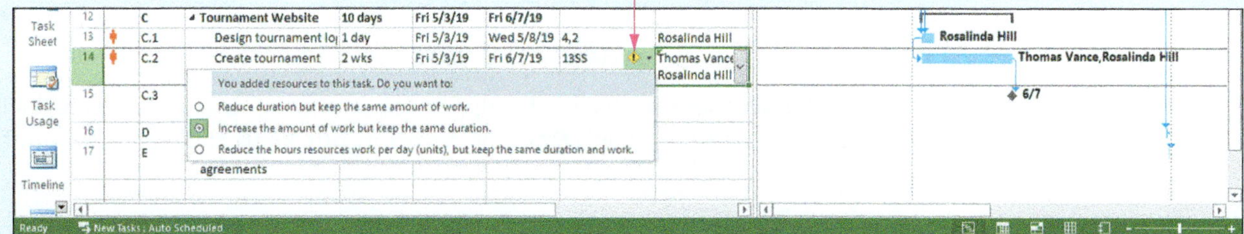

Microsoft Project 2016, Windows 10, Microsoft Corporation

Figure 25 Resource assignment warning

> **SIDE NOTE**
> **Overallocation**
> Note the overallocation symbol (red) in the Indicators column. You will adjust the overallocation of the resource in a later exercise.

f. Select **Reduce duration but keep the same amount of work.** Note the change of the duration of Task 14 to one week versus the original two-week duration. The total work is still 80 hours, but the time (duration) needed to complete the work is cut in half because two resources are assigned.

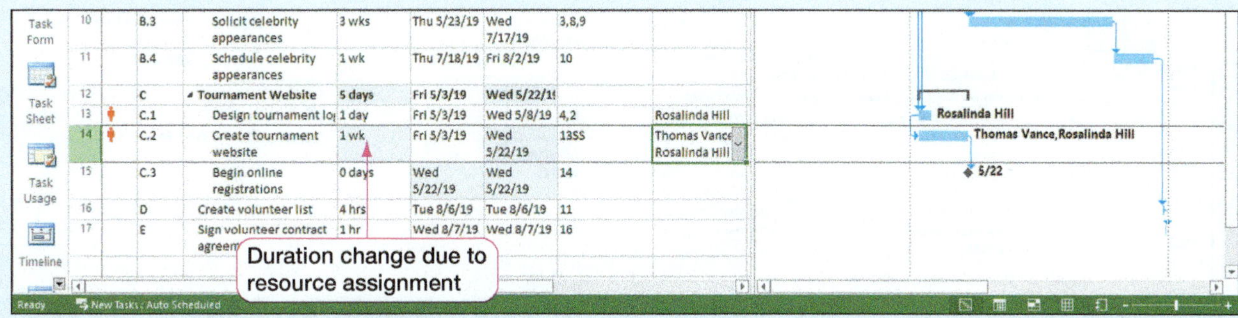

Microsoft Project 2016, Windows 10, Microsoft Corporation

Figure 26 Duration changed with resource assignment

> **SIDE NOTE**
> **Resource Assignments**
> It is good practice to assign a resource to a milestone task. The assignment ensures someone is responsible for overseeing the task.

g. Click **Begin online registrations** (Task 15), and then assign **Patti Rochelle** to the task.

h. Double-click **Solicit celebrity appearances** (Task 10), and then click the **Advanced** tab. Click to select the **Effort driven** check box to set the task to effort driven. Click **OK**.

i. With **Task 10** still selected, click the **Resource** tab, and then in the Assignments group, click **Assign Resources** .

j. Using the Assign Resources dialog box, click **Your Name**, and then click **Assign**. Click **Patti Rochelle**, and then click **Assign**. Note the change in the duration of Task 10 from three weeks to one and a half weeks due to the task being effort driven.

Troubleshooting

If the duration of Task 10 did not change to 1.5 weeks, make sure the task is set to effort driven by double-clicking the task, clicking the Advanced tab, and placing a check mark in front of Effort driven.

k. Click **Close** in the Assign Resources dialog box.

l. Click the **Warning** arrow in the upper left corner of the Task Name cell of Task 10, and then click **Reduce duration but keep the same amount of work**.

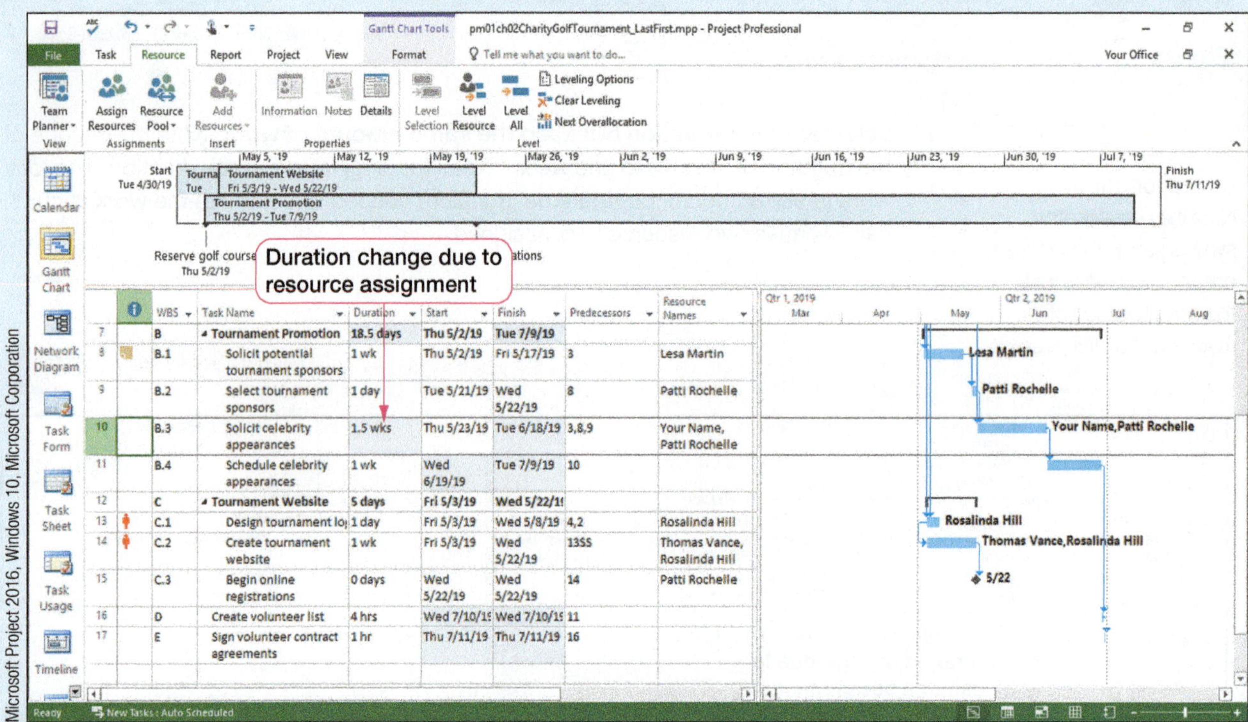

Figure 27 Task duration change

> **SIDE NOTE**
> **Effort Driven Task**
> Keep in mind that if resources are assigned to a task at the same time the duration will not change, even on an effort driven task.

m. **Save** the project.

Using the Work Task Form in Split View

Understanding how Project 2016 is calculating task durations and task work can be confusing. Project managers often find it useful to use the Task Details Form in split screen view. The Task Details Form in Split View allows you to see exactly how Project is distributing the work on a task as shown in Figure 28.

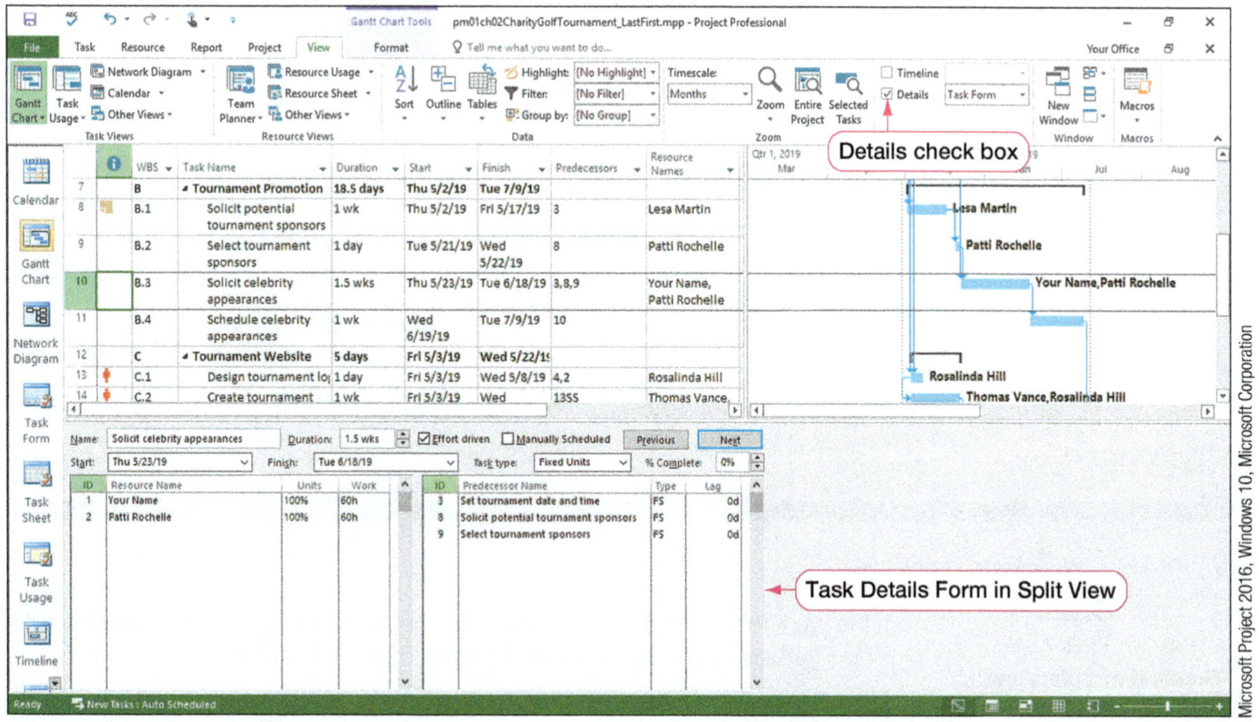

Figure 28 Task Details Form in Split View

In this exercise, you will change a duration of a task by using the Work form in Split view.

To Change a Duration Using the Work Form in Split View

a. Click **Solicit celebrity appearances** (Task 10) if necessary, and then click the **View** tab. In the Split View group, select the **Details** check box.

b. Right-click the **Task Details Form** in the lower pane of Gantt Chart view, and then click **Work**. You see that you are assigned 60 hours of work and Patti Rochelle is also assigned 60 hours of work. You also note the task has a check mark in the Effort driven check box.

SIDE NOTE

Split View

When selecting Details, Project may default to Resources & Predecessors form split view. Right-clicking the form allows you to change to Work form view.

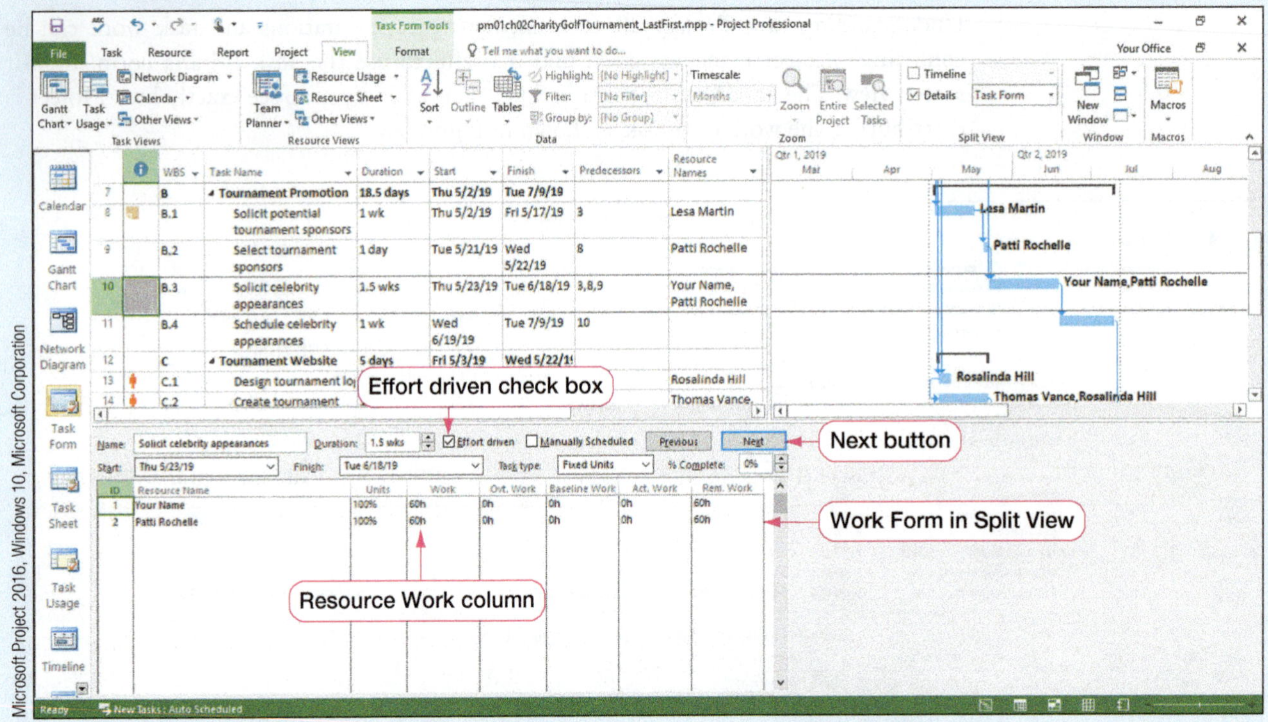

Figure 29 Work Form in Split View

SIDE NOTE

Timeline in Split View

Project 2016 will not display the Timeline in Split View.

c. In the Work form, click the **Next** button. **Schedule celebrity appearances** (Task 11) is now selected. Note the task has a 1-week duration (or 40 hours).

d. In the **Resource Name** column of the Work form, click in the first blank row in the Resource Name column. Click the **arrow**, and then click **Your Name**. Click in the blank row below Your Name, and then click **Barry Cheney**.

e. Click **OK** to assign both resources to this task. Notice in the Work form that both resources are assigned 40 hours of work. Although the task duration remains 1 week, the total of work hours has doubled to 80 hours because the task is not effort driven.

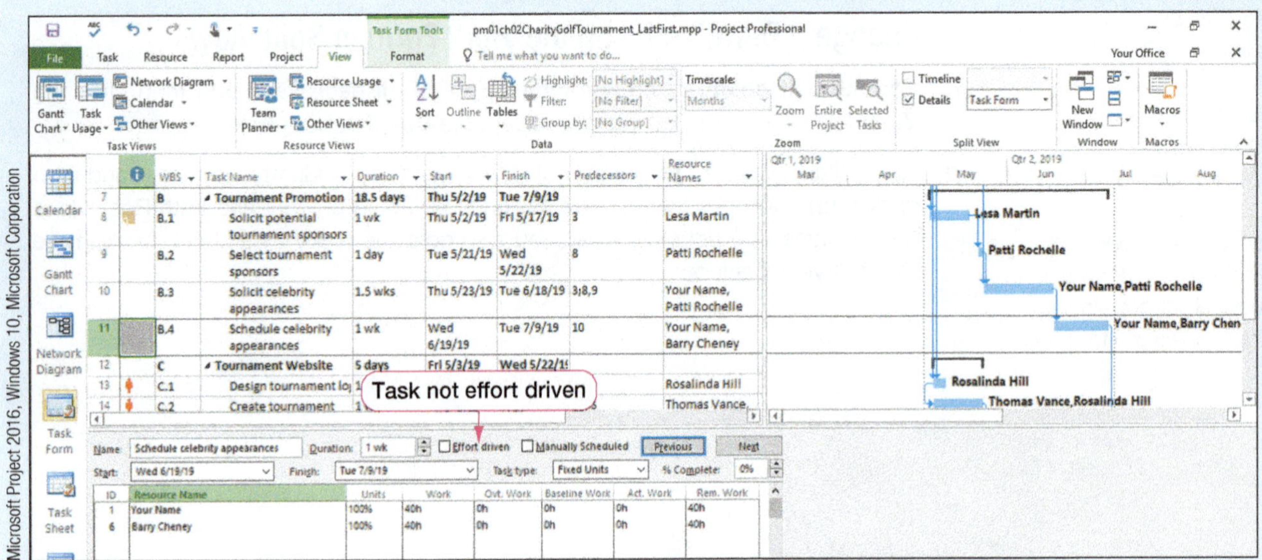

Figure 30 Work form with task not effort driven

f. With Task 11 still selected, click in the **Work** cell of **Your Name** row in the Work form. Type 10h, and then press Enter to change your work hours to 10 hours.

g. Next, click in the **Work** cell for **Barry Cheney**. Type 30h to change Barry's work hours to 30 hours. Click **OK**.

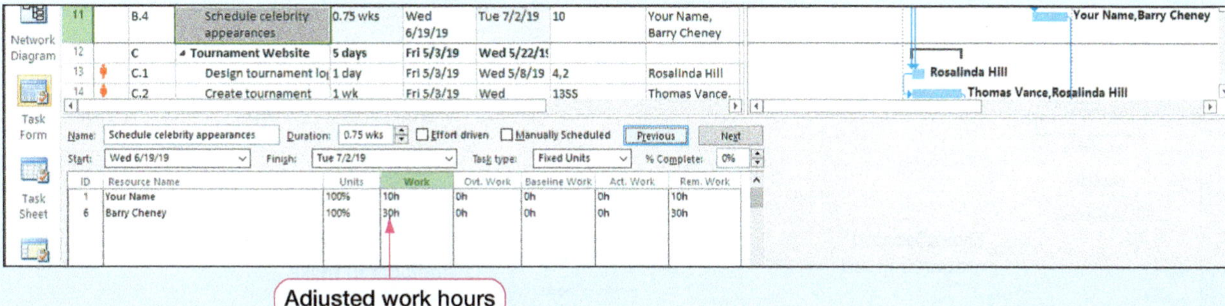

Microsoft Project 2016, Windows 10, Microsoft Corporation

Figure 31 Resource work hours manually adjusted

SIDE NOTE
Removing Split View
To remove the Split View group, you can also double-click the split bar between the Entry table and the Work form.

h. Note the change in the duration from 1 week to .75 weeks. By manually changing the work hours, you are creating an assignment similar to an effort driven task. Click **Next** five times to select Task 16.

i. Assign **Rosalinda Hill** to **Create volunteer list** (Task 16), and then click **OK**.

j. Click **Next** to move to **Sign volunteer contract agreements** (Task 17). Assign **Rosalinda Hill** to Task 17, and then click **OK**.

k. On the View tab, in the Split View group, click the **Details** check box to close the split view.

l. **Save** the project.

View Resource Assignments in the Team Planner View

After assigning resources, project managers may want to view how project team members are being assigned at a point in the project. This can be done by using Project's team planner. **Team Planner** is a Project view that shows a project's resources and tasks assigned to each resource. Each resource name appears on a separate row. In Team Planner view, you can drag task assignments from one resource to another resource to make adjustments to the resource assignment(s). Tasks associated with the individual resources appear on the same row as the resource name. Unassigned tasks appear at the bottom of the Team Planner view window. Resources identified in red are overallocated resources.

Viewing Resource Assignments in Team Planner View

You now want to view the resource assignments in your project plan. You will view all tasks assigned to you and view tasks assigned to other resources.

In this exercise, you will view resource assignments in the Team Planner view.

PM02.09

SIDE NOTE
Resource Assignments in Team Planner View
You can adjust resource assignments by clicking on a task in Team Planner view and dragging the task to a new resource.

To View Resource Assignments in Team Planner View

a. On the View tab, in the Resource Views group, click **Team Planner** to open Team Planner view.

b. Right-click **Your Name**, and then click **Scroll to Task**.

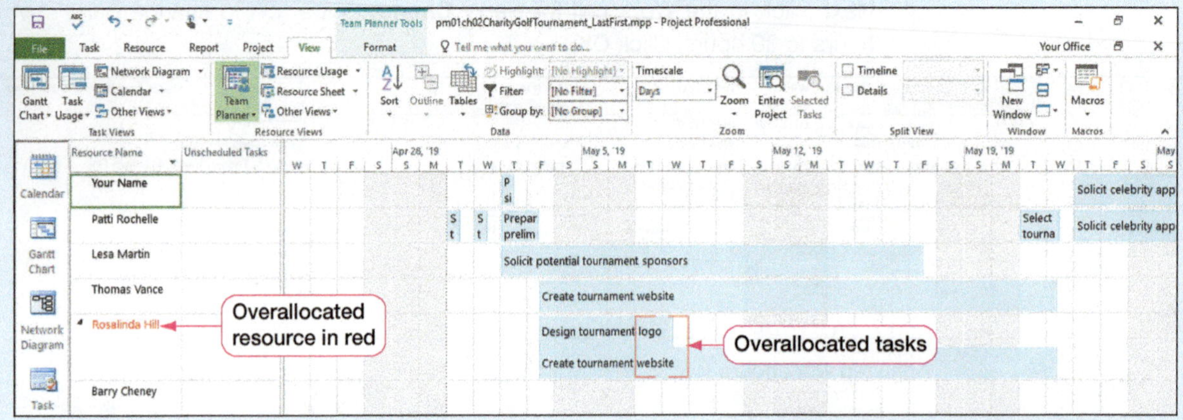

Microsoft Project 2016, Windows 10, Microsoft Corporation

Figure 32 Team Planner view

c. View the tasks assigned to you in Team Planner view. Use the horizontal scroll bar to view all tasks to which you are assigned. View the tasks assigned to others in Team Planner view.

d. Click **Gantt Chart** on the View Bar.

e. **Save** the project.

REAL WORLD ADVICE — Project Schedule and Resource Assignments

As you have learned, a project's schedule is calculated by Project based on things such as a project's calendar, task durations, task relationships, and resource assignments. However, project managers have the ultimate decision-making authority on the project's overall schedule. If Project is not creating a project schedule that makes sense to the project's needs, a project manager should review how the schedule is being created and make adjustments to the project calendar, task durations, task relationships, or resource assignments accordingly.

Enhance a Project Schedule with Elapsed Duration and Recurring Tasks

If you assign a task a duration of 48 hours, Project will schedule that task for 6 days of work (48 hours divided by an 8-hour work day). However, assume a task in your project needs 48 hours total without regard to the Project calendar. If this is the case, Project 2016 allows you to assign elapsed duration times. **Elapsed durations** ignore any project or resources working and nonworking times and schedules the task(s) to 24 hours a day.

Adding Elapsed Durations

You want to allow the online registration to be open for 6 weeks. Therefore, you will add the task and assign the task a 6-week duration to give participants time to register for the event. However, the project calendar allows for only 16 hours of work each week and does not account for the fact that participants can register any time of the day. Therefore, a 6-week duration will assign the task to last over 3 months, but you only want the registration open for 6 weeks. You decide to change the duration to elapsed time to accurately reflect how long you want online registration to remain open.

In this exercise, you will set a task duration to elapsed time.

PM02.10

To Set a Task Duration to Elapsed Time

a. Click **Create volunteer list** (Task 16), and then press Ins to insert a new task row. Add the task name **Accept online registrations**. Press Tab, and then type 10w to enter a task duration of 10 weeks. Press Tab three times, and then type 15 to assign a predecessor of Task 15. Press Tab. Note this task takes nearly 6 months to complete.

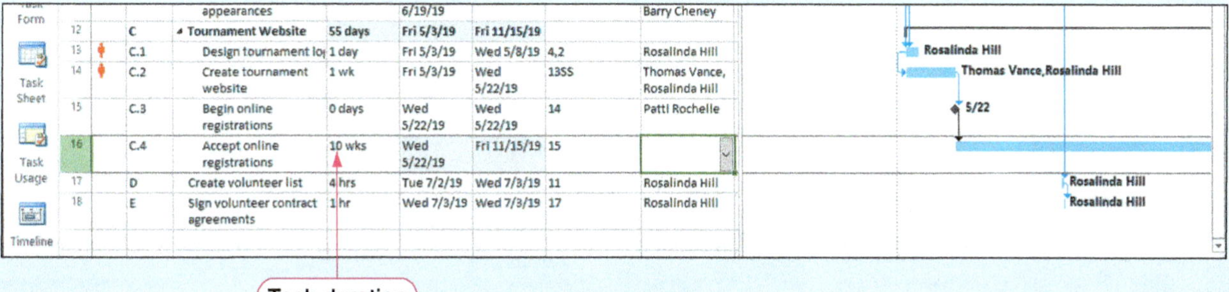

Microsoft Project 2016, Windows 10, Microsoft Corporation

Figure 33 Task duration

b. Click in the **Duration** column of Task 16, and then type 10ew to change the duration of the task to 10 elapsed weeks. Press Enter. Note the change to task Finish date of this task. Making the duration an elapsed time more accurately reflects the assignment of that task.

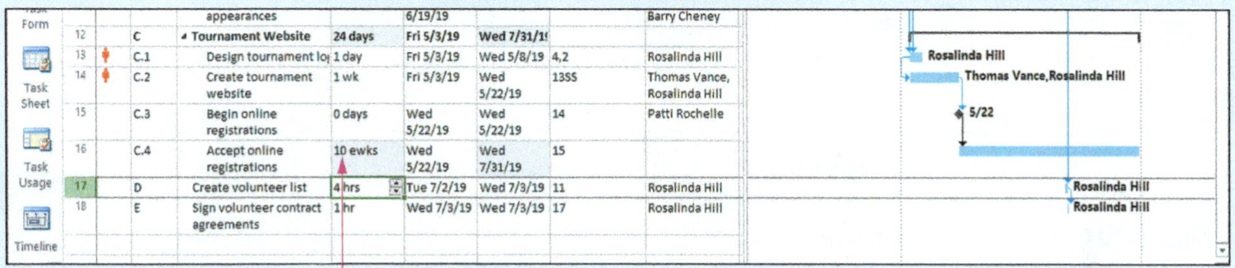

Microsoft Project 2016, Windows 10, Microsoft Corporation

Figure 34 Elapsed duration assigned to a task

SIDE NOTE

Overallocation

The overallocated indicator will appear on all tasks assigned to an overallocated resource.

c. Add **Your Name** as the resource to Task 16. The icon in the Indicators column shows overallocation. By assigning yourself to this task, you have overallocated yourself.

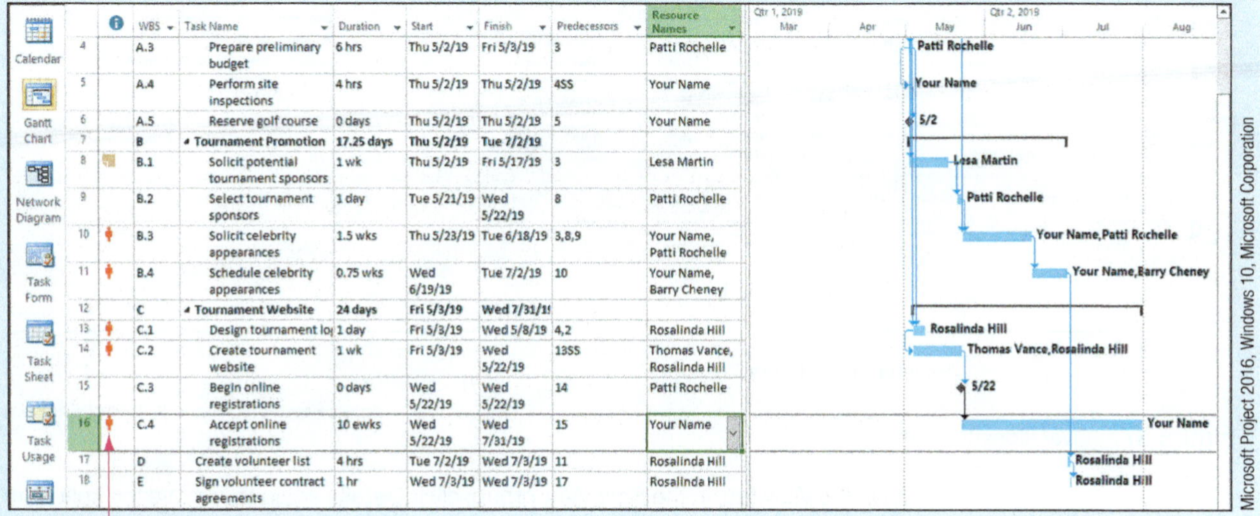

Microsoft Project 2016, Windows 10, Microsoft Corporation

Figure 35 Entry table with overallocated resources

d. With Task 16 still selected, open the Work form in **Split View** by clicking the **View** tab, and then in the Split View group, click **Details**. Note you are assigned to 1,680 hours of work on Task 16.

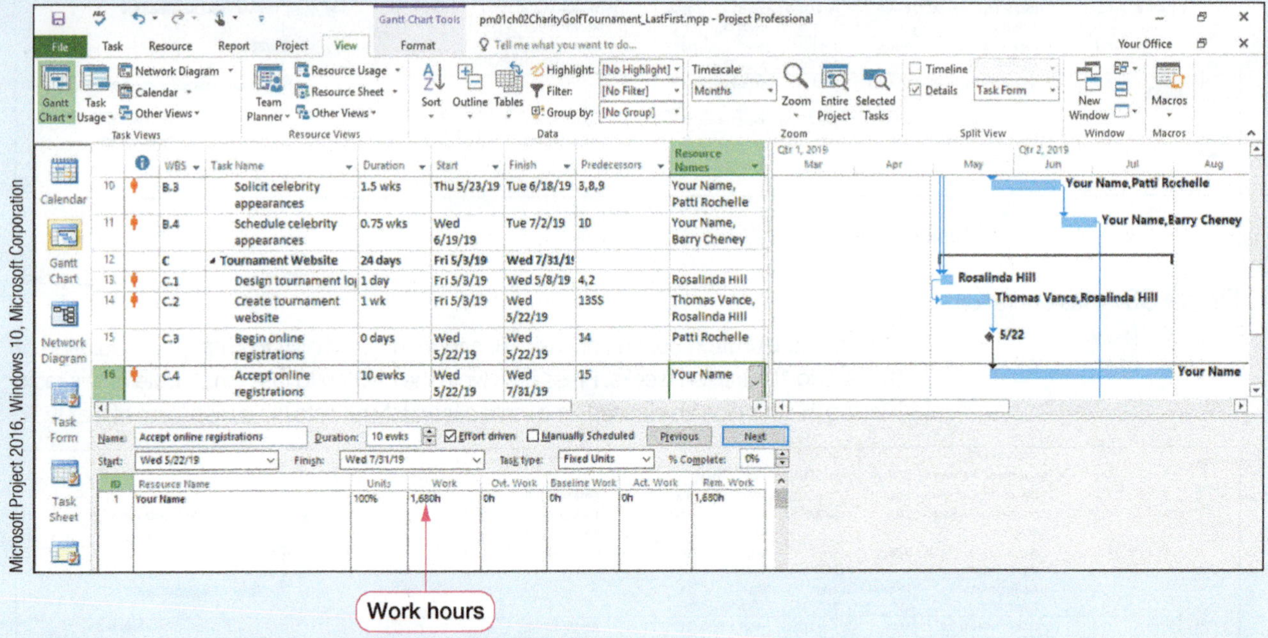

Figure 36 Work Form in Split View

> **SIDE NOTE**
> **Elapsed Duration**
> A task assigned an elapsed duration is displayed as a dotted line in the Gantt chart.

e. In the Split form, click in the Work column, and then type 0 since you do not need to spend time actually completing the task. Click **OK**. Note the overallocation on Task 16 is removed.

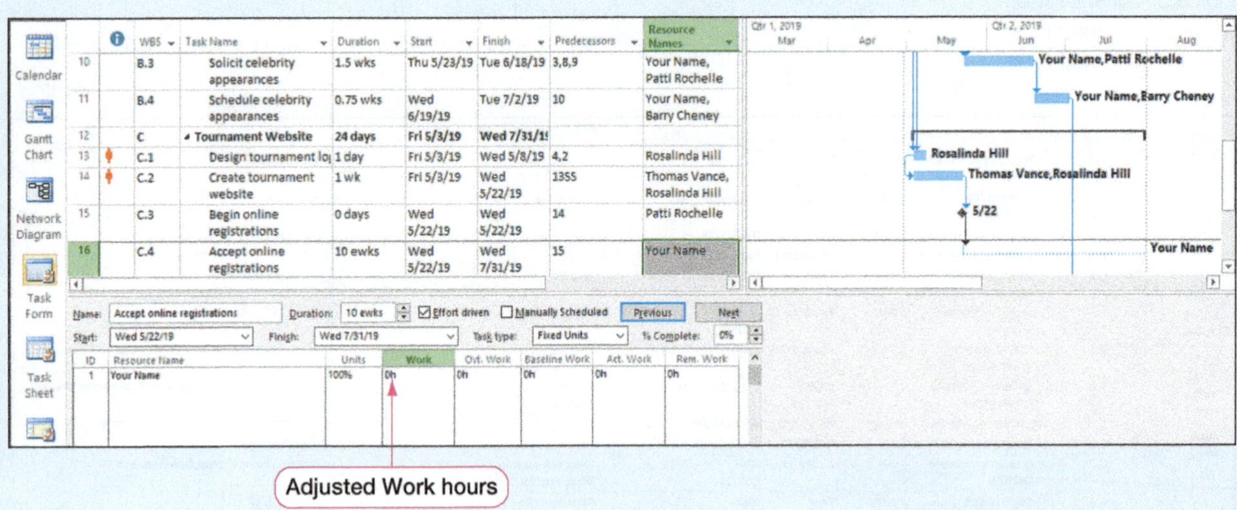

Microsoft Project 2016, Windows 10, Microsoft Corporation

Figure 37 Overallocation removed

f. On the View tab, in the Split View group, click **Details** again to remove the split form.

g. **Save** the project.

Adding a Recurring Task

There are also circumstances where you may do the same task over and over, such as a weekly status meeting. Tasks that have a regular occurrence can be entered into the Project software as recurring tasks. A **recurring task** is a task that repeats at regular intervals. For example, you may want to monitor online registrations every Wednesday to be sure the tournament is receiving enough registrations. Instead of setting up separate tasks each week, you could create a recurring task.

In this exercise, you will create a recurring task.

PM02.11

SIDE NOTE

Recurring Task

Recurring tasks are inserted as a summary task with the recurring tasks as individual task bars.

To Create a Recurring Task

a. Click in the Task Name column of row 19, the first blank row of the Entry table.

b. Click the **Task** tab, and then in the Insert group, click the **Task** button arrow. Click **Recurring Task** to open the Recurring Task Information dialog box.

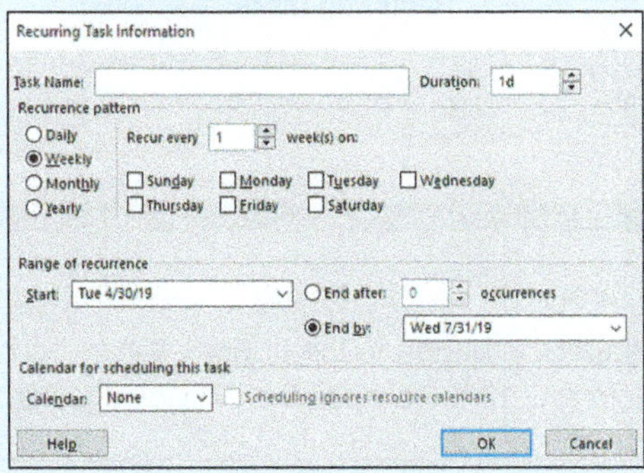

Figure 38 Recurring Task Information dialog box

c. Type the Task Name Monitor online registrations. Enter a duration of 1h.

d. If necessary, click **Weekly** under the Recurrence pattern. Set the task to recur every **1 week** on **Wednesday**. Set the Range of recurrence to start on **May 29, 2019** and end on **July 24, 2019**. Apply the **Standard Calendar** to the task.

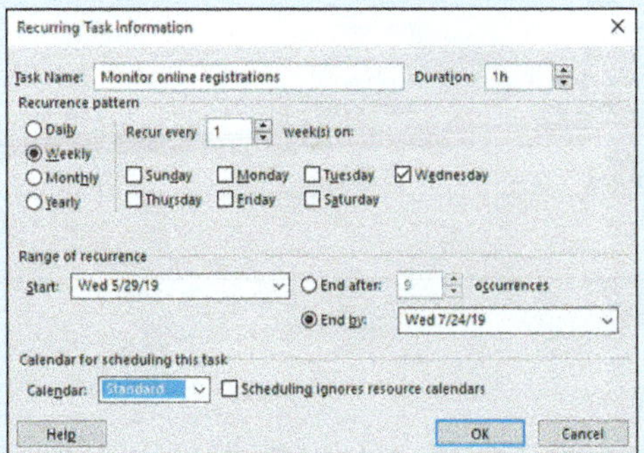

Figure 39 Recurring Task Information dialog box with task information

e. Click **OK.** A Recurring Task indicator appears in the Indicators column.

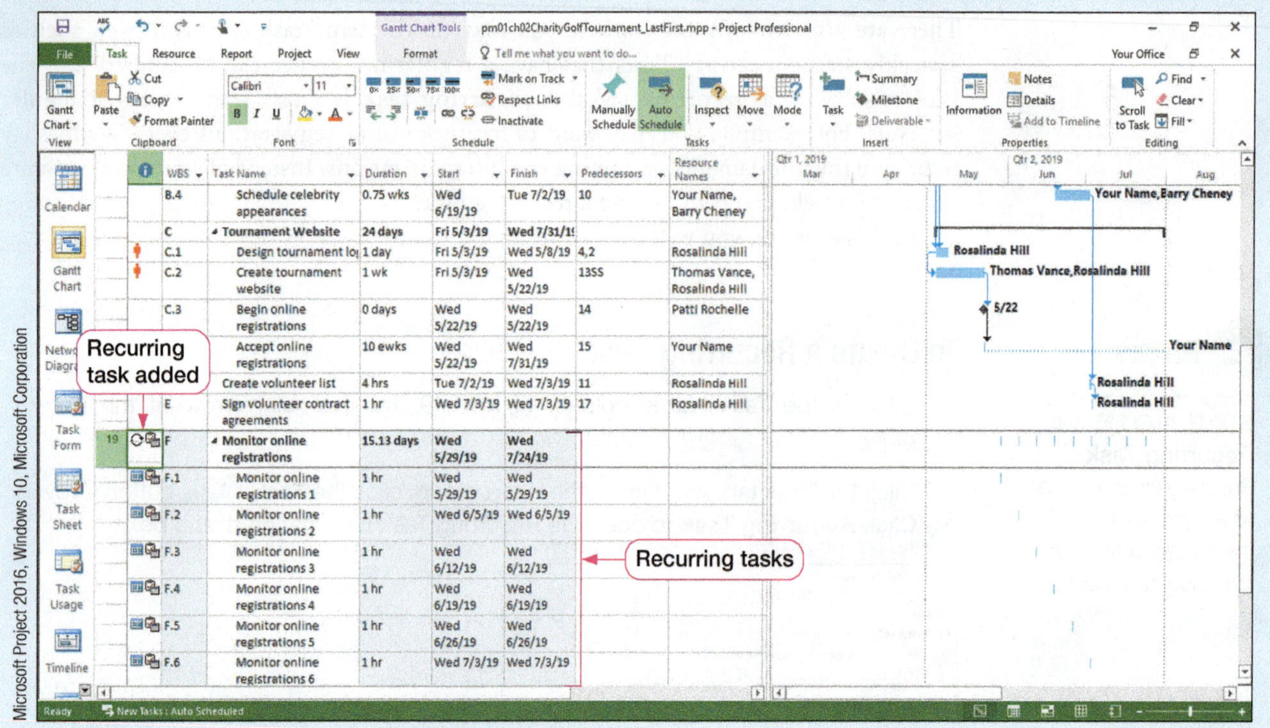

Figure 40 Entry table with recurring task information

f. Click the **Collapse** ◢ button in the upper left-hand corner of the name box of the recurring task in row 19 to collapse the individual tasks.

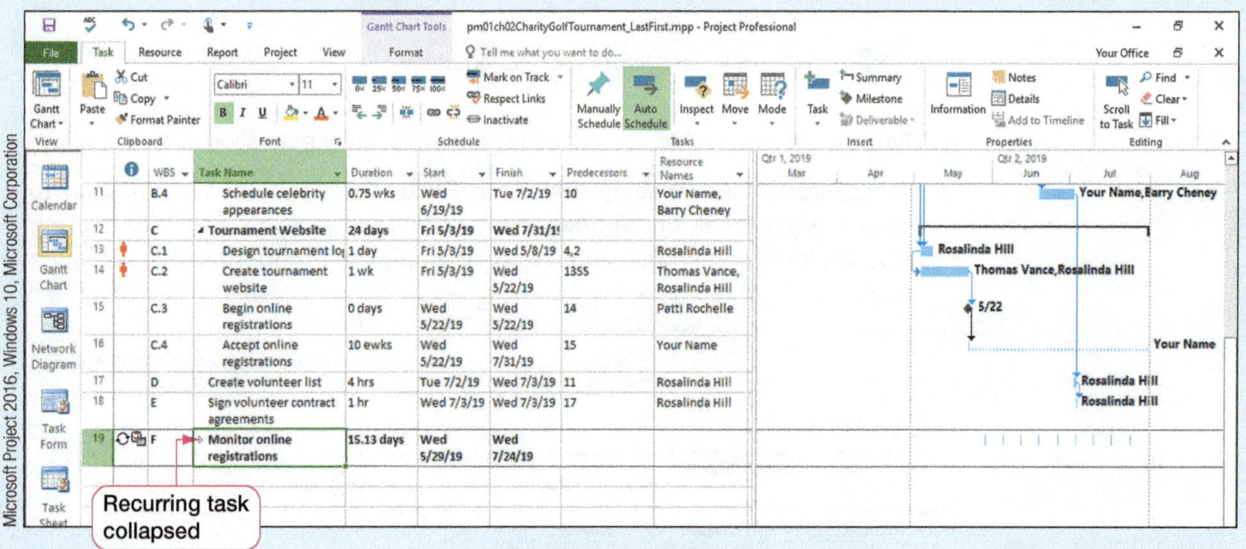

Figure 41 Recurring task collapsed

g. Click the **View** tab, and then in the Zoom group, click **Entire Project** to view the entire project plan in the Gantt chart.

h. **Save** the project.

Share Project Information

Communication is an integral part of a project manager's duties when managing projects. If a project manager is using Project 2016, project reports can be created. Project 2016 information can also be copied and pasted into other applications such as an Excel spreadsheet or a Word table. Information can also be exported to other applications or imported from other applications. Projects can be linked to other projects as well. Regardless of which method a project manager decides to use to share information, frequent project communication is good practice to be sure the entire project and project team stay on task.

The reporting features of Project 2016 have a new graphical appearance and many formatting capabilities. The reports now feature charts and images that better represent your project at a glance. You can add or remove elements in reports to fit your reporting needs. Project 2016 gives project managers dozens of pre-loaded reports that can be used immediately. Not only are these reports available, but they can also be customized to meet the project reporting needs. If a project manager does not find a report that works for a project, custom reports can also be created. Project allows for individual control of reports, from black and white to colors as well as chart effects.

Most of the reports available in Project are based on project status. To display the status of a project, a baseline must be set and the project is tracked. A baseline is a record of each task at a point in time from which you will track project progress. **Tracking** is recording the actual progress of the project's tasks (for example, identifying a task as completed or partially done). Baselines are set on the Project tab, and task tracking is done in the Schedule group on the Task tab.

REAL WORLD ADVICE **Setting a Project Baseline**

If your supervisor asks you how the project is going, you want to be sure to have an answer. Project managers who want the ability to run project reports to update the project status and determine where the project is compared to where the project should be will set a project baseline. As a snapshot of the original plan of the project, a baseline allows you to compare what should be happening with your project versus what is actually happening with your project.

Project 2016 includes five Dashboard reports. Dashboard reports display project progress relevant to an objective or process. Table 2 defines the five pre-determined Dashboard reports.

Report Name	Description
Burndown	This reports how much work you have completed and how much work you have left to complete.
Cost Overview	This report displays the current cost status of your project and its top level (Summary) to help you determine if your project is staying on budget.
Project Overview	This report displays how much of the project is complete as well as any upcoming milestones and tasks that are past due (late tasks).
Upcoming Tasks	This report displays the work that has been done during the current week, the status of any remaining tasks that were due, and which tasks may be starting in the next week.
Work Overview	This report displays how much work you have completed and how much you have left (such as burndown) as well as remaining availability of work resources.

Table 2 Dashboard reports

Creating Project Reports

In addition to Dashboard reports, there are also Resources, Costs, In Progress, and Custom reports. Although you have not set a project baseline and therefore have not started tracking your project, you still can explore the available reports for your project.

In this exercise, you will view reports in Project 2016.

PM02.12 To View Reports in Project

a. Click the **Report** tab. In the View Reports group, click the **Resources** arrow, and then select **Resource Overview**. Notice the graphical nature of the report and the features available to customize reports on the Report Tools Design tab.

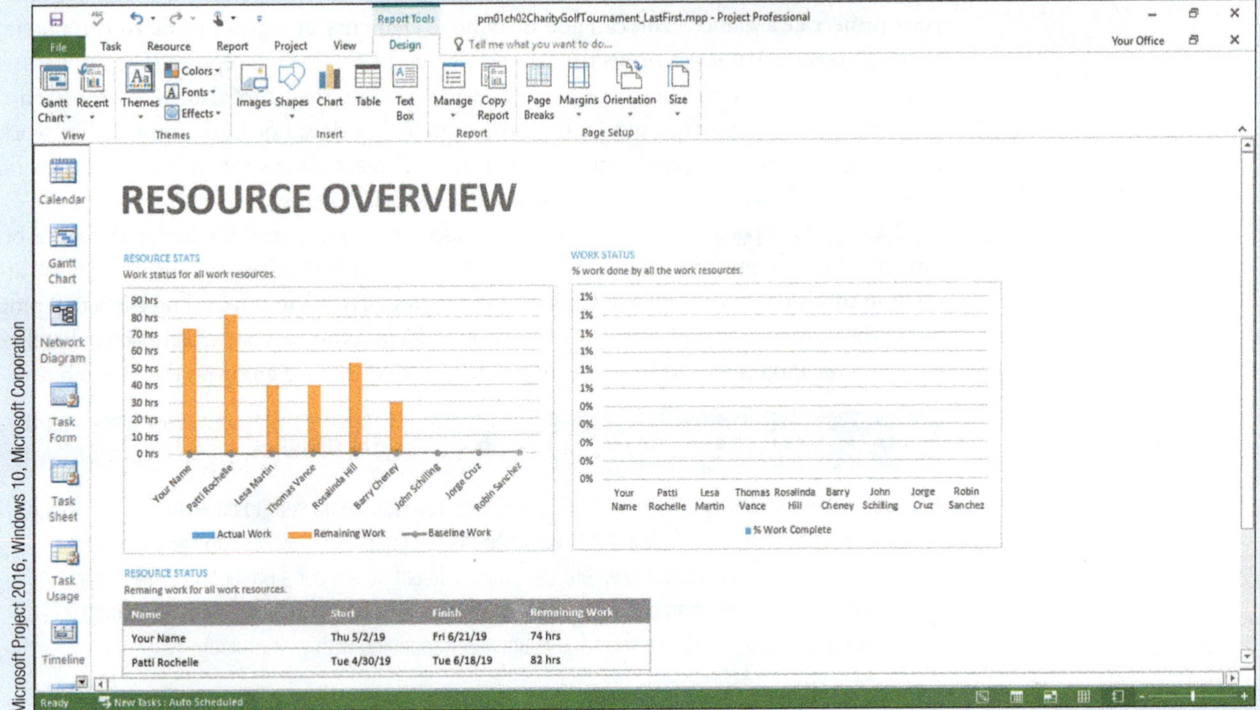

Figure 42 Resource Overview report

b. Click the **Report** tab. In the View Reports group, click the **Resources** arrow, and then select **Overallocated Resources** to view the overallocation for Rosalinda Hill.

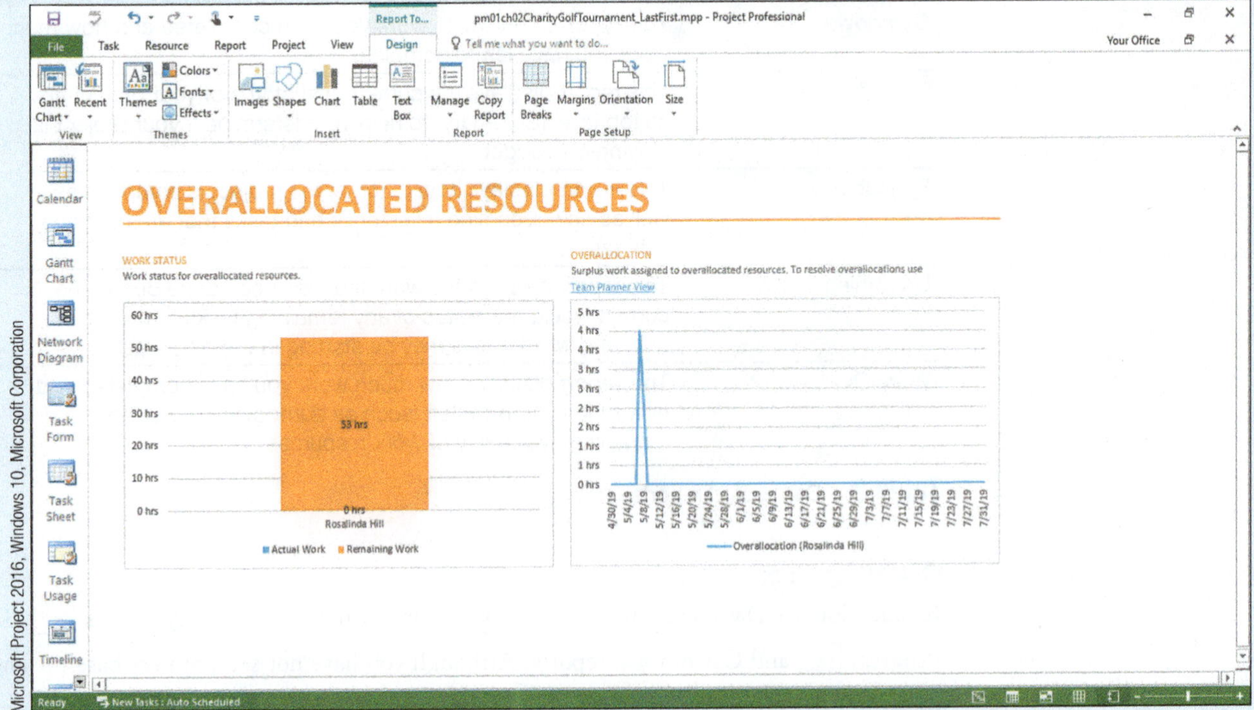

Figure 43 Overallocated Resources report

c. In the Overallocated Resources report, click the **Team Planner View** link to view the overallocation. You will see the overallocation occurs between the Design tournament logo task and the Create tournament website task.

d. Click **Gantt Chart** on the View Bar, and then select **Create tournament website** (Task 14) if necessary. Since there is a Start-to-Start relationship between Tasks 13 and 14, Rosalinda is being scheduled to work on two tasks as the same time. This is causing the overallocation.

e. Click in the Predecessors column of Task 14. Type 13, and then press Enter to remove the overallocation of Rosalinda.

Troubleshooting

If the overallocation is still present, make sure you delete the Start-to-Start relationship and the only predecessor for Task 14 is Task 13.

f. Click the **Report** tab. In the View Reports group, click the **Resources** arrow, and then select **Overallocated Resources**. You note there are no longer overallocated resources.

g. Click **Gantt Chart** on the View Bar.

h. **Save** the project.

Copy and Paste Project Information to Other Applications

A project manager is not limited to sharing project information through Project's reports. Project 2016 information can be shared by copying and pasting project information into another application such as Excel or Word. Since Excel is similar to Project's Entry table, pasting information into Excel will create a worksheet with columns and rows of data. When you paste information into Word, however, project information will be pasted into a table format.

Copying and Pasting Project Information to Excel and Word

You want to share your project information with other project team members who do not have knowledge of Project 2016. To make it easier for them to view the project's information, you will copy the information and then paste into Excel and Word.

In this exercise, you will copy data into an Excel workbook and into a Word document.

PM02.13

To Copy Data into an Excel Workbook and a Word Document

a. Click the **Select All** button in the upper left-hand corner of the Entry table.

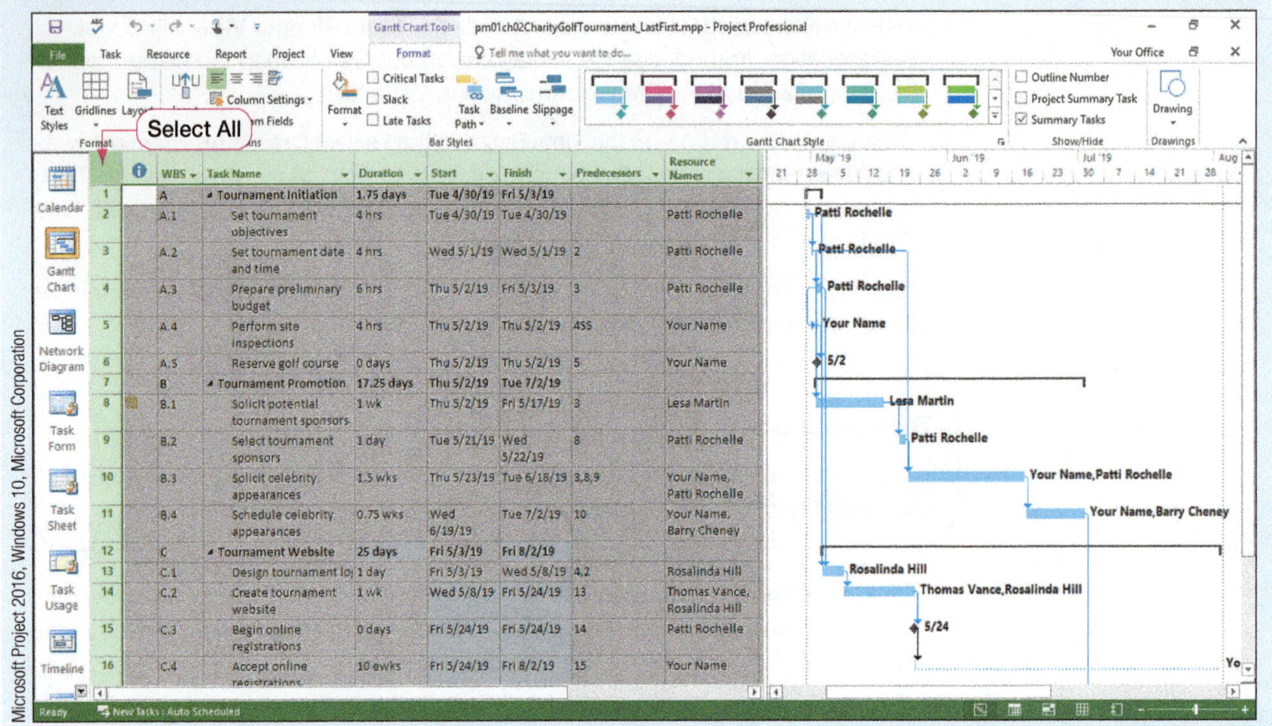

Figure 44 Entry table Select All button

SIDE NOTE
Microsoft PowerPoint
You could also paste a picture of your project into a PowerPoint presentation.

b. Click the **Task** tab, and then in the Clipboard group, click **Copy**.

c. While keeping your Project 2016 file open, locate and open **Excel 2016**. Select **Blank workbook** to create a blank Excel workbook.

d. If necessary, click in cell A1, and then press Ctrl + V to paste the project's Entry table data into Excel.

e. To adjust the width of Column B, right-click the column header for Column B. Click **Column Width**, and then type 35. Click **OK**.

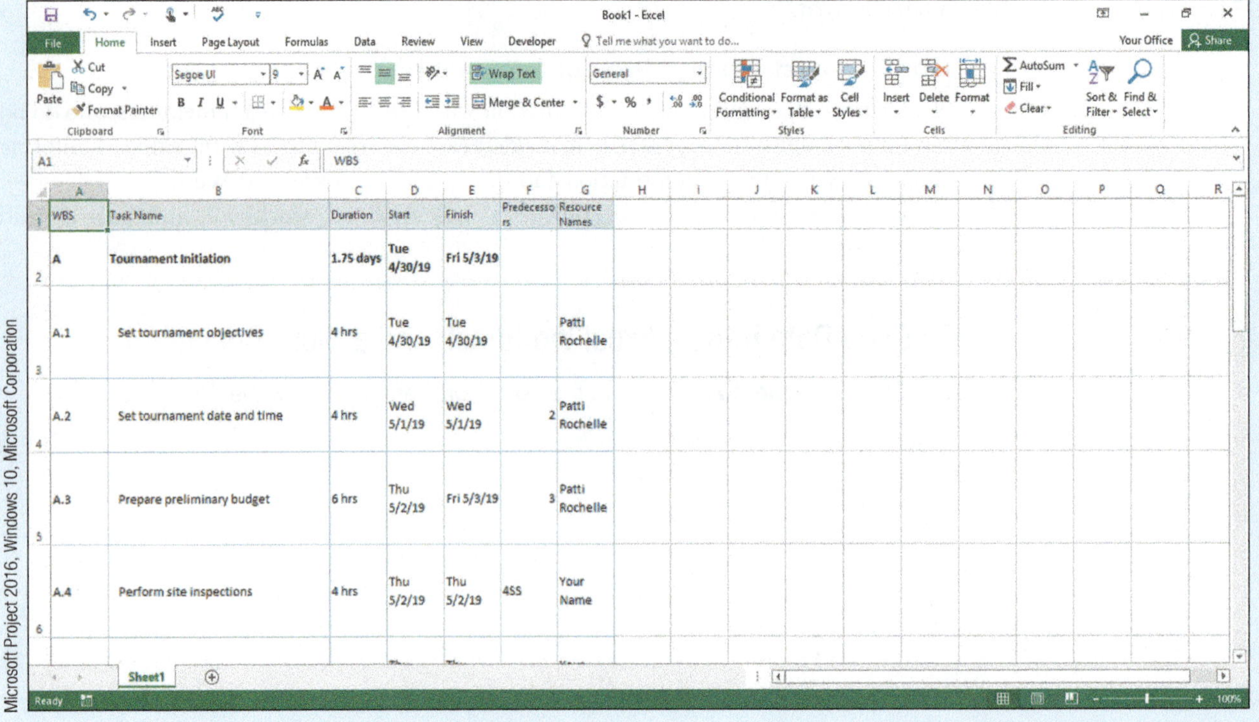

Figure 45 Project data pasted into an Excel workbook

f. Click the **File** tab, and then click **Save**. Click **This PC**, and then click **Browse**. Navigate to the location where you are storing your files.

g. In the Save As dialog box, click in the File name box, and then type pm01ch02 CharityGolfTournament_LastFirst, using your last and first name. Click **Save** to save the project task data in Excel format.

h. Click **Close** ✕ to close Excel 2016.

i. Locate and open **Microsoft Word 2016**. Select **Blank document** to create a blank Word document.

j. On the Home tab, in the Clipboard group, click **Paste** to paste your project's data into the document. Notice the project data is formatted as a Word table.

k. Click the **File** tab, and then click **Save**. Click **This PC**, and then click **Browse**. Navigate to the location where you store your files. In the Save As dialog box, click in the File name box, and then type pm01ch02CharityGolfTournament_LastFirst, using your last and first name. Click **Save** to save the project task data in Word format.

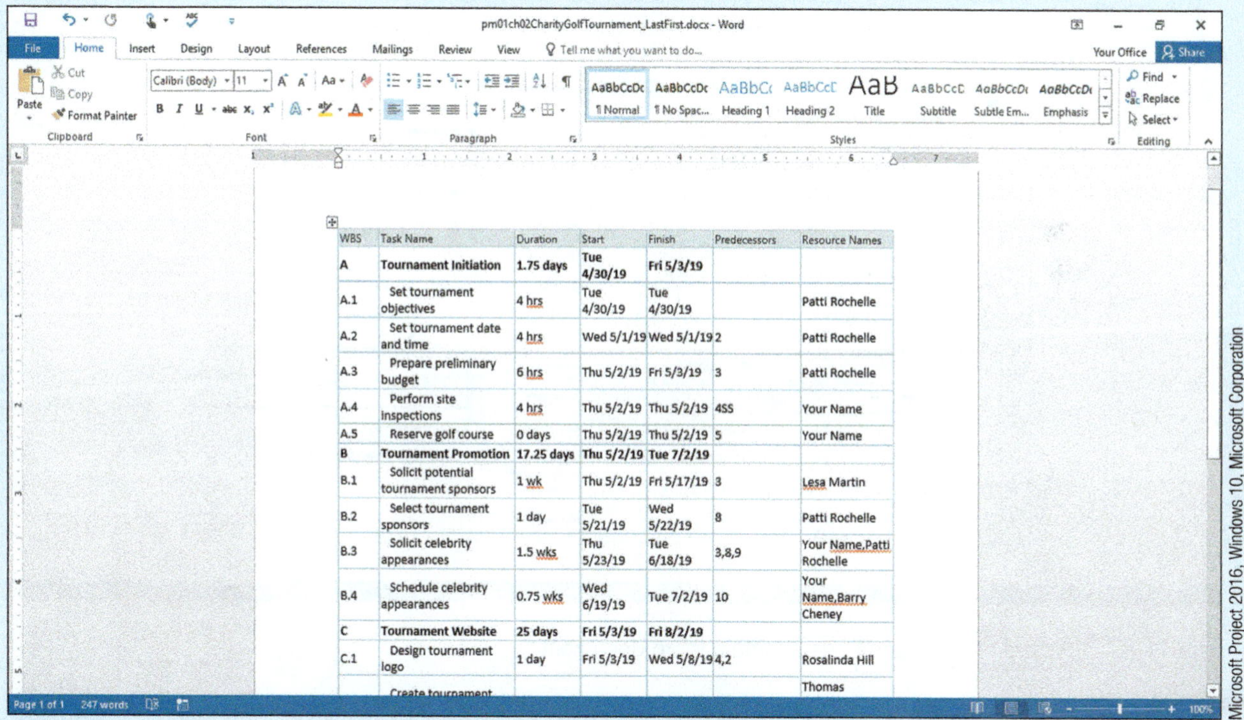

WBS	Task Name	Duration	Start	Finish	Predecessors	Resource Names
A	**Tournament Initiation**	**1.75 days**	**Tue 4/30/19**	**Fri 5/3/19**		
A.1	Set tournament objectives	4 hrs	Tue 4/30/19	Tue 4/30/19		Patti Rochelle
A.2	Set tournament date and time	4 hrs	Wed 5/1/19	Wed 5/1/19	2	Patti Rochelle
A.3	Prepare preliminary budget	6 hrs	Thu 5/2/19	Fri 5/3/19	3	Patti Rochelle
A.4	Perform site inspections	4 hrs	Thu 5/2/19	Thu 5/2/19	4SS	Your Name
A.5	Reserve golf course	0 days	Thu 5/2/19	Thu 5/2/19	5	Your Name
B	**Tournament Promotion**	**17.25 days**	**Thu 5/2/19**	**Tue 7/2/19**		
B.1	Solicit potential tournament sponsors	1 wk	Thu 5/2/19	Fri 5/17/19	3	Lesa Martin
B.2	Select tournament sponsors	1 day	Tue 5/21/19	Wed 5/22/19	8	Patti Rochelle
B.3	Solicit celebrity appearances	1.5 wks	Thu 5/23/19	Tue 6/18/19	3,8,9	Your Name,Patti Rochelle
B.4	Schedule celebrity appearances	0.75 wks	Wed 6/19/19	Tue 7/2/19	10	Your Name,Barry Cheney
C	**Tournament Website**	**25 days**	**Fri 5/3/19**	**Fri 8/2/19**		
C.1	Design tournament logo	1 day	Fri 5/3/19	Wed 5/8/19	4,2	Rosalinda Hill
	Create tournament					Thomas

Microsoft Project 2016, Windows 10, Microsoft Corporation

Figure 46 Project data pasted into a Word document as a table

l. Click **Close** ✕ to close Word, and return to your pm01ch02CharityGolf Tournament_LastFirst.mpp project file.

Copying Project Information as a Picture

Copying and pasting data from the Entry table works well since the Entry table is similar to Excel's column and row format. However, copying and pasting project data does not work well in all views. In this case, you may want to copy and paste a picture of the view into another application such as Microsoft Word or PowerPoint.

In this exercise, you will copy and paste a picture of the Gantt chart and the Timeline view in Project 2016 to Word 2016.

To Copy and Paste a Picture of the Gantt Chart and Timeline Views into Word

a. If necessary, click the **Gantt Chart** button on the View Bar. On the Task tab, in the Clipboard group, click the **Copy** arrow, and then select **Copy Picture**. The Copy Picture dialog box opens.

b. Verify **For screen** is selected, and then click **OK**.

c. Locate and open **Microsoft Word 2016**. Select **Blank document** to create a blank Word document.

d. On the Home tab, in the Clipboard group, click **Paste** to paste your project's data into the document.

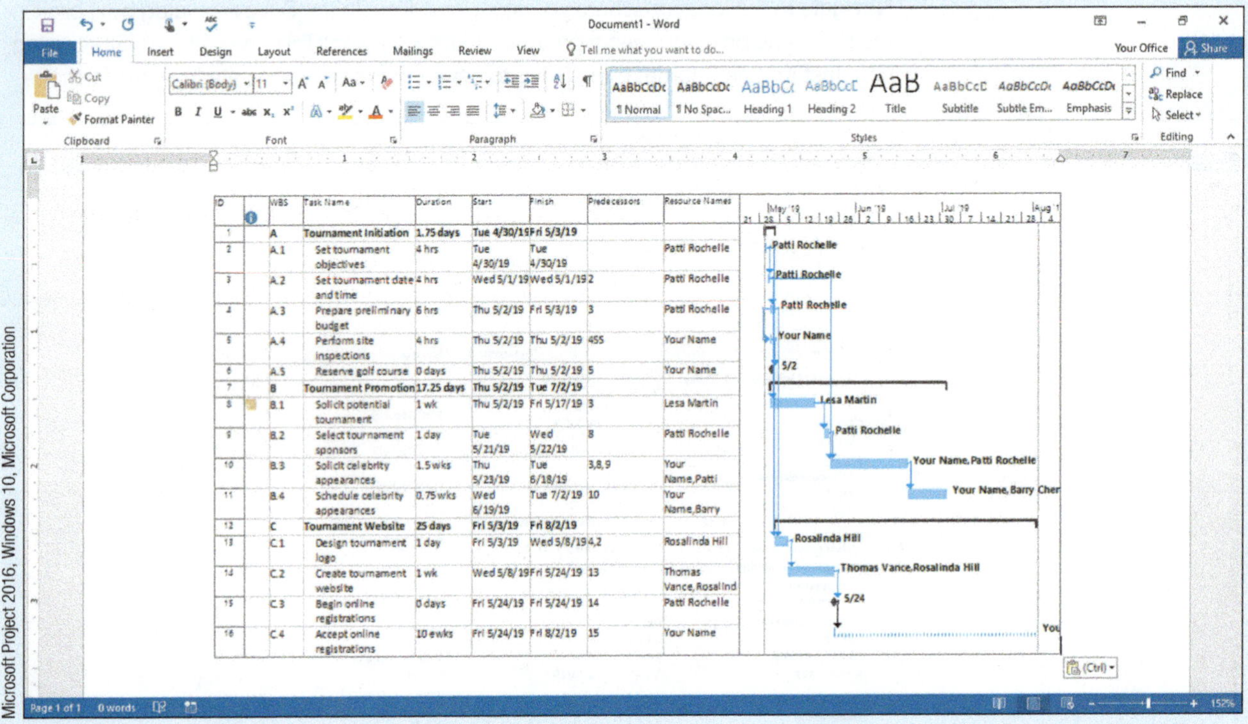

Figure 47 Picture of Gantt chart pasted into a Word document

e. Click the **File** tab, and then click **Save As**. Click **This PC**, and then click **Browse**. Navigate to the location where you store your files. Click in the File name box, and then type pm01ch02CharityGolfTournamentGanttChart_LastFirst using your last and first name. Click **Save** to save the Gantt chart picture in Word.

f. Click **Close** X to close the Word document.

g. On the Task tab, in the View group, click the **Gantt Chart** button arrow, and then click **Timeline**. This will display the Timeline view.

h. Click the **Timeline Tools Format** tab. In the Copy group, click **Copy Timeline**.

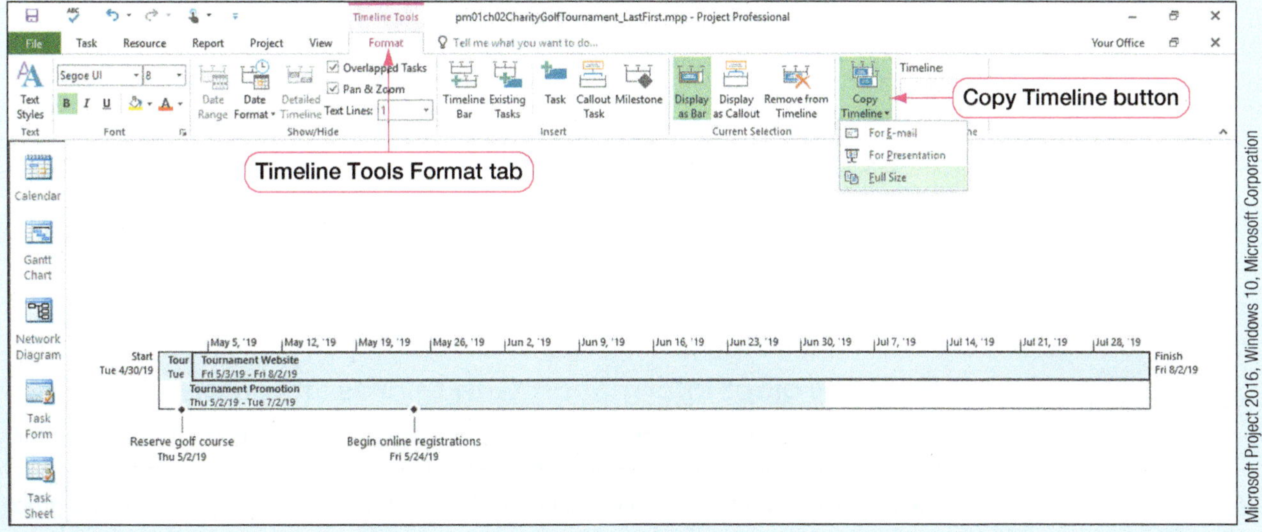

Figure 48 Timeline Tools Format tab

i. Select **Full Size**.

j. Once again, open **Microsoft Word 2016**, and then select **Blank document** to create a blank Word document.

k. In Microsoft Word, click the **Layout** tab. In the Page Setup group, click the **Orientation** button, and then select **Landscape**.

l. In the Page Setup group, click the **Size** button, and then select **Legal**.

m. Press Ctrl + V to paste a copy of the Timeline into Word.

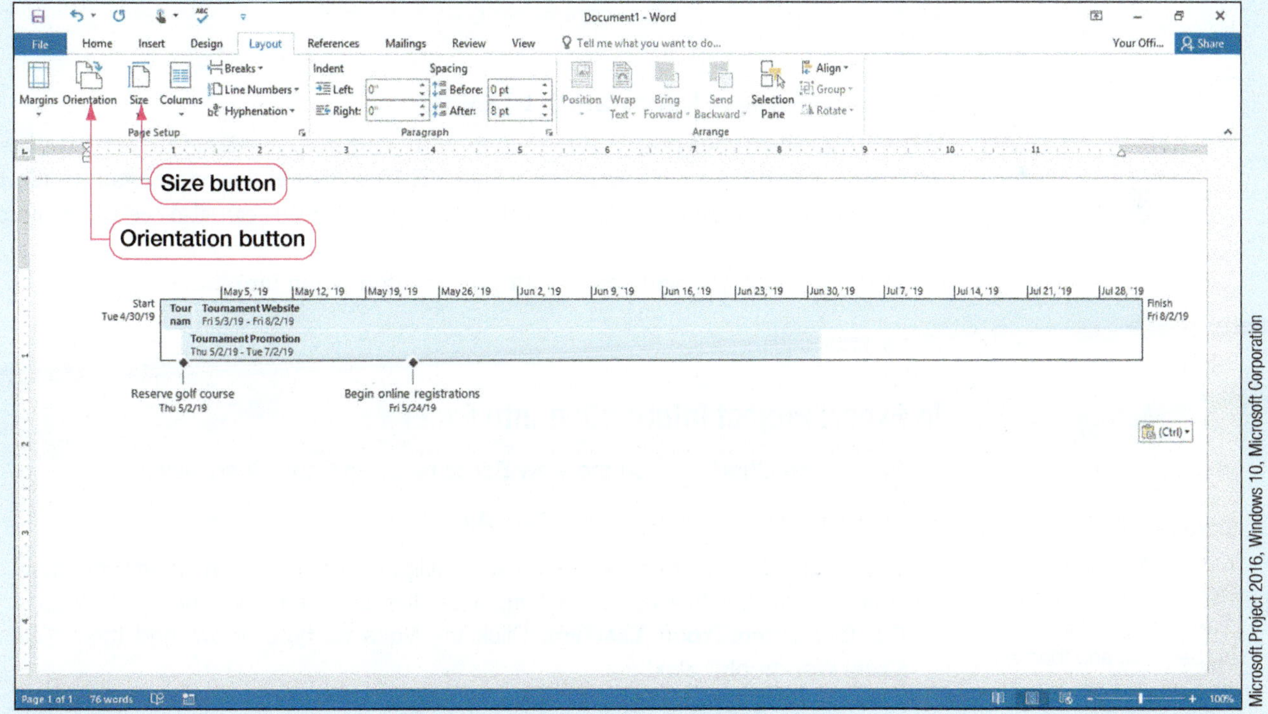

Figure 49 Picture of Timeline pasted into a Word document

n. Click the **File** tab, and then click **Save As**. Click **This PC**, and then click **Browse**. Navigate to the location where you store your files. Click in the File name box, and then type pm01ch02CharityGolfTournamentTimeline_LastFirst using your last and first name.

o. Click **Save** to save the Timeline data in Word, and then click **Close** ✕ to close Word.

p. Return to the Gantt Chart view.

Share Project Information with Microsoft Excel

There may be situations in which you need to share project information with other members of your project team or organization who do not have access to Project 2016. In this case, you can export your project data into Excel. When you begin the exporting process, the Export Wizard will take you through a series of steps to export all fields for project categories into a new format.

REAL WORLD ADVICE | **Analyzing Project Data with Excel**

Microsoft Excel 2016 is spreadsheet software that can be used for storing and analyzing data. Since projects often contain large amounts of data, project managers often find it useful to export project data into Excel and then use Excel's data analysis tools, such as PivotTables and advanced database management, to analyze a project's data. Data analyzed in Excel can be shared with project team members and/or project stakeholders and can be used to make strategic project decisions.

Exporting Project Information to Excel

You want to share your project information with your project team, but you have been informed some do not have access to Project 2016 software. Therefore, you decide to export your project data into Excel so that your project team can also see the project's tasks.

In this exercise, you will export your project information into Excel.

PM02.15

SIDE NOTE
Save as PDF
You can also save your Project file as a PDF by clicking the File tab, clicking Save As, and then in the Save as type: box, selecting PDF Files (.pdf).

To Export Project Information into Excel

a. Click **Gantt Chart** on the View Bar to return to Gantt Chart view.

b. Click the **File** tab, and then click **Save As**.

c. Click **This PC**, and then click **Browse**. Navigate to the location where you store your files. In the File name section, enter the project name pm01ch02CharityGolfTournamentExport_LastFirst. Click the **Save as type** arrow, and then click **Excel Workbook(*.xlsx).**

d. Click **Save**. The Export Wizard dialog box opens.

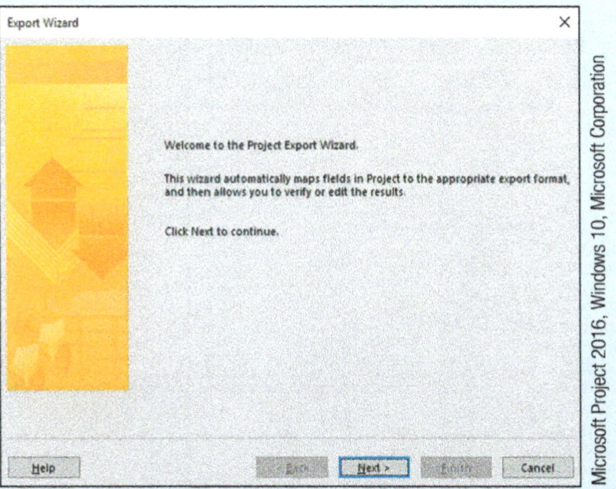

Figure 50 Export Wizard dialog box

e. Click the **Next** button. Click the **Project Excel Template** button.

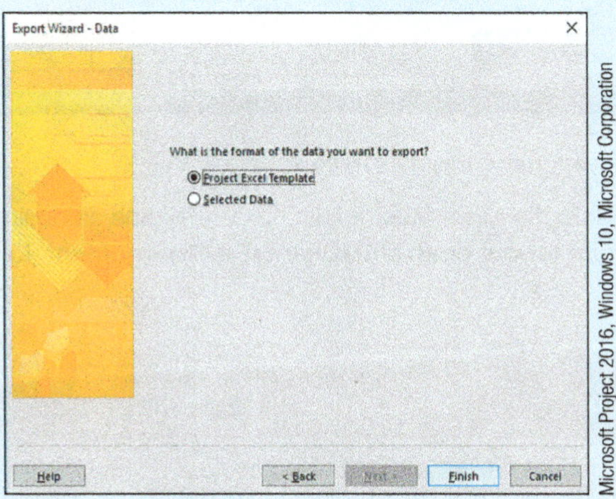

Figure 51 Export Wizard – Data dialog box

f. Click **Finish**. Your project data is exported to Excel.

g. Use File Explorer to navigate to the location where you store your data files. Double-click **pm01ch02CharityGolfTournamentExport_LastFirst.xlsx** to open the charity golf tournament file in Excel.

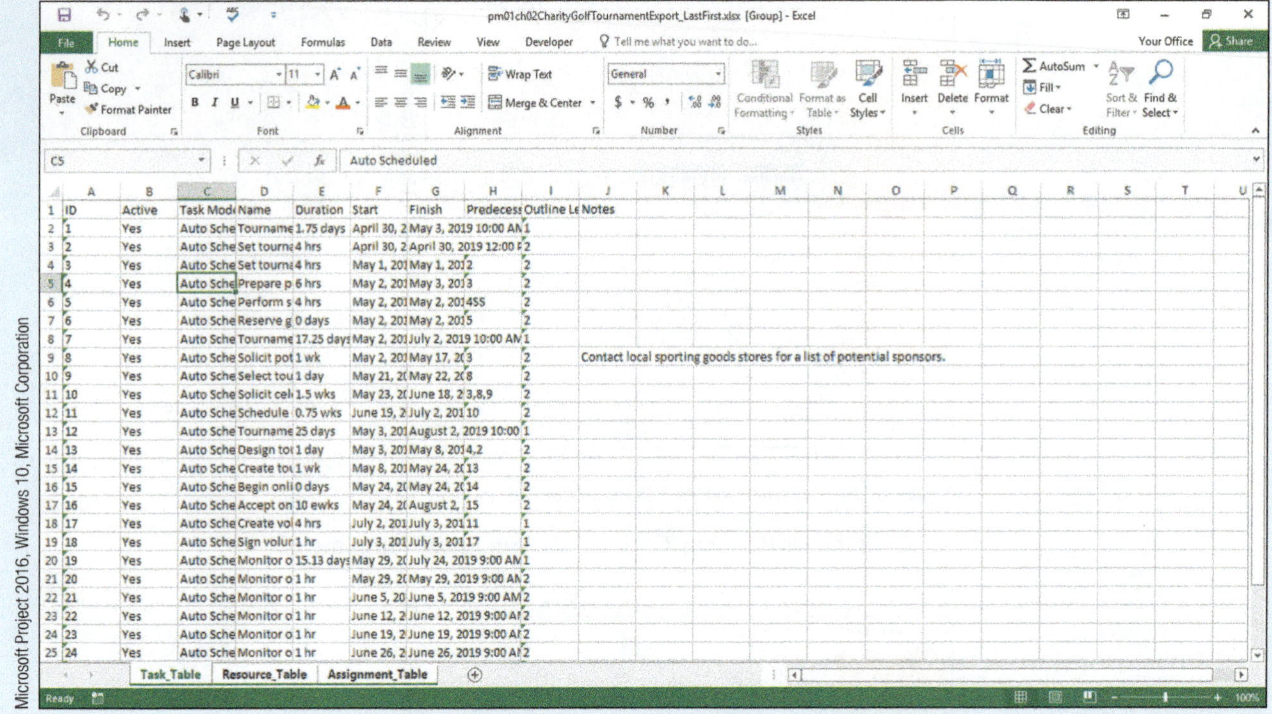

Figure 52 Excel workbook with exported Project 2016 data

h. Explore the sheet tabs, adjust column widths as desired, and then **Close** ✕ Excel. Return to your **pm01ch02CharityGolfTournament_LastFirst.mpp** project file.

QUICK REFERENCE — Exporting Project Data to Excel 2016

1. Select the File tab, and then click Save As.
2. Click This PC and then click Browse to navigate to where you store your files.
3. Click in the File name box, and then enter a name for the exported data.
4. Click the Save as type arrow, and then click Excel Workbook.
5. Click Save to open the Export Wizard dialog box.
6. Click the Next button.
7. Click the Project Excel Template button.
8. Click Finish.

Importing Project Information from Excel

Although information can be copied into Project from another application such as Excel, importing information into Project is more flexible by allowing for data to be imported that does not exactly match. By importing data from Excel, you can use the Import/Export Wizard to assist in bringing in field data into a new project or a current project.

REAL WORLD ADVICE **Sharing Data with Project Partners**

It is not uncommon for projects to be a collaboration of efforts between more than one organization or project team. For example, a project may rely on collaboration with an external vendor. Whenever working with someone outside your organization, it may be difficult to obtain their project schedule in a format that works with your project, especially if they are not using Project 2016.

If an external vendor is using Project 2016 for its schedule needs, the vendor may not want to give you its entire project schedule because it may contain costing and salary information that is private to its organization. If this is the case, you can request an Excel file with tasks and start and finish dates that you can then import directly into your project plan. If the vendor is also using Project 2016, it may actually be exporting the data from Project 2016 to Excel to get you an Excel file, which you can then import back into Project 2016.

In this exercise, you will import project information from Excel.

To Import Project Information from Excel

a. With your Project file open, click the **File** tab, and then click **Open**.

b. Click **Browse**, and then navigate to the location of your student data files. Click the file type list arrow next to the File name box, and then click **Excel Workbook**. Click **pm01ch02CharityGolfTournamentTasks.xlsx**, and then click **Open** to open the Import Wizard dialog box.

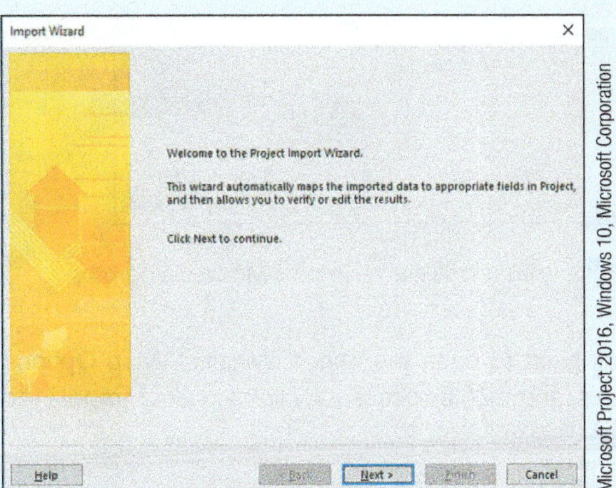

Microsoft Project 2016, Windows 10, Microsoft Corporation

Figure 53 Import Wizard dialog box

c. Click **Next** to open the Import Wizard – Map dialog box, and then if necessary, click **New map**.

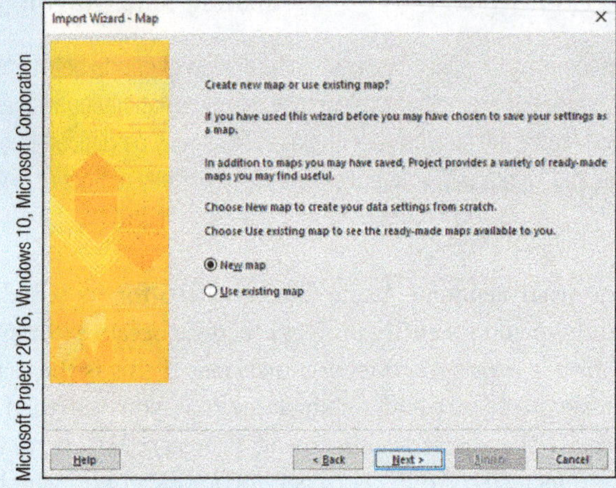

Figure 54 Import Wizard – Map dialog box

d. Click **Next** to open the Import Wizard – Import Mode dialog box. Click **Append the data to the active project.**

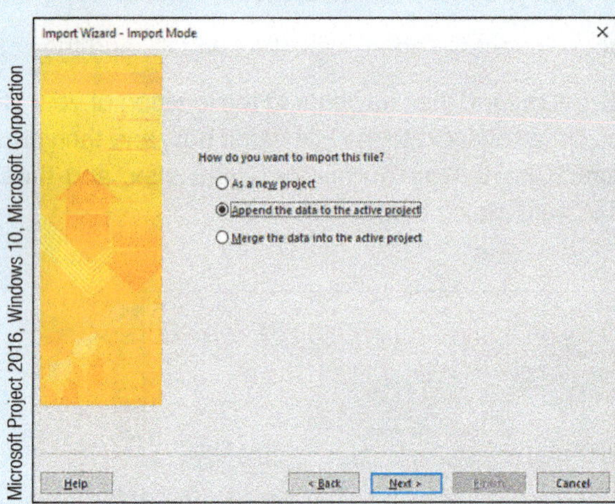

Figure 55 Import Wizard – Import Mode dialog box

e. Click **Next** to open the Import Wizard – Map Options dialog box. Click to select **Tasks**, and then if necessary, click to select **Import includes headers**.

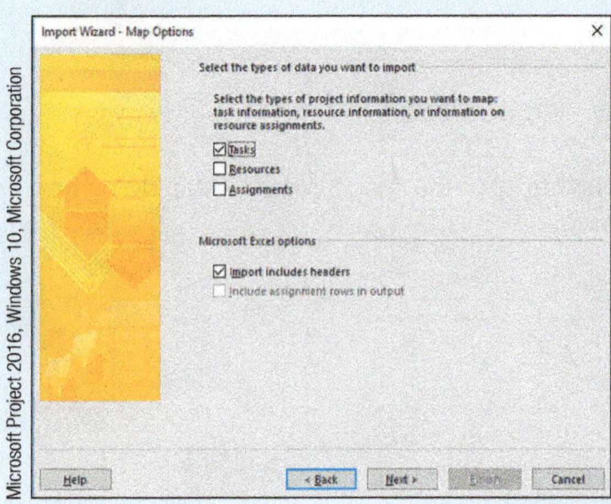

Figure 56 Import Wizard – Map Options dialog box

f. Click **Next** to open the Import Wizard – Task Mapping dialog box.

g. In the Import Wizard – Task Mapping dialog box, click the **Source worksheet name** arrow, and then click **TaskData**.

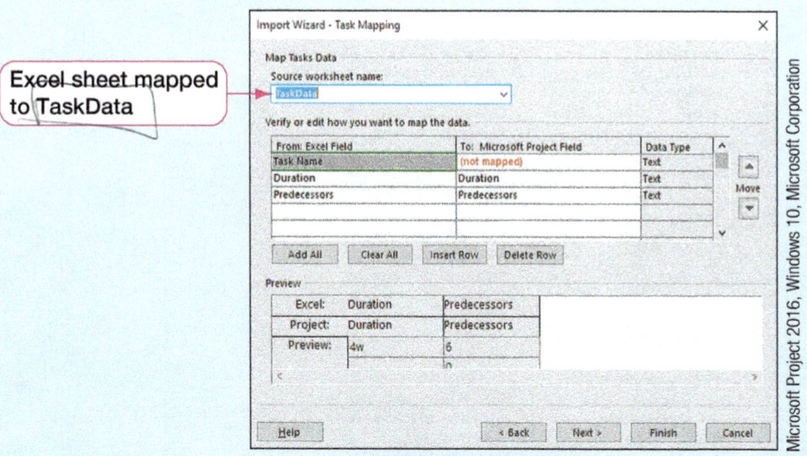

Figure 57 Import Wizard – Task Mapping dialog box

SIDE NOTE

Finding Column Names

When searching for column names, you can type the first letter of a column name to filter for only columns starting with that letter.

h. In the **To: Microsoft Project Field**, view the Task Name row that has the text (not mapped). Click the **(not mapped)** field list arrow, and then scroll until you see Name. Click **Name**. The Duration and Predecessors were automatically mapped.

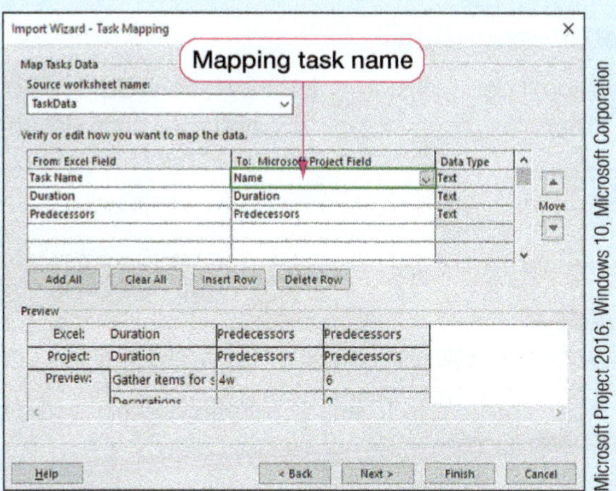

Figure 58 Import Wizard – Task Mapping dialog box with tasks mapped

i. Click **Finish**. Tasks from Excel have been imported into your project starting at row 29.

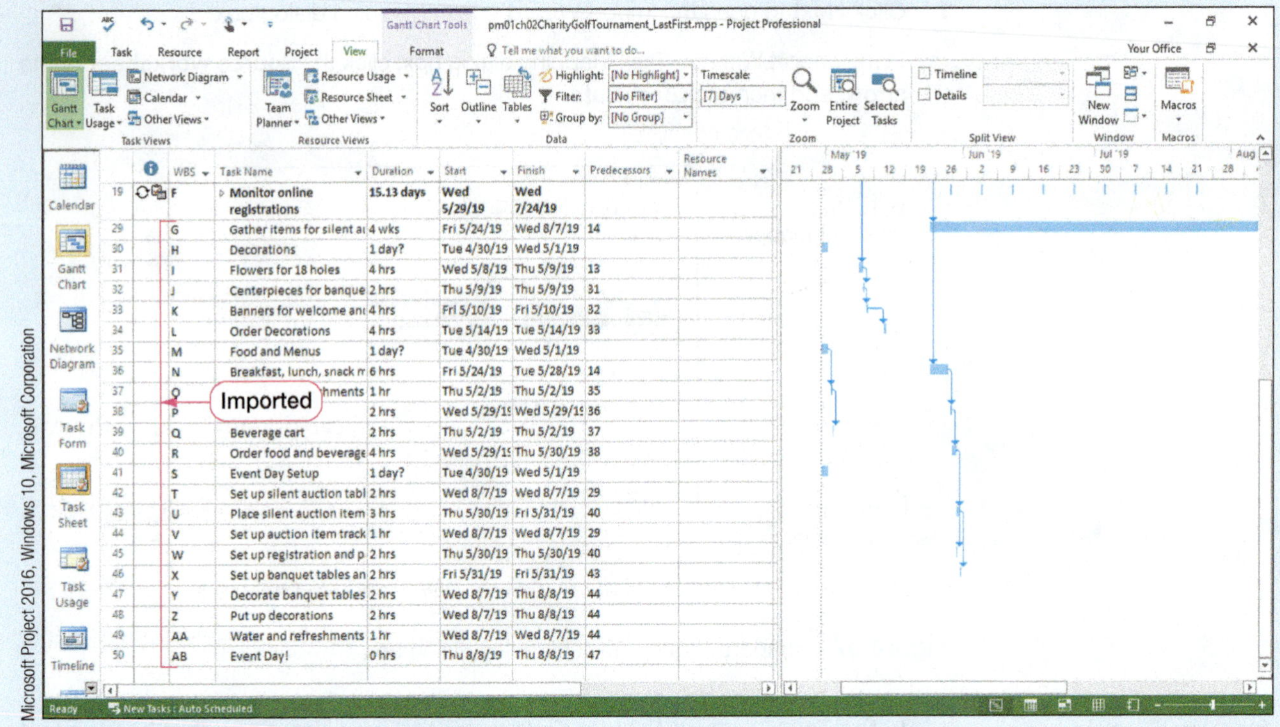

Figure 59 Entry table with tasks imported

j. **Save** the project.

> **Troubleshooting**
>
> If the appended tasks do not start with a WBS code of G, click the Project tab. In the Properties group, click WBS, and then click Renumber.

QUICK REFERENCE — Importing Excel 2016 Data into Project

1. With a Project file open, click the File tab, and then click Open.
2. Click Browse, and then navigate to the location where you store your files. Click the file type list arrow in the Open dialog box, and then click Excel Workbook.
3. Click the Excel workbook from which you want to import data, and then click Open.
4. Click Next.
5. In the Import Wizard – Map dialog box, click the New map option button, and then click Next.
6. In the Import Wizard – Import Mode dialog box, click Append the data to the active project, and then click Next.
7. In the Import Wizard – Map Options dialog box, click Tasks, and if necessary, click Import includes headers, and then click Next.
8. In the Import Wizard – Task Mapping dialog box, click the arrow on the Source worksheet name, and then click Sheet1—or other sheet name that contains the data you wish to import.
9. Verify or edit how you want to map the data portion. All tasks should be mapped.
10. Click Finish.

Adjusting Imported Project Tasks

Imported tasks may not have the proper formatting, task relationships, or resource assignments. Therefore, you will modify the imported tasks to meet your project's needs.

In this exercise, you will adjust the imported tasks from Excel.

To Adjust the Imported Tasks from Excel

a. Select the **task names** in rows **29–50**. Click the **Gantt Chart Tools Format** tab, and then in the Columns group, click **Wrap Text** twice.

b. Click the **Task** tab. Select **Tasks 31–34**, and then in the Schedule group, click **Indent Task** to make the tasks subtasks of Decorations (Task 30).

c. Select **Tasks 36–40**, and then in the Schedule group, click **Indent Task** to make the tasks subtasks of Food and Menus (Task 35).

d. Select **Tasks 42–49**, and then in the Schedule group, click **Indent Task** to make the tasks subtasks of Event Day Setup (Task 41).

e. Click **Food and Menus** (Task 35). Note the WBS code is inaccurate.

f. Click the **Project** tab, and then click **WBS**. Click **Renumber**, be sure **Entire project** is selected, and then click **OK**.

g. Click **Yes**.

SIDE NOTE

Effort Driven Tasks

Remember, new tasks have been set to effort-driven scheduling.

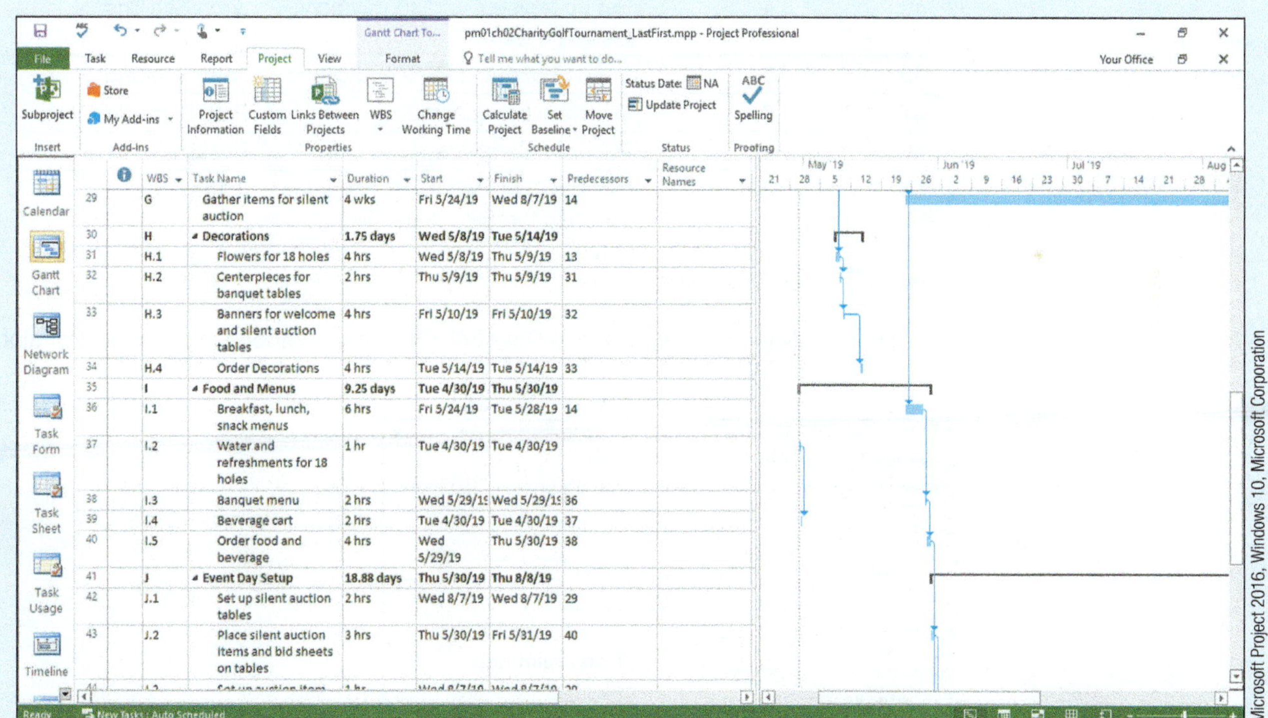

Figure 60 Imported tasks in a Work Breakdown Structure

h. Assign resources to the imported tasks as shown below.

Row	WBS Code	Task Name	Resource
		Decorations	
31	H.1	Flowers for 18 holes	Your Name
32	H.2	Centerpieces for banquet tables	Your Name
33	H.3	Banners for welcome and silent auction tables	Your Name
34	H.4	Order decorations	Your Name
		Food and Menus	
36	I.1	Breakfast, lunch, and snack menus	Robin Sanchez
37	I.2	Water and refreshments for 18 holes	Thomas Vance
38	I.3	Banquet menu	Robin Sanchez
39	I.4	Beverage cart	Thomas Vance
40	I.5	Order food and beverage	Robin Sanchez
		Event Day Setup	
42	J.1	Set up silent auction tables	John Schilling
43	J.2	Place silent auction items and bid sheets on tables	Lesa Martin
44	J.3	Set up auction item tracking at payment table	Patti Rochelle
45	J.4	Set up registration and payment welcome table	John Schilling
46	J.5	Set up banquet tables and chairs	John Schilling
47	J.6	Decorate banquet tables	Patti Rochelle
48	J.7	Put up decorations	Rosalinda Hill
49	J.8	Water and refreshments placed at 18 holes for the golfers	Jorge Cruz

Table 3 Resource Assignments

i. Double-click **Order decorations** (Task 34). Click the **Advanced** tab. Set a Constraint date of 8/2/19.

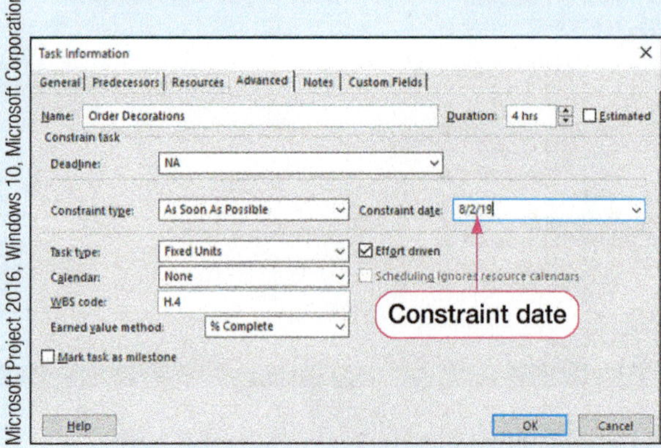

Microsoft Project 2016, Windows 10, Microsoft Corporation

Figure 61 Task Information dialog box

j. Click **OK**. Double-click **Order food and beverage** (Task 40). Click the **Advanced** tab. Set a Constraint date of 8/2/19, and then click **OK**. Note the calendar indicators in the Indicators column.

k. Click in the Resource Names column for **Gather items for silent auction** (Task 29). Assign **Lesa Martin** and **Your Name**. Notice the duration of the task does not change when you assign two resources at the same time even though the task is an effort driven task.

l. Select the **View** tab, and then click the **Details** check box to add Split form view. Since you are only monitoring the silent auction donations, set the Work hours to 0 for Your Name resource. Click **OK**. This removes your overallocation.

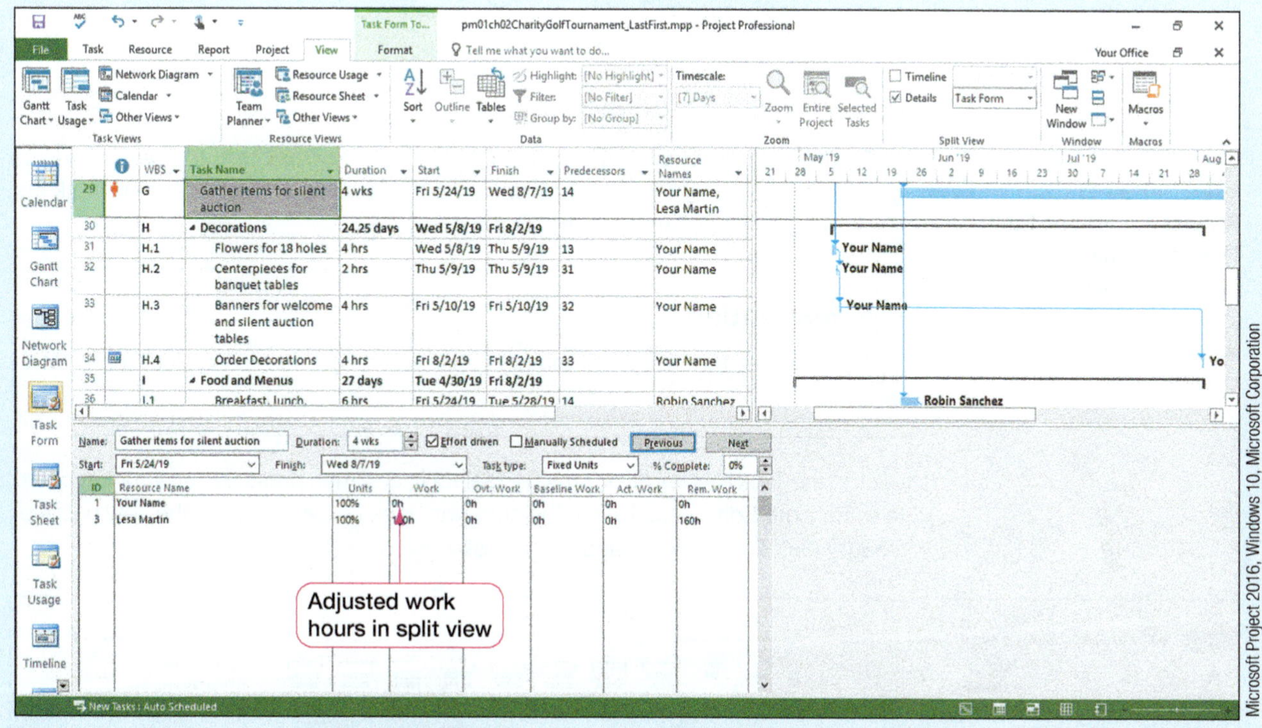

Microsoft Project 2016, Windows 10, Microsoft Corporation

Figure 62 Work form in Split View

m. Lesa Martin is still overallocated because the work for Tasks 29 and 43 is scheduled on the same day. Scroll down, and then select **Place silent auction items and bid sheets on tables** (Task 43). Click in the Predecessors column, and then type 42. This will remove Lesa's overallocation.

n. Select the **View** tab, and then in the Split View group click **Details** to remove the split view.

o. **Save** the project.

QUICK REFERENCE

1. With your project plan open, click the Task tab.
2. In the Insert group, click the Task button arrow.
3. Click Import Outlook Tasks.
4. In the Import Outlook Tasks dialog box, click the expand button for the Folder: Tasks to display tasks in Outlook.
5. Click the check box for each task you want to import (or click Select all to select all tasks).
6. Click OK.

Adding a Project Summary Task

Once project tasks have been added, a WBS has been created, and project resources are assigned, project managers may want to view overall project information. It is often helpful for project managers to see the overall start and finish date of a project as well as the entire project duration. This information can be displayed at the top of the Entry table by adding a project summary task bar. A **Project Summary Task** summarizes the timeline of your project and displays the total duration of your project. The same information can be found in the Project Information dialog box.

In this exercise, you will add a project summary task.

SIDE NOTE

Project Summary Task

The total duration of the project summary task is total hours worked represented in days, not total calendar days.

To Add a Project Summary Task

a. In Gantt Chart view, click the **Gantt Chart Tools Format** tab. In the Show/Hide group, click to select **Project Summary Task**. View the Project Summary Task bar (Task 0) in the Entry table and the Gantt chart.

> **Troubleshooting**
>
> If you do not see the Project Summary Task, you may need to scroll up until you see row 0.

b. Click in the Task Name cell of **Task 0** to select it, and then press F2 on your keyboard to switch into Edit mode. Delete the summary task name and enter the new name of Charity Golf Tournament, and then press Enter.

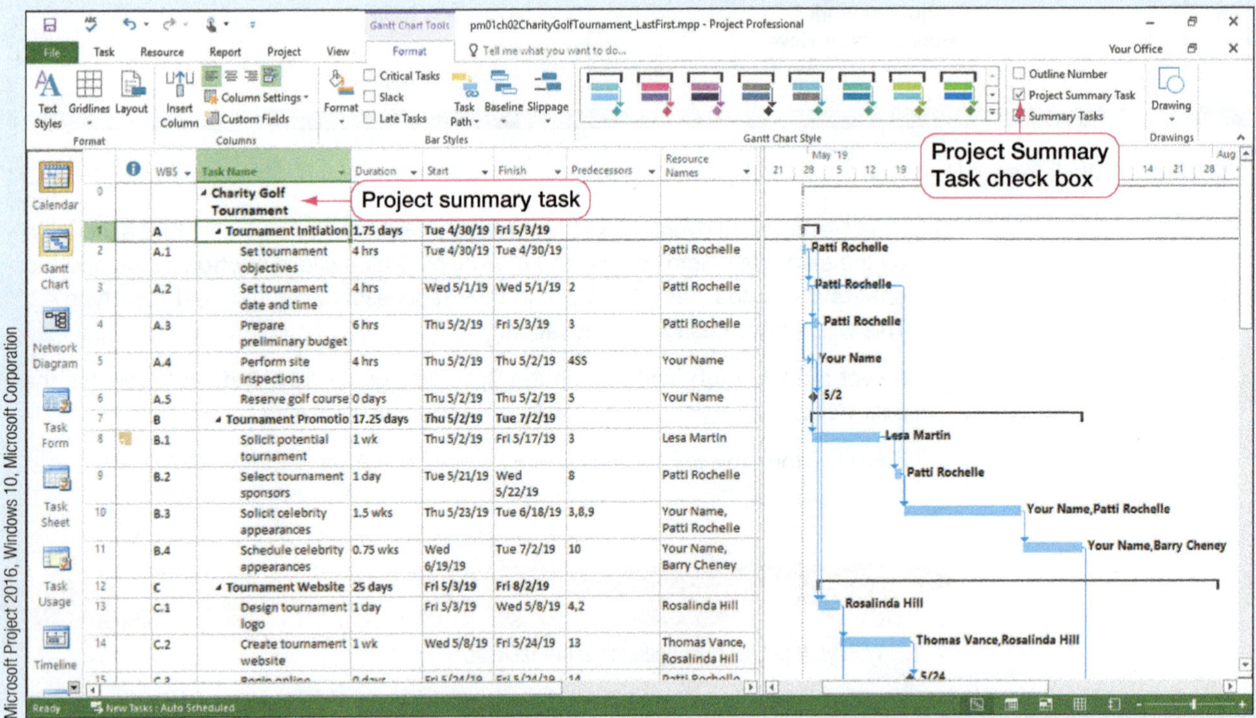

Figure 63 Project summary task

c. Click the **Project** tab. In the Properties group, click **Project Information** to open the Project Information dialog box.

d. Click the **Statistics** button. View the project statistics and note they are the same as those displayed on the project summary task.

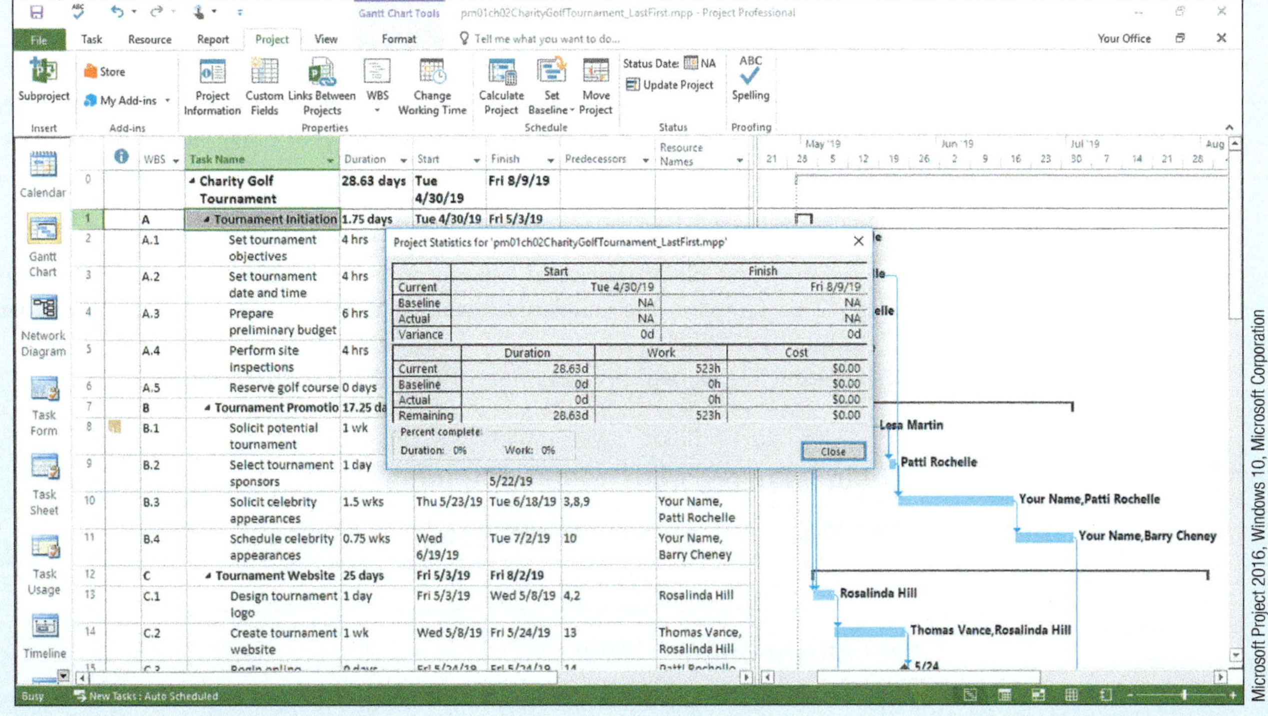
Microsoft Project 2016, Windows 10, Microsoft Corporation

Figure 64 Project Statistics

e. Click **Close** on the Project Statistics dialog box. Click **Save**, and then close your Project 2016 file but leave Project open.

Linking Excel Data to Project

Instead of copying, pasting, importing, or exporting data, there may be situations in which you want to link data to Project 2016 so you do not create a copy of the data. Another advantage of linking data is that if the data is updated in the source document (such as Excel), it is automatically updated in the destination file (such as Project) or vice versa. If data is updated in the source document but the destination document is closed, the destination document will be updated the next time it is opened.

A disadvantage of linking files is that the source file and the destination file must accompany each other if they are emailed, moved, or shared. Otherwise, you will "break a link" and get an error in the destination file. Another disadvantage is that you cannot create a map as you can when you import data into Project.

QUICK REFERENCE | **Linking Excel Data to Project**

1. Select and copy the data in Excel you want to link to Project.
2. In Project, click a cell in the Entry table where you wish to insert the data.
3. Select the Task tab.
4. In the Clipboard group on the Task tab, click the Paste button list arrow, and then click Paste Special.
5. Click Paste Link, and then select Microsoft Excel Worksheet.
6. Click OK.

Data linked to another source is indicated by a link graphic in the lower right-hand corner of a cell.

Use and Create Project Templates

A **Project template** is a Project file that contains sample project information such as tasks, durations, resources, and other project data. Templates can help you get started with your project if you are new to the Project 2016 software or the project management process. Templates can also help create consistency in your organization if projects are based on a standard template.

Creating a Project Plan from an Existing Project Template

When you opened a blank project in Chapter 1, you were opening the Blank Project template. This template has standards (defaults) in place such as project Start date, project manually scheduled, etc.

In this exercise, you will begin a project from a Project 2016 template.

PM02.19

To Begin a Project from a Project Template

a. Click **File** if necessary, and then click **New**.

Troubleshooting

If the Project 2016 software is closed, you will need to reopen Project 2016.

b. In the right pane of the New window, click in the **Search** box, and then enter simple project plan. Press Enter. The Simple project plan template appears.

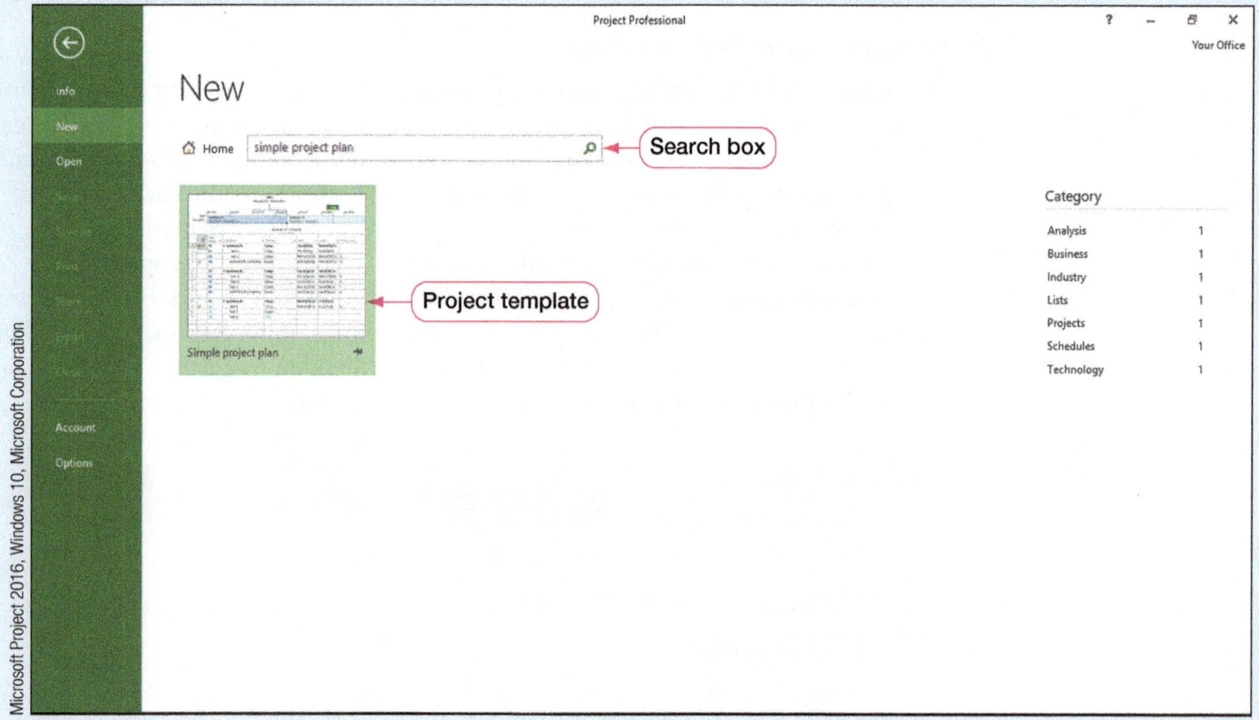

Figure 65 New project window with Simple project plan template

c. Click **Simple project plan** to open the Simple project plan template window. Note how you can preview the template before downloading it.

> **Troubleshooting**
>
> If you double-clicked the Simple project plan icon, you will go directly to a new project and not to the template preview window.

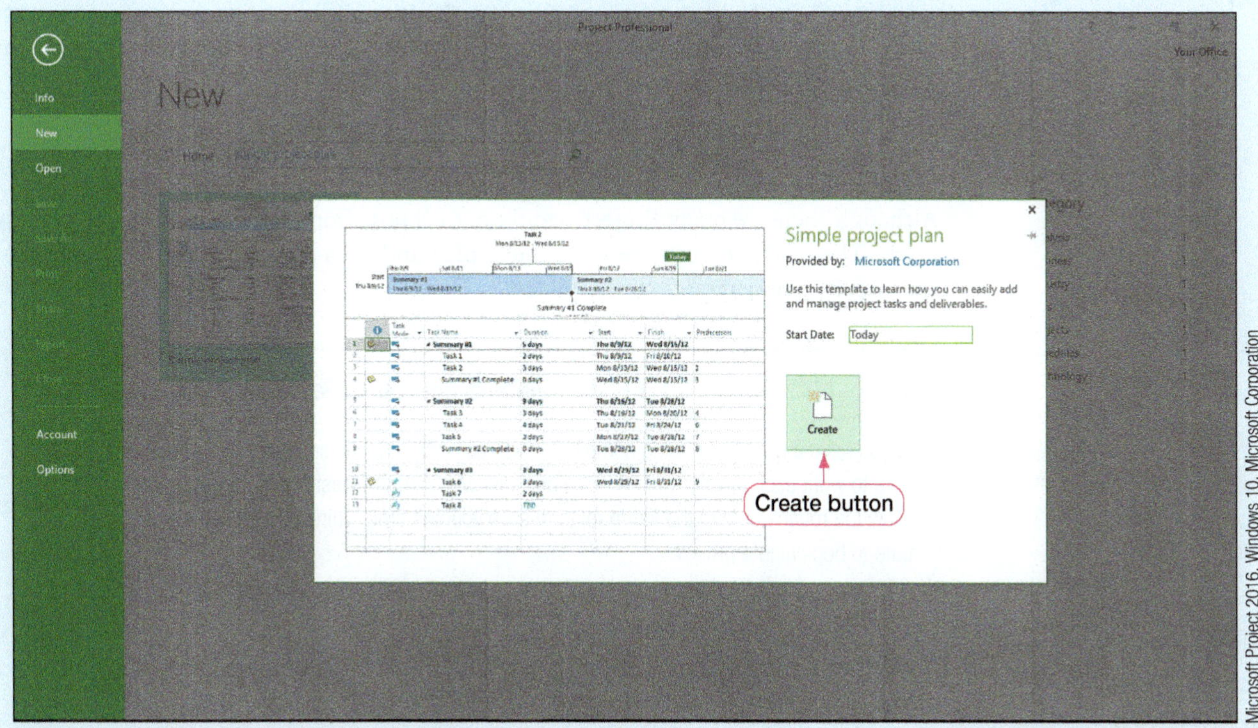

Figure 66 Simple project plan template preview window

d. In the Simple project plan window, click **Create**.

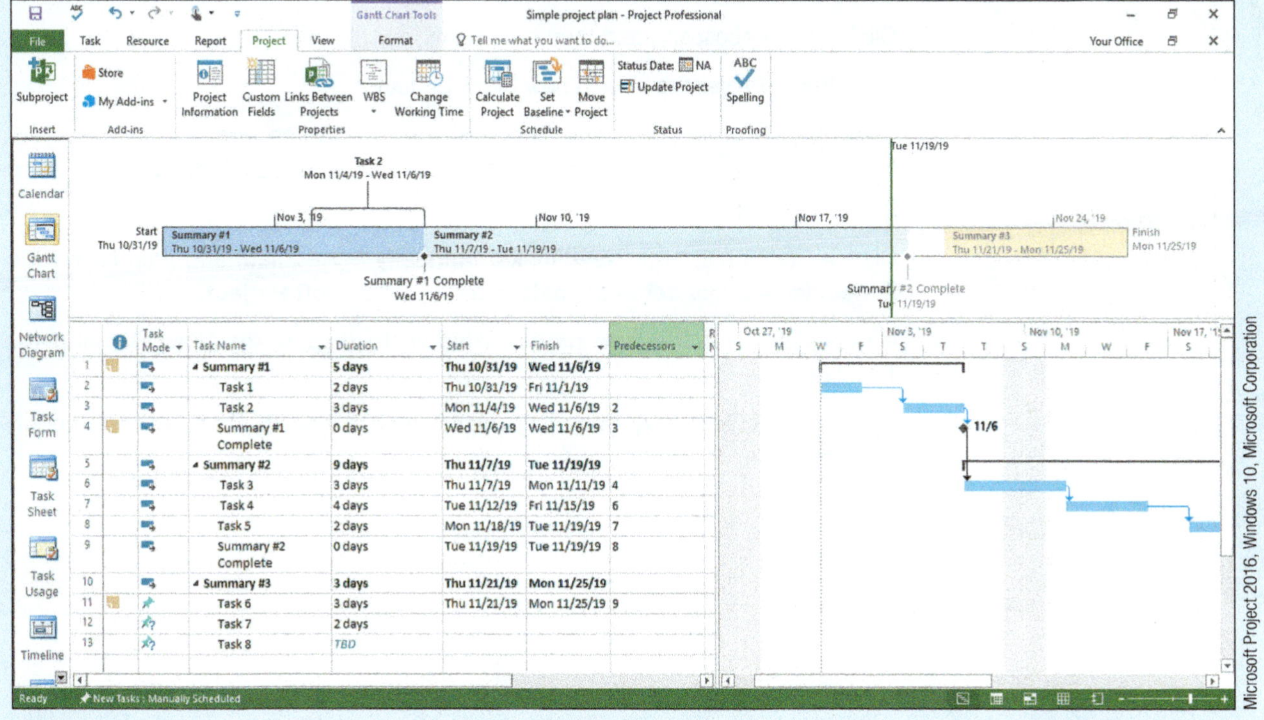

Figure 67 Simple project plan in Gantt Chart view

e. Explore the newly created project plan. Note the Summary task and subtask structure. Also view the notes in the Indicators column. Note some tasks are set to schedule manually while others are set to auto scheduled.

f. Click the **File** tab, and then click **Save As**. Click **This PC**, and then click **Browse**. Navigate to the location where you are saving your files.

g. In the Save As dialog box, click in the File name box, and then type pm01ch02 SimpleProjectPlan_LastFirst using your last and first name. Click **Save**, and then **close** the project file.

Creating a Custom Project Template

Although there are many Project templates to choose from, they may not fit your project needs. Therefore, you can create a project plan and then save your plan as a template to use on future projects.

CONSIDER THIS | Would You Like to Save Time Planning a Project?

Do you have a routine for doing something such as getting ready for school? Or do you take the same route to work each day because it is the quickest way with the least amount of traffic? It is likely you follow the routine or take the same route to save yourself time. Think of a Project template as a fast route to beginning a project.

Since Painted Paradise Resort does a lot of event planning, you have decided to create a project template for planning events.

In this exercise, you will create a project template.

To Create a Project Template

a. Click **File** if necessary, and then click **New**.

b. Click **Blank Project** to open a new blank project.

c. Click the **Project** tab, and then in the Properties group, click **Project Information** to verify the project is set to Schedule from **Project Start Date**. Click **OK**.

d. On the Status bar, click **New Tasks: Manually Scheduled**, and then click **Auto Scheduled - Tasks dates are calculated by Microsoft Project**.

e. If necessary, set the new project window to display the View Bar and the Timeline.

f. Enter in the following summary tasks and subtasks, but do not supply durations.

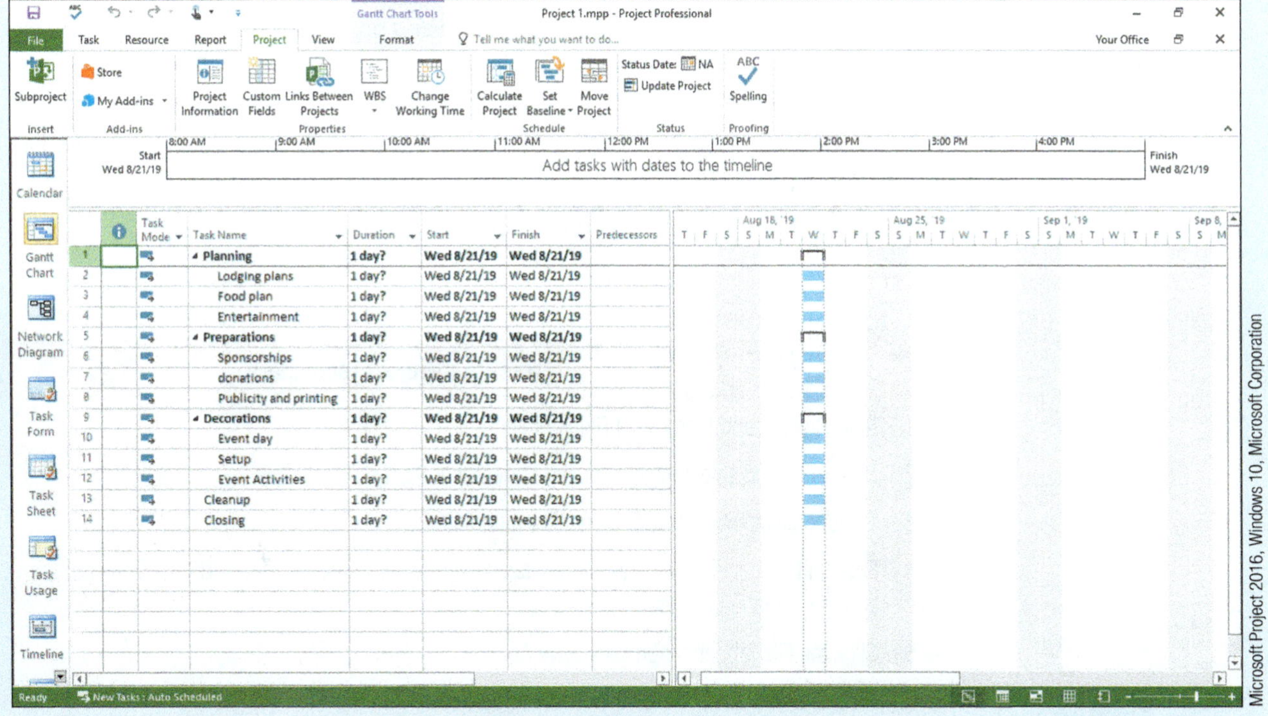

Microsoft Project 2016, Windows 10, Microsoft Corporation

Figure 68 Template tasks

g. Click the **File** tab, and then click **Save As**. Click **This PC**, and then click **Browse** and navigate to where you store your files. In the File name box, enter pm01ch02EventTemplate_LastFirst.

h. Click the **Save as type** arrow, and then click **Project Template**.

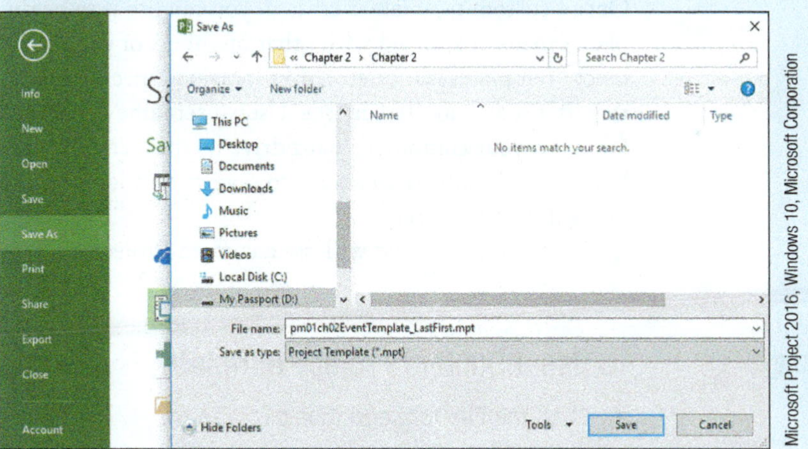

Microsoft Project 2016, Windows 10, Microsoft Corporation

Figure 69 Save As dialog box

i. Click **Save** to open the Save As Template dialog box. Since you have only added the summary task information, you do not need to check any of the boxes on the Save As Template dialog box.

j. Click **Save**. The template is now saved and the template .mpt file extension should appear in the title bar.

k. Click the **File** tab, and then click **Close** to close the template.

QUICK REFERENCE	Create a Project Template

1. Start Project, and then select Blank Project.
2. Determine and select the scheduling standard of Start or Finish date.
3. Select project scheduling of manual or automatic.
4. Enter in the main headings (summary tasks) and other structure in the WBS that may be common among projects.
5. Click the File tab, and then click Save As.
6. Browse to the location where you store your files.
7. Type a name for the template in the File name box.
8. Click the Save as type arrow, and then click the Project Template option.
9. Click Save, and then click Save again.

Using a Custom Project Template

Once a custom template is created, you can use it to begin a future project plan. The template can also be shared with other members of your organization for project plan consistency. Templates can be stored in locations specified by the creator or a Templates folder that is usually located in the Users\username\AppData\Roaming\Microsoft\Templates folder on your computer's hard drive or company network drive. The AppData folder is hidden by default. If you want to save to this location, you will need to display Hidden items in File Explorer.

In this exercise, you will use a custom Project 2016 template.

To Use a Custom Project Template

a. Click the **File** tab, and then click **Open**.

> **Troubleshooting**
>
> If Project 2016 is not open, open Project 2016, and then in the left pane, click the Open Other Projects link.

b. Click **This PC**, and then browse to the location where you store your files. Click the **file type** arrow, and then click **Project Templates**.

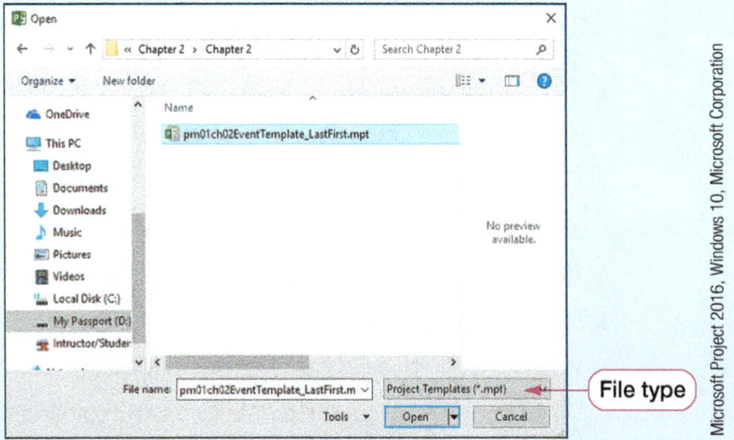

Microsoft Project 2016, Windows 10, Microsoft Corporation

Figure 70 Open dialog box for Project Template search

c. Click **pm01ch02EventTemplate_LastFirst.mpt** from the available templates list, and then click **Open**.

d. Click **File**, and then click **Save As**. Click **This PC**, and then navigate to the location where you store your files. Verify the Save as type is **Project**, and then click **Save**. A new project file named **pm01ch02EventTemplate_LastFirst.mpp** is created.

Troubleshooting

If the Save as type is Project Template, click the Save as type arrow, and then select Project.

e. Close the template, and then click **Close** ✕ to close Project.

f. Submit your files as directed by your instructor.

Concept Check

1. What is the best Project view for identifying the critical path?
2. What is a Work Breakdown Structure?
3. Define a work resource, material resource, and cost resource.
4. What is the purpose of the Team Planner view?
5. Explain how resource assignments can change task durations.
6. How is elapsed time different than duration?
7. What is the purpose of the Overallocated Resources report?
8. When copying Project 2016 data to paste in other applications, what is the difference between selecting Copy from the Clipboard group of the Task tab and Copy Picture from the Clipboard group of the Task tab?
9. Identify at least two ways of sharing information between Project 2016 and Excel 2016.
10. Why would a project manager use a Project 2016 template to begin a project?

Key Terms

Cost resource 70
Crashing 77
Effort driven scheduling 76
Elapsed duration 84
Indenting 63
Leveling 77
Material resource 70
Outdenting 63
Overallocated 77
Project Summary Task 106
Project template 108
Recurring task 87
Resource Sheet view 70
Slack 60
Subtask 63
Summary task 63
Team Planner 83
Tracking 89
Work Breakdown Structure (WBS) 62
Work resource 70

Visual Summary

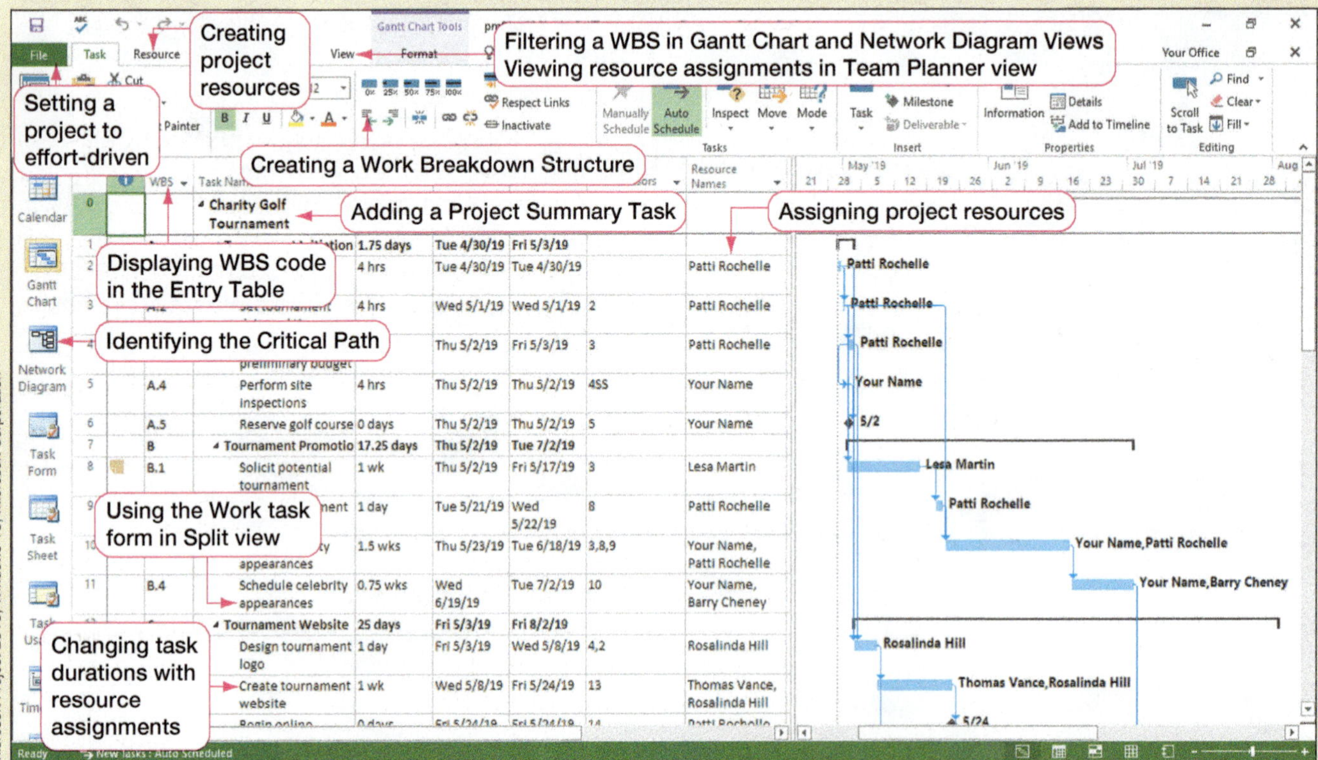

Figure 71

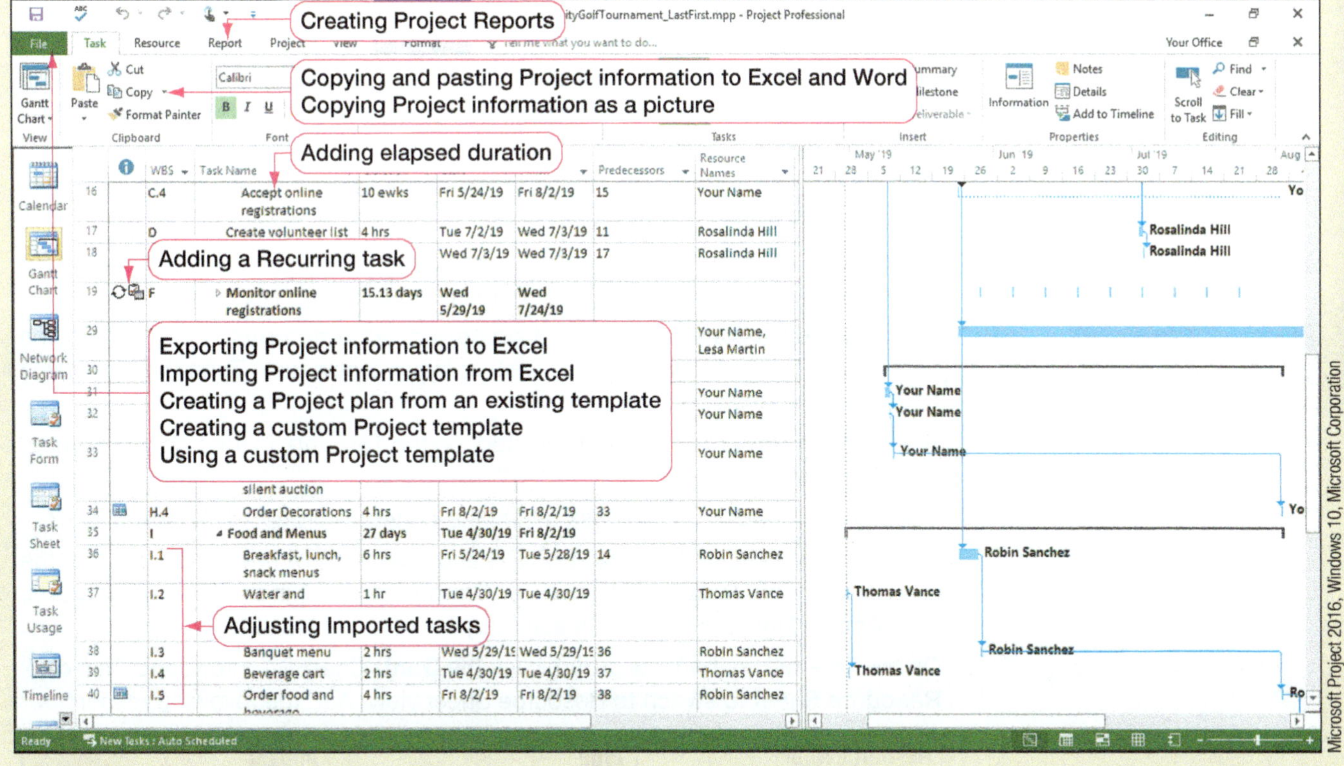

Figure 72

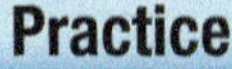

Practice

Student data file needed:

pm01ch02BloodDrive.mpp

You will save your files as:

pm01ch02BloodDrive_LastFirst.mpp

pm01ch02BloodDrive_LastFirst.xlsx

pm01ch02BloodDrive_LastFirst.docx

Organizing a Blood Drive at Your Community College

IT Information Technology

You continue working with the student senate of your community college by planning a blood drive to promote a cause that saves millions of lives each year. You created your initial task list using Microsoft Project. Now you will create a Work Breakdown Structure, assign your project team members' duties, and work with adjusting the project schedule to fit your project needs. The blood drive will occur on October 10, 2019. You and your project team are available to work on this project Wednesday through Friday, 8:00 AM to 12:00 PM.

a. Navigate to the location of your student data files and open **pm01ch02 BloodDrive.mpp**. Save the Project file as pm01ch02BloodDrive_LastFirst.mpp using your last and first name.

b. You want to be sure you have enough volunteers for the number of appointments set, so you decide to check each week on the appointment list by adding a recurring task. Select **Check site arrangements** (Task 10). Click the **Task** tab if necessary, and then in the Insert group, click the **Task** list arrow.

c. Click **Recurring Task**. Type the task name Check appointment list. Type a duration of 1h. Set a recurrence pattern of **Weekly** on **Wednesday**. Enter a Start date of 10/2/19 and an End by date of 10/9/19. Click **OK**.

d. Click **Select blood drive campus location** (Task 1), and then press Ins on your keyboard to insert a new task. Type the task name Event planning, and then press Enter.

e. Select **Tasks 2–5**, and then on the Task tab, in the Schedule group, click **Indent Task**. Tasks 2–5 become subtasks of Event planning (Task 1).

f. Click **Plan promotional strategies** (Task 6). On the Task tab, in the Insert group, click the **Task** button to insert a new task. Type the task name Event preparation, and then press Enter.

g. Click **Event preparation** (Task 6), and then on the Task tab, in the Schedule group, click **Outdent Task**.

h. Select **Tasks 7–18**, and then on the Task tab, in the Schedule group, click **Indent Task**. Tasks 7–18 become subtasks of Event preparation (Task 6).

i. Click **Post directional arrows and posters around campus** (Task 19). On the Task tab, in the Insert group, click **Task** to insert a new task. Type the task name Event day, and then press Enter.

j. Select **Event Day** (Task 19), and selected, on the Task tab, in the Schedule group, click **Outdent Task**.

k. Select **Tasks 20–21**. On the Task tab, in the Schedule group, click **Indent Task**.

l. Click the row selector for **Task 1**. Press and hold the Ctrl key, and then click the row selectors for **Task 6** and **Task 19**. On the Task tab, in the Properties group, click **Add to Timeline** to add the summary tasks to the timeline.

m. On the Task tab, in the View group, click the **Gantt Chart** list arrow, and then click **Resource Sheet** to switch to Resource Sheet view. Add the following resources.

Resource Name	Type	Initials
Your Name	Work	YN
Emma Jones	Work	EJ
Joseph Ramirez	Work	JR

n. Click **Gantt Chart** on the View Bar to return to Gantt Chart view. Click the **Resource** tab, and then in the Assignments group, click **Assign Resources**. Using the Assign Resources dialog box, assign the resources to the tasks as follows.

Task Name	Resource Names
Event planning	
Select blood drive campus location	Your Name
Set blood drive goal	Your Name
Form a recruitment team	Your Name
Divide team roles and duties	Joseph Ramirez, Your Name
Event preparation	
Plan promotional strategies	Joseph Ramirez
Create promotional materials	Joseph Ramirez
Contact local businesses	Joseph Ramirez
Publicize the blood drive	Joseph Ramirez, Your Name
Schedule appointments	Emma Jones
Check appointment list	Your Name
Check site arrangements	Joseph Ramirez
Get visitor parking passes	Your Name
Email visitor parking passes	Your Name
Email appointment reminder messages	Your Name
Event day	
Post directional arrows and posters around campus	Your Name

o. Next, you need to remove your overallocation. Click **Email appointment reminder messages** (Task 18).

p. Click the **View** tab. In the Split View group, click **Details**. Right-click the split form, and then select **Work**. In the Work column, change your work hours to 0h. On the View tab, in the Split View group, click **Details** again to remove the split view.

q. Click the **Gantt Chart Tools Format** tab, and then click **Project Summary Task** to add a project summary task (Task 0). Change the name of the project summary task (Task 0) to Blood Drive.

r. Right-click the **Task Name** column, and then click **Insert Column**. Scroll through the list, and then click **WBS**. Adjust the WBS column width as necessary.

s. Click the **Project** tab, and then click **WBS-Define Code**. Define the code with Level 1) **Numbers**; Level 2) **Uppercase Letters**; Level 3) **Lowercase Letters**.

t. Right-click the **Task Mode** column, and then click **Hide Column**.

u. Select the **Task Name** column. Click the **Gantt Chart Tools Format** tab, and then in the Columns group, click **Wrap Text** twice.

v. Click the **Select All** button in the upper left of the Entry table. On the Task tab, in the Clipboard group, click **Copy**. Open a blank Excel workbook, and then on the Home tab, in the Clipboard group, click **Paste**.

w. If necessary, select the columns in the Excel workbook containing pasted data. On the Home tab, in the Cells group, click **Format**, and then click **AutoFit Column Width**. Increase the width of Column B as desired.

x. Save the workbook in the location where you store your files as pm01ch02BloodDrive_LastFirst. Close Excel.

y. In Gantt Chart view, click the **Task** tab. In the Clipboard group, click the **Copy** arrow, and then select **Copy Picture**. Ensure For screen and Selected rows are selected. Click **OK**. Open a blank Word Document, and then press Ctrl + V to paste a picture of the Gantt Chart view into Word. Save the document in the location where you store your files as pm01ch02BloodDrive_LastFirst. Close Word.

z. Save your project, exit Project 2016, and then submit your files as directed by your instructor.

Problem Solve 1

Grader Project

Student data files needed:

 pm01ch02JobSearchPortfolio.mpp

 pm01ch02JobSearchPortfolio.xlsx

You will save your files as:

 pm01ch02JobSearchPortfolio_LastFirst.mpp

 pm01ch02JobSearchPortfolio_LastFirst.xlsx

Sales & Marketing

Planning Your Job Search Portfolio

You have started planning your professional portfolio to use during the interview process since you will be graduating in May 2019 from your program of study at your local college. You have an initial list of tasks already added into a Project file. Now you will add summary tasks, import tasks from Excel, and assign resources to your project to complete your project plan.

a. Navigate to the location of your student data files and open **pm01ch02JobSearch Portfolio.mpp**. Save the Project file as pm01ch02JobSearchPortfolio_LastFirst.mpp.

b. Select **Purchase portfolio supplies** (Task 1), and then insert a new task. Name the new task Portfolio planning. Indent Tasks 2–11 to make them subtasks of Task 1.

c. Select **(Task 12)**. Insert a new task, and then name the task Interview planning. **Outdent** Task 12.

d. Indent Tasks 13–16 to make them subtasks of Interview planning (Task 12).

e. Select **Write resume** (Task 5), and then insert a new task. Name the task Resume. **Outdent** Task 5.

f. Move **Send resumes to potential employers** (Task 14) to the Task 9 position. Note how the task becomes a subtask of Task 5.

Troubleshooting

If Send resumes to potential employers (Task 9) did not become a subtask of Task 5, then select the task and indent it.

g. Your project resources are saved in an Excel workbook. Import the resources from the **pm01ch02JobSearchPortfolio.xlsx** data file. (Hint: Select File, Open, and look for the Excel data file. Select New map; Append the data to the active project; select Resources as the type of data to import; for the Map Resources Data, select Sheet1; for the Resource Name field, select Name.)

h. Switch to **Resource Sheet** view to view the added resources. Change the "Your Name" resource to your **first and last name**.

i. Return to **Gantt Chart** view, and then in a method of your choice, assign the resources as shown.

Task Name	Resource Names
Portfolio Planning	
Purchase portfolio supplies	Your Name
Get an unofficial transcript	Your Name
Identify references	Your Name
Resume	
Write resume	Your Name
Edit resume	James Yang, Your Name
Create a resume in PDF format	Your Name
Send resumes to potential employers	Your Name
Conduct online job search	Your Name
Write a cover letter	Your Name
Gather work examples for portfolio	Your Name
Compile portfolio	Your Name
Interview Planning	
Obtain interview attire	Your Name
Obtain brief case for interviewing	Your Name
Conduct a mock interview	Career Resource Center

j. The resource assignments have resulted in overallocation. To remove the overallocation, view the **Team Planner**. If necessary, right-click **Your Name**, and then select **Scroll to Task**. From the Team Planner view, you can see the overallocation is occurring on April 4.

k. Return to **Gantt Chart** view. Double-click **Obtain interview attire** (Task 15), and then set a Start No Earlier Than Constraint date of 2/13/19.

l. Click **Obtain brief case for interviewing** (Task 16). If necessary, click the **Task** tab. In the Properties group, click **Details**.

m. Right-click the Split View, and then click **Work**. Change your work hours of Obtain brief case for interviewing to 0 hours. The overallocation has now been corrected.

n. Insert a WBS column to the left of the Task Name column. Adjust the WBS column width as necessary.

o. Define the WBS code with Level 1) **Numbers (ordered)**; Level 2) **Uppercase Letters (ordered)**; Level 3) **Lowercase Letters (ordered)**.

p. View the critical path in the **Network Diagram** view, and then return to **Gantt Chart** view.

q. Export the project data to an Excel workbook, using the Project Excel Template, with the file name pm01ch02JobSearchPortfolio_LastFirst.

r. If necessary, return to your pm01ch02JobSearchPortfolio_LastFirst.mpp project file. Filter the project to display Summary Tasks. Select the summary tasks, and then add them to the Timeline.

s. Save your project with the Entry table filtered, exit Project 2016, and then submit the project files as directed by your instructor.

Perform 1: Perform in Your Career

Student data file needed:

 pm01ch02BusinessPlan.mpp

You will save your files as:

 pm01ch02BusinessPlan_LastFirst.mpp

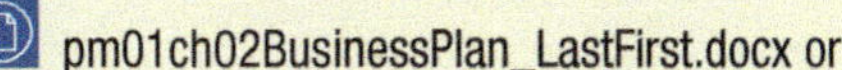 pm01ch02BusinessPlan_LastFirst.docx or

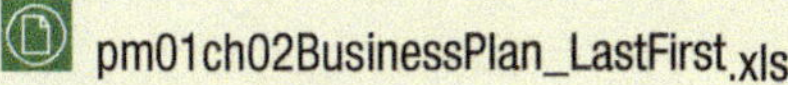 pm01ch02BusinessPlan_LastFirst.xlsx

Preparing a Business Plan

You have a start to your new virtual assistant business plan in Project 2016. You have decided to add more detail to your plan by creating a Work Breakdown Structure and adding project resources. You also want to share your data with family members who do not have Project 2016 software, so you will export the project into Word or Excel.

a. Navigate to the location of your student data files and open **pm01ch02 BusinessPlan.mpp**. Save the Project file as pm01ch02BusinessPlan_LastFirst.mpp.

b. Create a minimum of **two work resources**. Assign resources to each of your subtasks.

c. If necessary, correct any **overallocation** of your resources by changing resource assignments, modifying task relationships, setting task constraints, or modifying work hours.

d. Create a Work Breakdown Structure with a minimum of **three logical summary tasks**.

e. Add a **WBS** column, and then define a WBS code.

f. If necessary, hide the **Task Mode** column.

g. Add the project's summary tasks to the **Timeline**.

h. **Share** your data in a Word document or Excel workbook. As directed by your instructor, explain why you chose Word or Excel and what steps you took to share the project's data.

i. **Save** your project, and then submit your files as directed by your instructor.

Business Unit Capstone

This business unit had two outcomes:

Outcome 1

Get started using Project 2016 by creating a project schedule, modifying a project calendar, and exploring how project is scheduling tasks.

Outcome 2

Use Project to modify project tasks, create and edit task dependencies, and prepare a project for printing.

In Business Unit 1 Capstone, students will demonstrate competence in these outcomes through a series of business problems at various levels from guided practice, problem solving an existing project, and performing tasks to create new projects.

More Practice 1

Student data file needed:

 pm01BathroomRemodel.mpp

You will save your files as:

 pm01BathroomRemodel_LastFirst.mpp

 pm01BathroomRemodelTemplate_LastFirst.mpt

Bathroom Remodel Project

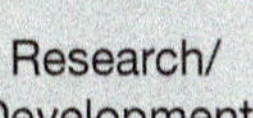

Research/ Development   Sales & Marketing

The Painted Paradise Resort & Spa takes great pride in its high-quality guest rooms. After management reviewed guest satisfaction survey results, it was determined that 20 bathrooms need to be updated. To keep the projects on task, you have been asked to create a bathroom remodel template that can be used on all the remodeling projects.

a. Start Microsoft Project 2016, and then open **pm01BathroomRemodel** from the location where you store your files. Save the file as pm01BathroomRemodel_LastFirst, using your last and first name.

b. Click the **Project** tab, and then in the Properties group, click **Project Information**. Set the project start date to 7/08/19. Click **OK**.

c. On the Project tab, in the Properties group, click **Change Working Time**. Click the **Work Weeks** tab, and then click Details. Set Mondays to nonworking time. Adjust the working times of Tuesday-Friday to **10:00 AM–6:00 PM**. Set Saturdays to working time of **8:00 AM–12:00 PM**. Click **OK**, and then close the Change Working Time dialog box.

d. Click the **Task** tab, and then select **Tasks 2–4**. In the Schedule group, click **Indent Task** to indent the tasks. This makes Tasks 2–4 subtasks of Task 1.

e. Select **Tasks 6–8**, and then in the Schedule group, click **Indent Task** to indent the tasks. This makes Tasks 6–8 subtasks of Task 5.

f. Select **Tasks 9–15**. On the Task tab, in the Insert group, click **Summary** to create a summary task. Name the summary task Selecting Materials.

g. Select **Tasks 2–4**. On the Task tab, in the Schedule group, click **Link the Selected Tasks** to link the tasks in a Finish-to-Start relationship.

h. Select **Tasks 4 and 6**, and then in the Schedule group, click **Link the Selected Tasks**. Double-click the link line between Tasks 4 and 6 in the Gantt chart. In the Task Dependency dialog box, change the Type to **Start-to-Start (SS)**.

i. Select **Tasks 6–8**, and then create a **Finish-to-Start relationship** between the tasks.

j. Select **Task 8**, press and hold the Ctrl key, and then select **Task 10**. Create a **Finish-to-Start relationship** between the tasks.

k. Select **Tasks 10–16**, and then create a **Finish-to-Start relationship** between the tasks.

l. Click the **View** tab, and then in the Data group, click the **Filter** arrow. Select **Summary Tasks** to filter for the project's summary tasks. Using the row selectors, select the Summary Tasks.

m. Click the **Task** tab, and then in the Properties group, click **Add to Timeline** to add the summary tasks to the Timeline.

n. Click the **View** tab, and then remove the filter.

o. Double-click **Selecting Materials** (Task 9). In the Summary Task Information dialog box, click the **Notes** tab. Add the note Consider purchasing in bulk.

p. Right-click the **Task Mode** column, and then click **Hide Column** to remove the column from the Entry table.

q. Right-click the **Task Name** column, and then click **Insert Column**. Click **WBS** to add the WBS column to the Entry table. Adjust the width of the WBS column as necessary.

r. Click the **Project** tab. In the Properties group, click **WBS**, and then click **Define Code**. Define the WBS code first by **Uppercase Letters**, then by **Lowercase Letters**, and then by **Numbers**.

s. Click the **File** tab, and then click **Print**. Click the **Page Setup** link. Click the **Header** tab, and then click the **Right** tab. Type your name in the right-side header. Click the **Back** button to exit Backstage view.

t. Click the **Gantt Chart Tools Format** tab, and then in the Show/Hide group, click **Project Summary Task**. Select the **Project Summary Task (Task 0)**, and then press the F2 key. Rename the Project Summary Task Bathroom Remodel Template.

u. Select the **Task Name** column. On the Gantt Chart Tools Format tab, in the Columns group, click **Wrap Text** twice. If necessary, widen the Finish column to view all the Finish Dates.

v. Save the project.

w. Since this will be a template, you will not assign resources. Save the project as a Project template. Name the template pm01BathroomRemodelTemplate_LastFirst. Do not remove any of the data items from the template.

x. Exit Project, and then submit the project files as directed by your instructor.

Problem Solve 1

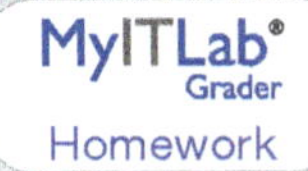

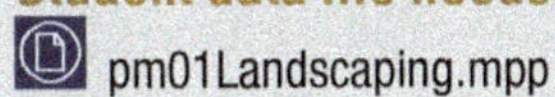

Student data file needed:

pm01Landscaping.mpp

You will save your files as:

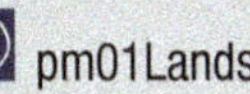

pm01Landscaping_LastFirst.mpp

pm01Landscaping_LastFirst.xlsx

Sales & Marketing

Production & Operations

Landscaping Project

You are the manager of the buildings and grounds crew at the Painted Paradise Resort & Spa. You have been assigned to update the landscaping around the resort property. Although you will hire an outside contractor to complete most of the work, you were given a Project file to use from a former landscaping job completed at the resort. When you open the file, you notice there are several errors in the project such as overallocation, types of relationships, calendar, length of project, and resource assignments. However, you believe it is easier to correct the Project file instead of creating a new project.

a. Navigate to the location where you store your files and open **pm01Landscaping**. Save the file where you store your files as pm01Landscaping_LastFirst, using your last and first name.

b. Using the Project tab, set the project start date to **April 1, 2019**.

c. Set all current project tasks to Auto Scheduled by selecting the tasks, and then on the Task tab, in the Tasks group, click **Auto Schedule**. Set new project tasks to be Auto Scheduled.

d. Due to the heat of the afternoon, the laborers won't work past 1:00 PM. Adjust your project calendar to the work times of 7:00 AM–1:00 PM Monday–Friday. Set May 27, 2019, as a calendar exception. Name the exception Memorial Day. Set July 4–5, 2019, as an additional calendar exception. Name the exception Fourth of July.

e. Switch to Resource Sheet view and replace Your Name with your actual first and last name. You notice resource overallocation on the project plan. One reason there is overallocation is that you are assigned to summary tasks as well as subtasks, which is causing Project to double-schedule you. Remove yourself as a resource from all summary tasks.

f. After removing your name as a resource from the summary tasks, you are still over-allocated. Review the project. Note that Task 7, Drawings, has a start date before Task 5, Determine budget. Create a Finish-to-Start (FS) relationship between Task 5 and Task 7.

g. Create an FS relationship between Task 6 and Task 12.

h. Create an FS relationship between Task 11 and Task 22.

i. On the Task tab, in the View group, click the **Gantt Chart** button arrow to switch to Resource Sheet view. Add an additional work resource of General contractor. Assign the initials of GC.

j. Add a third resource of General labor. Enter the initials of GL. Assign the Max. Units of 300% to give you the availability of assigning three workers to each task. Return to Gantt Chart view.

k. On the View tab, in the Split View group, select **Details**. Right-click the **Details** pane, and then select **Work**.

l. Select **Drawings (Task 7)**. Assign yourself **0 hours** of work. Assign **General contractor** as an additional resource.

m. Repeat Step l for Tasks 8 and 9.

n. Remove yourself as a resource from Tasks 12–20.

o. Change Task 10, Permits and approvals, to an effort driven task. Click the Resource Names arrow for Task 10, and select **General contractor** to assign the additional resource to the task. If a warning symbol appears, select **Reduce duration but keep the same amount of work**. The duration of Task 10 is now 3.5 days.

p. Select **Task 12, Mark utility lines**. Assign one **General labor** resource. Select **Task 13, Removal of plants as needed**. Assign three **General labor** resources by entering **300%** in the Units column of the Work split form.

q. Assign three **General labor** resources for Tasks 14–16.

r. Select **Task 17**, and then assign the **General contractor** resource.

s. Select **Task 18**, and then assign three **General labor** resources.

t. Select **Task 19**, and then assign one **General labor** resource.

u. Select **Task 20**, and then assign three **General labor** resources.

v. Select **Tasks 22–23**, and then add the **General contractor** as an additional resource.

w. Close the split view. Hide the Task Mode Column. Add a **WBS** column, and then adjust the width of the WBS column. Change the WBS code so tasks are first identified by uppercase letters and then by numbers.

x. Filter the Entry table for Summary Tasks. Add the four summary tasks to the Timeline. Remove the filter.

y. On the Gantt Chart Tools Format tab, add a **Project Summary Task** to your project, and then rename the task Landscaping.

z. Add your name as a right-side header of the Gantt chart. Save the project.

aa. Export your project data to Excel by selecting the **File** tab, clicking **Save As**, and then in a location where you store your files, saving the project as an Excel workbook with the file name pm01Landscaping_LastFirst.xlsx, using your last and first name. Export the data as a Project Excel Template.

bb. Submit your project files as directed by your instructor.

Critical Thinking Why would you assign a resource to a task and then adjust the resource work hours to zero on that task? How does this affect the resource's availability on other tasks?

Problem Solve 2

Student data file needed:

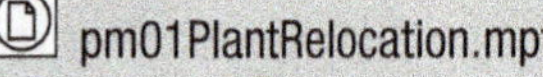
pm01PlantRelocation.mpt

You will save your files as:

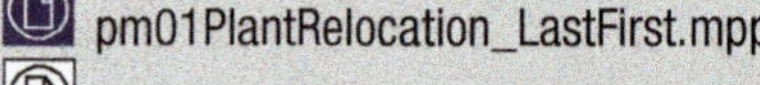
pm01PlantRelocation_LastFirst.mpp
pm01PlantRelocationTemplate_LastFirst.mpt

Manufacturing Project

Sales & Marketing

Production & Operations

Your company, Falu Fabricating, Inc., has grown over the past ten years, and the old production shop floor no longer has adequate space for your current production needs. Your company has acquired another location, and you have been put in charge of the team to plan the relocation. A Project template has been started for you, but it contains overallocated resources. You will fix the overallocated resources to determine the earliest date your company could begin production in the new facility.

a. Navigate to the location where you store your files and open **pm01PlantRelocation.mpt** template file. Save the file in the location where you store your files as a Project file with the name pm01PlantRelocation_LastFirst, using your last and first name.

b. Switch to Resource Sheet view, and then change the resource Your Name to your first and last name. Return to Gantt Chart view.

c. On the Resource tab, in the View group, click **Team Planner**. Right-click your name, and then click **Scroll to Task**. View the resource overallocations, and then click **Gantt Chart** on the View Bar.

d. Select **Task 5, Computers and other technology**. Open the split view. Right-click the split form, and then select **Work**. Assign yourself 0 hours of work for Task 5.

e. Select **Task 6**, **Office equipment**, and then assign yourself 0 hours of work for Task 6.

f. Change the Predecessor of Task 6 to 5. Change the Predecessor of Task 8 to 6.

g. Select **Task 10**. Change the hours of work for each resource to 40 hours. You notice this decreased the duration of this task to one week. You know the team won't be able to work all 40 hours in one week so you want to extend the finish date of the task. Double-click **Task 10** to open the Task Information dialog box. On the General tab, change the finish date to 9/30/19.

h. You note there is still overallocation of one resource. To correct the overallocation, add Task 11 as an additional predecessor to Task 13.

i. Close the split view. If necessary, display the **Timeline**. Filter the project for **Summary Tasks**. Add the Summary Tasks to the **Timeline**. Remove the filter.

j. Hide the Task Mode and Indicators columns. Wrap text as necessary in the Task Name column.

k. Add a **Project Summary Task**. Change the name of the Project Summary Task to Plant Relocation.

l. Display the Critical Tasks on the Gantt chart.

m. Zoom the project to **Entire Project**.

n. Add your name in the right header of the Gantt Chart view, Calendar view, and Network Diagram view.

o. Save the project.

p. Save the project as a Project Template with the file name pm01PlantRelocationTemplate_LastFirst.mpt.

q. Switch to Resource Sheet view, click Select all in the upper left corner of the Resource Sheet, and then press Del to remove all the resources from the project template. Save the template, exit Project, and then submit your files as directed by your instructor.

Perform 1: Perform in Your Life

Student data file needed:	You will save your files as:
No data file needed	pm01Construction_LastFirst.mpp
	pm01ConstructionTemplate_LastFirst.mpt

Basement Construction Project

Production & Operations

You built a new home two years ago but didn't have the funds to finish the lower level. You believe you have saved enough to complete this project. You will be finishing approximately 8,000 square feet. The lower level already has the electrical and the plumbing in place and has passed inspection. You will plan for the construction of walls, bathroom, cabinetry, flooring, and finishing touches such as painting and trim. Identify your project resources—those who will help you with your project. Determine if you will do the work by yourself or hire outside contractors to assist with some of the work. Determine if you will need to rent any equipment. Decide if you have to consider neighborhood restrictions or any zoning regulations.

a. Start a new Project 2016 file. Save your project as pm01Construction_LastFirst.

b. Select a start date or a finish date. Explain to your instructor why you selected either a start or finish date.

c. Select a task scheduling mode of auto scheduled or manually scheduled. Explain to your instructor which mode you selected and why.

d. Set your project tasks to effort-driven.

e. Adjust the project calendar to reflect appropriate working times and days for your project needs.

f. Enter a minimum of 30 task names and task durations.

g. Add a minimum of three milestones.

h. Create a minimum of three summary tasks to develop a Work Breakdown Structure (WBS).

i. Add the summary tasks to the timeline.

j. Link project tasks. Give consideration to appropriate task relationships. Not all tasks should have a Finish-to-Start relationship.

k. Create a minimum of three resources, including yourself as one of the resources. Assign resources to the tasks as appropriate. If necessary, use the split view to adjust work hours.

l. Remove any overallocation of resources.

m. View the critical path in the Network Diagram. Add your name to the right header of the Network Diagram.

n. Add your name to the right header of the Gantt Chart view.

o. Hide the Task Mode column. Add the WBS column. Define the WBS code.

p. Add a task note to at least one task.

q. Add a Project Summary Task. Give the Project Summary Task an appropriate name.

r. Zoom to see the Entire Project.

s. Display Critical Tasks on the Gantt chart, and then save your project.

t. Save your project as a Project template with the file name pm01ConstructionTemplate_LastFirst. Switch to Resource Sheet view, click Select all in the upper left corner of the Resource Sheet, and then press Del to remove all the resources from the project template.

u. Save and close the template, exit Project, and then submit your files as directed by your instructor.

Perform 2: Perform in Your Career

Student data file needed:

 pm01ConventionPlan.xlsx

You will save your file as:

 pm01ConventionPlan_LastFirst.mpp

Sales & Marketing

Convention Planning Project

The organization you work for sells and services life-saving devices for water safety. Next summer, your organization is hosting a one-day convention to promote new and improved life-saving devices in your industry. You have been asked to plan this convention. Because you know planning a convention involves many steps and that many resources will be involved, you decide to use Project 2016 to plan the event. You had entered your list of tasks in Excel 2016, so to save time, you will import these tasks into Project. Because you have not yet set a date for the convention, but know it must be in the summer of 2019, you will schedule your project by Start Date and use Project to help you predict when the event should be scheduled. Because there are many tasks and task relationships, you will set your project to Auto Schedule.

a. Open a blank project file, and then save the project as pm01ConventionPlan_LastFirst, using your last and first name, in the location where you store your files.

b. Set the start date of the project to August 5, 2019.

c. Set the project's new tasks to **Auto Scheduled**.

d. Set new tasks to **effort-driven**.

e. Display the View Bar and the Timeline, if necessary.

f. Adjust the project calendar to make the available work hours on Fridays 8:00 AM–12:00 PM only.

g. Add at least one calendar exception of your choice.

h. Browse to the location of your student data files, and then **import** the tasks from the **pm01ConventionPlan** workbook.

i. Adjust column widths as necessary. Wrap text as necessary. Hide the Task Mode column, and then add the WBS column. Define the WBS code. Renumber the WBS code for the entire project.

j. Select **Tasks 1–13**, and then insert a summary task. Name the summary task Convention Initiation.

k. Select **Tasks 15–43**, and then insert a summary task. Name the summary task Convention Planning.

l. Select **Tasks 45–48**, and then indent the tasks to make them subtasks of Task 44, Setup starts.

m. Select **Task 50**, and then insert a blank task. Name the new blank task Convention Close Out. Indent Tasks 51–57 to make them subtasks of Convention Close Out, Task 50.

n. After reviewing the tasks, assign logical task relationships. Consider relationships such as Start-to-Start, Finish-to-Finish, or Finish-to-Start.

o. Add your name as a resource, and then assign resource initials and a resource group. Create a minimum of four more resources with resource initials, and then assign the resources to a group. Sort the resources by Group.

p. Assign resources to tasks as you see appropriate. Give consideration to tasks having more than one resource assignment.

q. Adjust resource assignments or work hours to remove any overallocation that may have occurred during resource assignments.

r. Add a Project Summary Task, and then give the Project Summary Task a descriptive name.

s. Add the project's summary tasks to the project's Timeline.

t. Add your first and last name to the right-side header of the Gantt Chart, Network Diagram, and Calendar views.

u. Zoom for the Entire Project.

v. Save the project, exit Project, and then submit the file as directed by your instructor.

Glossary

A

Auto Scheduled a scheduling option where the project schedule is calculated based on the project's calendar, project tasks and task durations, task dependencies, resource assignments, and any constraint dates assigned to tasks.

B

Backstage view location where you manage your project file and perform tasks such as saving, printing, and setting project options.

Baseline a record of each task at a point in time from which you will track project progress.

C

Calendar view a view that displays tasks as bars on a calendar in a monthly or weekly format.

Constraint a limitation set on a task.

Cost resource independent cost associated with a task; costs that are not based on work, such as equipment needed to complete a task or airfare or lodging for travel.

Crashing adding more work resources to a project to get the project tasks done faster and shorten the project's duration.

Critical path tasks (or a single task) that determine the project's Finish date (or Start date).

Critical task a task that must be completed on time in order to meet the project's Finish date (or Start date).

Current date today's date as determined by your computer's clock.

E

Effort-driven scheduling a method of scheduling in Project in which the duration of a task is shortened as resources are added or lengthened as resources are removed from a task.

Elapsed durations ignores any project or resources working and nonworking times and schedules the task(s) to 24 hours a day.

Entry table used to enter task information and is located to the left of the Gantt chart; contains columns and rows similar to Microsoft Excel 2016.

F

Finish date the date Project 2016 uses to schedule tasks that will calculate the project's Start date.

G

Gantt chart the graphical representation of the tasks listed in the Entry table; tasks are shown against a timeline displayed as horizontal bars in which the length of the bar is determined by the activities' durations and start/finish dates.

Gantt Chart view lists task details in the Entry table on the left side of the window and displays each task graphically in the Gantt Chart on the right side of the window.

I

Indenting moves a task to the right in the Entry table and makes it a lower level task in a Work Breakdown Structure.

Indicators column a column in the Entry table view that will display an icon that provides further information about a task, such as task constraint, task calendar, or task note.

L

Lag time moves a successor task forward in time so the Start dates between the tasks are further apart.

Lead time moves a successor task back in time so the two tasks overlap and the Start date between the tasks gets closer.

Leveling a process of correcting overallocated resources to ensure no resource is assigned more hours than available work hours.

M

Manually Scheduled a scheduling option where task dates are not calculated or adjusted by Project's scheduling engine, even if changes to related tasks are made.

Material resource a consumable resource such as supplies that is used up as a project progresses.

Milestone a task that is used to communicate project progress or mark a significant point in a project.

N

Network Diagram view displays tasks in a detailed box along with clearly representing task dependencies with link lines; also displays critical path.

Night Shift calendar assigns a schedule that is sometimes referred to as the "graveyard" shift schedule of Monday night through Saturday morning, 11:00 PM to 8:00 AM, with an hour off for break.

Nonworking day a day during which Project will not schedule work to occur.

Note acts as a sticky note for a task providing further information or instructions regarding a task.

O

Outdenting moves a task to the left in the Entry table and makes it a higher level task in a Work Breakdown Structure.

Overallocated when a resource is assigned to more work than available working hours.

P

Predecessor task a task that must be completed before the next task can start.

Project goal the desired result of a project upon completion.

Project Information dialog box the dialog box used to update various aspects of a project such as the project's start date, status date, current date, and project base calendar.

Project management a process of initiating, planning, executing, monitoring, and closing a project's tasks and resources in order to accomplish a project's goal.

Project manager the person responsible for overseeing all the details of the project plan.

Project Summary Task summarizes the timeline of your project and displays the total duration of your project.

Project template a Project file that contains sample project information such as tasks, durations, resources, and other project data.

Q

Quick Access Toolbar a series of small icons for commonly used commands that appear in the top-left corner of the Project 2016 window.

R

Recurring task a task that repeats at regular intervals.

Resource work, a material, or a cost associated with a project task.

Resource Sheet view a view commonly used to create resources and present resource information.

Row selector the box containing the row number of a task in the Entry table.

S

Scope what must be completed to deliver a specific product or service.

Select All a button that selects all tasks and task information in the Entry table.

Slack the time a task can be delayed from its scheduled start date without delaying the project.

Split bar separates the Entry table and the Gantt chart.

Standard calendar Project's default base calendar of 40 hours a week from 8:00 AM to 12:00 PM and 1:00 PM to 5:00 PM.

Start date the date Project 2016 uses to schedule tasks that will calculate the project's Finish date.

Status date the date set to run reports on a project's progress.

Subtask a related task that further defines the summary task.

Successor task a task that has a predecessor.

Summary task a task listed in bold in the Entry table associated with a group of tasks that logically belongs together.

T

Task an activity that is completed to reach a project goal.

Task dependency a relationship between tasks that defines which task(s) have to finish before the next task(s) can start.

Task duration prediction of time it will take to complete a task.

Task Information the dialog box that includes all the details for a single task.

Task Mode column a column in the Entry table that indicates the mode in which Project will schedule tasks, either manually or automatically.

Task Name column a column in the Entry table where the name of each task is entered.

Team Planner a Project view that shows a project's resources and tasks assigned to each resource.

Timeline a visual representation of the project from start to finish.

Timescale displays the unit of measure that determines the length of the Gantt bars in the Gantt chart.

Tracking recording the actual progress of the project's tasks.

24 Hours calendar a calendar that assigns a schedule with continuous work such as a project that must work around the clock.

V

View Bar a vertical bar on the left-hand side of the Project window that contains buttons for quick access to different Project views.

W

Work Breakdown Structure (WBS) a method of organizing tasks in a hierarchical structure.

Work resource the person and equipment that needs to be used to complete a project task.

Index

Bold page numbers indicate definitions.

E

F

G

I

J

L

M

N